本书为2021年江西省社会科学规划一般项目"英汉多模态叙事绘本图文互补机制研究"的研究成果，同时得到2019年江西省社会科学规划重点项目"南昌汉代海昏侯国遗址外宣英译研究"的支持。

邱晴 著

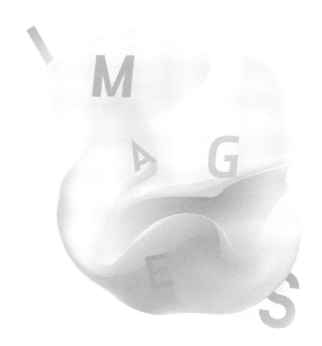

社会符号学视角下的图文互补研究

A Social Semiotic Approach to Visual-Verbal Complementarity in
Chinese Children's Picture Books

中国社会科学出版社

图书在版编目（CIP）数据

社会符号学视角下的图文互补研究:英文/邱晴著. —北京：中国社会科学出版社，2021.9
ISBN 978 - 7 - 5203 - 8634 - 0

Ⅰ.①社… Ⅱ.①邱… Ⅲ.①儿童故事—图画故事—文学研究—中国—英文 Ⅳ.①I207.8

中国版本图书馆 CIP 数据核字（2021）第 123370 号

出 版 人	赵剑英
责任编辑	陈肖静
责任校对	刘 娟
责任印制	戴 宽

出　　版	中国社会科学出版社
社　　址	北京鼓楼西大街甲 158 号
邮　　编	100720
网　　址	http://www.csspw.cn
发 行 部	010 - 84083685
门 市 部	010 - 84029450
经　　销	新华书店及其他书店

印　　刷	北京君升印刷有限公司
装　　订	廊坊市广阳区广增装订厂
版　　次	2021 年 9 月第 1 版
印　　次	2021 年 9 月第 1 次印刷

开　　本	710×1000　1/16
印　　张	17.75
插　　页	2
字　　数	282 千字
定　　价	108.00 元

凡购买中国社会科学出版社图书，如有质量问题请与本社营销中心联系调换
电话：010 - 84083683

Preface

I take great pleasure in writing this preface for Dr. Qiu Qing's monograph *A Social Semiotic Approach to Visual-Verbal Complementarityin Chinese Children's Picture Books*. This book is based on the author's doctoral thesis, which was completed under my supervision, so I am very pleased to know that it is to be formally published.

This book aims to explore the visual-verbal complementarityin Chinese children's picture books. This is a significant topic in multimodality research. As we know, communication in the modern worldmore often consists of a variety of semiotic modes instead of just language. As a result, there is currently a consensus that communications which draw on more than one semiotic resource are playing apredominant role in information dissemination. Children's picture books, as a typical kind of multimodal texts, are highly valued in the initiation and education of children. As research data, they are perceived as an extremely good site to explore how the visual and verbalsemiotic resources are co-deployed in order to make meaning.

This research is informed by Halliday's Systemic Functional Linguistics (SFL), and the data analyzedincludes ten Chinese children's picture bookswritten by different authors. From a social semiotic approach, the studyexplores how the visual and verbal semiotic resources are co-deployed to make different strands of meaning, i. e. to construct representational meanings, to establish interpersonal relationships and to create coherent and meaningful texts. Apart from adopting the analytical tools from Halliday's functional grammar, the study also incorporates Painter et al. 's (2013) visual narrative framework, Royce's (1999, 2007) intersemiotic complementarity framework in the actual analysis. In addition, drawing on the concept of "instantiation" and recent research in this dimension, the book also looks into the differencesin the affordance of meaning by each modality used in the picture books, with interesting findings. For example, it is found that there is more interpersonal commitment in the image than in the verbal text. Ideationally, there is a divergence in the commitment of meaning due to the different sharing of semantic load by each of the modes.

Thebookis well organized and clearly presented. It is of high academic quality as it has both theoretical and practical significance. This is attributable to Qiu Qing's diligence and devotion to academic research. During her years as a PhD candidate at Sun Yat-sen University, she read extensively in the field of SFL and linguistics in general, and was very active in participating in all the seminars and symposia that were organized by the SFL Research Group. She benefited greatly from discussions with world renowned linguists such as Professor M. A. K. Halliday, Professor Ruqaiya Hasan and Professor Geoff Thompson, who, as guest professors, often came to visit the university.

I offer my warmest congratulations to Dr. Qiu Qing and best wishes for her future academic career. I also hope that readers will find this book a useful reference in multimodality research.

Professor Chang Chenguang

Sun Yat-sen University

Acknowledgements

I would deliver my sincere and deep-felt gratitude to those who have inspired, guided, and helped me throughout the preparation, composition and improvement of this book.

First of all, I would express my heartfelt appreciation to Professor Chang Chenguang. As an agreeable man full of wisdom, insight and initiative, he has taught me a lot as to the inspirational ideas towards life as well as professional and academic competence. My sincere appreciation is also dedicated to Professor M. A. K. Halliday, Professor Ruqaiya Hasan and Professor Geoff Thompson for their generous guidance and invaluable suggestions which have nurtured me for the past years. My deep appreciation also extends to Professor Huang Guowen for his academic inspiration and guidance in life.

My gratitude goes to the faculty members of the Jiangxi Normal University as well, especially to my postdoctoral advisor, Professor Dong Shenghong, for his constant help and support. And I also greatly indebted to Professor Huang Hui, the dean of School of Intercultral Studies, who has always inspiring me with her insightful advice and encouragement.

Last but not the least, I would thank my family. My heart is always filled with the profound affection from my parents. My father, Professor Qiu Dongsheng, is an unfailing torchlight in the voyage of my life, guiding me through all the twists and turns; my mother Li Yuying, an English professor, is always available whenever I am in a low mood or in need of academic help. Throughout the years, they fill me with their unconditional love, immense encouragement and meticulous care. The years also witness the ever-growing understanding and love between my husband, Dr. Hu Yong and me. For his love, care, help, kindness and tolerance I have nothing to give in return, but my lifelong company and affection.

Content

List of Figures

List of Tables

List of Illustrations

List of Abbreviations

GSP   Generic Structure Potential

MDA   Multimodal Discourse Analysis

SFG   Systemic Functional Grammar

SFL   Systemic Functional Linguistics

SF-MDA   Systemic-functional Multimodal Discourse Analysis

Chapter One Introduction

1.1 Introductory remarks

Today's media-oriented world takes us into an era of images. Language rarely stands alone in various discourses (spoken and written) in people's lives, whether they are adults or children. Children's picture books, as a special type of multimodal reading material, exert enormous influences on young children. This book aims to explore the ways in which linguistic and visual semiotic resources are combined to make meaning within Chinese children's picture books. On the one hand, it intends to examine the collaboration of the two semiotics, visual and verbal, to synergistically make meaning, probing into the convergence in the creation of overall meaning. On the other hand, it aims to analyse the different affordances for meaning of each semiotic, exploiting divergence between verbal and visual semiotics by comparing their relative contributions to the overall meaning. To frame the present study, this chapter begins with a brief introduction of the background of the book (e.g. studies on children's picture books and multimodality as well as instantiation), which is immediately followed by the data description. The aims and significance of the research will be demonstrated, with research questions outlined and the research focus specified. In the end of the chapter, an overview of the research organisation will be provided.

1.2 Studies on children's picture books

Children's picture books play a fundamental part in the lives, entertainment, as well as education of children in some distinctive ways (e. g. Nodelman & Reimer 2003). First and foremost, picture books serve as a useful tool for early literary education and as an essential medium which introduces the young children to the literary world (whether via reading or being read to), contributing to the significant preparation for the child's future school literacy and success. Secondly, picture books, especially in the forms of a narrative, are generally perceived as a foundational vehicle for passing on social and cultural values from one generation to another, providing the child reader the entry into the "highly valued realm" of literature (Meek 1998). Moreover, children's picture books are regarded as a key means for socialisation and enculturation which constitute an important instrument for conveying sociocultural values. They convey (overtly or covertly) ideological messagesof social values, cultural values and the world (including material world and depicted world) to the young child (Stephens 1992).

In recent years, children's picture books have gradually become a popular subject of academic study in various researches. Among these studies on children's literacy, there are a wide range of approaches to picture books analysis with different research focus, such as cultural studies (e. g. Bradford, 1998; Dong 2006); developmental psychology (e. g. Schwarcz 1982; Nikolajeva & Scott 2001); literature and education of children (e. g. Hunt 1994, 1999; Lewis 2001; Stephens 1992) and so on (A more detailed review of the studies on children's picture books will be provided in Chapter 2). In most of the studies, the visual aspects within children's picture book have been considered as secondary and their relations to the verbal text are ignored. In recent years, a number of critics have been carried outto recall the attention to how the two semiotic resources (visual and verbal) work together to create meaning in children's picture books (e. g. Moebius 1986; Nodelman, 1988; Nikolajeva & Scott, 2000). Inspired by such tendency, this book conducts a social semiotic analysis of the synergistic cooperation between verbal and visual semiotics to make meaning within Chinese children's picture book.

1.3　Multimodality and instantiation

With the development in modern technology of communication, interactions and communicative exchanges between one and another consist of a variety of semiotic modes (e. g. images, music, sound, gesture, action, etc.), all of which contribute to the creation of meanings (Kress & van Leeuwen 2006; Kress 2010). It is generally-held that the meaning-making process in a text is necessarily multimodal, since that "it is no longer sufficient to deconstruct and analyse the use of verbal language in a text… [but] the operation of other semiotic resources must also be factored in as contributing to the total meaning made in the text" (Lim 2007: 195). As an emerging concept, the notion of "multimodality" covers such relevant changes in the views towards the multisemiotic nature of texts in present-day society. There is a growing consensus that communications which draw on more than one semiotic resource "are assuming their central role in information dissemination in the modern world" (Bateman 2008: 2). As a typical form of multimodal texts, there are two different modes (visual and verbal semiotic resources) co-deployed in children's picture books to make meaning and to exert influence on the child reader. In order to achieve a systemic and comprehensive account of the synergy of images and words, this research draws on the theoretical framework of social semiotics[1] (Halliday 1978/2001; Hodge & Kress 1988; Kress & van Leeuwen 2006) developed by Systemic Functional Linguistics (SFL) to probe into the multisemiotic nature of children's picture books.

Over the past decades, most research in SFL has focused on the development of two hierarchies (realisation and rank) and two complementaries, whereas the study on other complementary hierarchies (instantiation and individuation) is relatively less developed (see Martin 2008: 484). Instantiation refers to the relation between the meaning potential that inheres in the systems

---

[1]　It is also defined as "systemic functional semiotics" (Unsworth 2008: xvi).

of language and the actual text as instance. In children's picture books, instantiation is concerned with the relation between the totality of meaning choices of two semiotic systems and the specificity of the individual text (a bimodal text consists of verbal and visual texts). In order to systematically explain the interrelations between verbal and visual semiotics, the SFL dimension of instantiation (e. g. Halliday & Mattiessen 2004) and Martin's articulated notion of "commitment" (e. g. Martin 2008, 2010) have been applied to analyse the different commitments of meaning between the two semiotic systems within Chinese children's picture books, aiming to track the way in which different-semiotic systems (visual and verbal) are instantiated in the bimodal text and to compare their relative contributions to the overall meaning.

1.4　Data description

The choices of these picture books as the data are primarily based on a common theme which is closed related to Chinese custom and traditional culture. The selection of the sample texts covers ten preeminent Chinese children's picture books with extensive readership, written by well-known authors and artists within the field of Chinese picture book writing. Each book is written by a different author so that the conclusions will not be attributed to some kind of individual style or to particular language used by one specific author. Although there are a variety of Chinese characteristics, the study selects the picture books in relation to the most representative aspect of Chinese culture: the Spring Festival.

These ten Chinese picture books are presented in terms of title (both Chinese and English title), name of author, and year of publication (see Table 1 – 1).

Table 1 – 1　　　　**The data of the present study**

Year of Publication	The Authors	The Titles
2007	熊亮 Xiong Liang	《年》 *The Monster Nian*
2008	余丽琼, 朱成梁 Yu Liqiong; Zhu Chenliang	《团圆》 *Reunion*

Continued

Year of Publication	The Authors	The Titles
2011	孙肇志 Sun Zhaozhi	《过年啦》 *Happy New Year*
2012	王早早，李剑 Wang Zaozao；Li Jian	《辞旧迎新过大年》 *On the Spring Festival*
2013	柳垄沙 Liu Longsha	《年兽来了》 *The Monster Nian is Coming*
2013	朱世芳，话小屋 Zhu Shifang；Hua Xiaowu	《春节》 *The Spring Festival*
2013	高竞男，王芳 Gao Jinnan；Wang Fang	《年》 *Nian*
2014	郑春华 Zheng Chunhua	《邮递员叔叔的奇遇》 *The Adventure of the Postman*
2015	朱慧颖 Zhu Huiyin	《年》 *Nian*
2015	刘嘉路 Liu Jialu	《斗年兽》 *A Battle with Nian*

1.5　Objectives and significance of the study

Informed by a social semiotic perspective, the book aims to elaborate the synergistic cooperation between verbal and visual semiotic resources in Chinese children's picture booksin the hope of providing a comprehensive account and to contribute insights useful for the better understanding of how any individual Chinese children picture book makes meaning and the meanings construed by each modality (visual or verbal) converge with or diverge from that of the other. Overall, the book intends to address the following research questions:

(1) How are the three strands of meanings construed by choices from both verbal and visual semiotic systems in Chinese children's picture books?

(2) How are cohesive relations construed between visual and verbal semiotic sys-

tems within the picture books?

(3) To what degrees are meanings in verbal system and visual system taken up in the process of creating the story as a meaningful whole? And what are the differences between the commitments of verbal and visual semiotic resources in these picture books?

The first research question is concerned with both the verbal and visual choices for construing representations, to establish interpersonal relationships and to create coherent messages. Inspired by SFL theory and its metafunctional diversity, the analyses in this book are metafunctionally oriented and meaning choices are organised into three broad semantic domains (ideational, interpersonal and textual). To be more specific, this research aims to explore the ways in which meanings are construed by verbal and visual semiotic systems within Chinese children's picture books. To facilitate the study, theoretical frameworks are drawn from the field of systemic functional approaches to multimodality, in particular, SFL theory (Halliday 1994/2000; Halliday & Matthiessen 2004) for the analysis of linguistic semiotics and the visual narrative framework (Painter & Martin 2011; Painter et al. 2013) for the exploration of visual semiotics. Detailed discussion on the basic tenets of SFL and visual narrative framework that underpin the theoretical construct of this research will be provided in Chapter 3.

The second question deals with the ways in which verbal and visual semiotics are collaborated to make meanings within Chinese children's picture books. The focus of the research is not only placed on accounting for how any individual Chinese picture book makes meaning, but also on the interrelation and synergy between visual and verbal modalities. To achieve these ends, the intersemiotic complementarity framework as proposed by Royce (e. g. 1999, 2007) is applied to explore how verbal and visual semiotic systems cohere with each other to synergistically create coherent and meaningful messages.

In analysing the intermodal relations in Chinese children's picture books, this research delves into the different affordance of meaning related to each mode by focusing on the SFL dimension of instantiation (e. g. Halliday & Matthiessen 2004). Since picture books as a type of complex bimodal text instantiate meaning choices from both verbal and visual semiotic systems, the investigation of how choices combine across different modalities, and how they diverge in affording different degrees of meaning comes to the fore. The notion of commitment (Martin 2008, 2010) is drawn on to consider different affordances for meaning of verbal and visual semiotic resources and to track the way in which each of them is instantiated in the bimodal text, as well as to explore whether the commitment of each semiotic (visual or verbal) diverges from or converges with that of the other.

As implicated in the research questions, the book is significant from both theoretical and practical grounds: on the one hand, the book contributes to the theoretical orientation by extending the social semiotic account of the visual semiotic resources and exploring how the visual semiotic can be considered in relation to the verbal semiotic to synergistically construe different strands of meaning in Chinese children's picture books. On the other hand, the book contributes to the practical orientation by enriching the linguistic studies of Chinese picture books with a complementary study on visual narratives. Although there are some new emerging studies on picture books (e. g. Guijarro & Sanz 2009; Painter et al. 2013; Tian 2010), the foci of attention given to Chinese picture book narratives is rare, thus the present study will fill in the gap by providing a systematic account of verbal and visual semiotic resources and the interplay between them in Chinese picture books. Furthermore, the research examines the different commitment (as a perspective on the cline of instantiation) of meaning as manifested by both verbal and visual semiotic resources when they are co-instantiated in the Chinese children's picture book texts, consequently, expanding and broadening the application scope of SFL. Since the studies on the SFL dimension of instantiation are primarily centred upon the relation between the meaning potential that inheres in the system of language and the actual linguistic text, this research extends the analysis of instantiation to the non-verbal semiotic system.

1.6 Organisation of the book

The book is organised into seven chapters.

Chapter One as the introductory chapter has outlined a general introduction of the present research, introducing the research background, data description, aims and significance, as well as the organisation of the book.

Chapter Two focuses on the review of the relevant studies on children's picture books. In this chapter, some of the major literature which examines the different studies on children's picture books is reviewed with a particular focus on the interplay between verbal and visual components within children's picture books. In addition, the chapter introduces the concept of "multimodality", the concept of "narrative" as well as the notion of "story family" in order to facilitate the analysis of Chinese children's picture books.

Chapter Three is devoted to the theoretical framework and methodological implications of the book. In this chapter, some basic tenets of SFL relevant to the present study (e. g. the stratification, the cline of instantiation, themetafunctional diversification) are introduced. As a general and appliable linguistic theory (e. g. Halliday 2008; Huang 2006; Chang & Liao 2010), SFL has been widely extended to the analysis of non-verbal semiotic systems (e. g. O'Halloran 2005, 2008; O'Toole 1994). Therefore, the models for analysing visual semioticresources that are derived from the SFL theory and the social semiotic theory (Kress & van Leeuwen 2006; Painter et al. 2013) are examined and explained in detail, which provide the research a useful analytical tool for analysing visual elements within Chinese children's picture books. Furthermore, the chapter places a particular focus on the interrelations among different semiotic systems, in particular, relations between verbal and visual semiotics (e. g. O'Halloran 2005, 2008; Martinec & Salway 2005; Royce's 1999, 2007).

Chapter Four is primarily concerned with the interpersonal meanings construed in the picture book narratives. It then explores the visual and verbal choices for writers (and illustrators) to establish engagement between various participants in the picture books, including both the interactions between different depicted characters and the alignments between represented characters and the child reader. To this end, the chapter examines the interpersonal intersemiotic complementarity between verbal and visual semiotic systems which establish engagement and affinity within an exemplar. Moreover, there is a scrutiny of the different affordance for meaning of verbal and visual semiotics in relation to interpersonal meaning and their relative contribution to the whole meaning in the last part of this chapter.

Chapter Five deals with the ideational choices available to the writer/illustrator to represent the narrative reality and different participants within Chinese picture books. In this chapter, ideational cohesive relations between verbal and visual semiotics are analysed by examining various ideational cohesive devices. Apart from the cohesive relations between the two modalities within the picture book, the chapter also conducts an account of the difference between the two semiotic resources by explicating the degree to which each commits ideational meanings in the exemplar.

Chapter Six is devoted to the analysis of textual choices available to the writer/illustrator to create coherent and meaningful messages. The textual features of visual components are identified throughout the picture books in the chapter, and a systematic analysis of compositional intersemiotic complementarity between verbal and visual semiotic systems is also conducted. This chapter concludes with an analysis of different commitment of meaning for both verbal and visual semiotics in the exemplar book and their relative contribution to overall meaning when they are co-instantiated in a particular instance (in this case a bimodal text).

Chapter Seven summarises the major findings of the book and thereby draws the conclusion. It also presents the general significance, implications and limitations of the present study and the suggestion for the future work.

Chapter Two   Literature Review

2.1   Introduction

As the primary concern of this book is the interplay and synergy of visual and verbal semiotic resources within Chinese children's picture books, this chapter reviews relevant studies on children's picture books and on approaches to multimodality. It first makes an overview of the concept of multimodality and three main lines of research that examine the process of making meaning by various semiotic resources within multimodal ensembles. Some of the major literature which examines the different studies on children's picture books is then reviewed with a particular focus on the interplay of verbal and visual components within children's picture books. In addition, the concept of "narrative" (Labov & Waletzky1967) and "story family" (Martin & Rose 2008) are also introduced to facilitate the analysis of Chinese children's picture books.

2.2   Approaches to multimodality

Unlike the more conservative views of text focusing on its linguistic nature, text in recent years is preferentially perceived as a "semiotic object" in which different modes or semiotic resources co-occur to create meanings in combination (Fowler 1986; Kress 2000). According to Fairclough (1995), the existence of multi-semiotic texts exerts an enormous influence in our daily lives in modern society:

> I think it is necessary to move further towards this view than I have done in these pa-
> pers, where a text is mainly understood as written or spoken language. A strong argument
> for doing so is that texts in contemporary society are increasingly multi-semiotic; texts
> whose primary semiotic form is language increasingly combine language with other semiotic
> forms⋯[And] written (printed) texts are also increasingly becoming multisemiotic texts,
> not only because they incorporate photographs and diagrams, but also because the graphic
> design of the page is becoming an ever more salient factor in evaluation of written texts.
>
> (Fairclough 1995: 4)

Alongwith the acceleration of modern technology of communication, we are engaged in social interactions which are composed of more than one mode. Instead of merely keeping an eye on the verbal semiotic, recent developments in multimodal studies place a particular focus on the multi-semiotic texts involving some other non-verbal semiotics, such as on visual images (e. g. Kress & van Leeuwen 1996, 2001, 2006; O'Toole 1990, 1994; Royce & Bowcher 2007), on spatial design (e. g. Martin & Stenglin 2007; Ravelli 2006), on sound and music (e. g. van Leeuwen 1999), actions (e. g. Martinec 1998, 2000, 2004; Hood & Forey 2007), on mathematical symbolism (e. g. O'Halloran 2005, 2007); on film and media (e. g. Baldry 2004; Baldry & Thibault 2006; Thibault 2000) and so on. Among these studies, three main lines of research that examine the process of making meaning by various semiotic resources within multimodal ensembles are outlined: social semiotic multimodal analysis, multimodal discourse analysis and multimodal interactional approach (see Jewitt 2009: 28).

2.2.1　Social semiotic multimodality

The social semiotic approach to multimodality emergesessentially from Halliday's (1978/2001) social semiotic theoryof language, Barthes's (1977) idea of semiotics and studies of interactional sociology (e. g. Goffman 1983; Bateson 2000; Jewitt 2009). In the distinctive work *Language as Social Semi-*

otic, Halliday (1978/2001) has explicated the importance for investigating language in its social context and for interpreting texts as complex signs which serve as the material instantiation of three kinds of social meaning. By utilising Halliday's semiotic approach and SFL as its theoretical cornerstone, a comprehensive framework has been established by Kress and van Leeuwen (1996, 2006) to investigate how these meanings/functions are realised in visual images via a series of concepts such as modality, framing and composition (A detailed discussion of their visual grammar will be provided in Section 3.3.1). *Reading Images* (Kress & van Leeuwen 1996) as a pioneering work on the construction of visual grammar generates a set of semiotic network systems, demonstrating the semiotic resources of image in play and how they represent different kinds of meaning. They go on to point out that semiotic resources of images are also assumed to convey representational meaning, to design and establish interpersonal meaning between different participants involved, and to form coherent messages. In Halliday's account (1978/2001, 1994/2000), representational meaning, interpersonal meaning, and textual meaning are realised through the traditional modes of language (speech and writing), however, nowadays, both verbal and non-verbal components are perceived as essential element for the construction of meaning (Kress 2010; Kress & van Leeuwen 1996; Ventola & Moya 2009).

In their framework for visual grammar, Kress and van Leeuwen (1996, 2006) provide a set of taxonomic diagrams (or system networks) which display the visual semiotic resources. These systems are established to map out the choices available to the members of a given community to simultaneously create three different strands of meaning (representational, interpersonal, and compositional) and to explore their meaning potential when they are used in a given context of communication (van Leeuwen 2009). Although initiated and developed by SFL and theory of social semiotic, Kress and van Leeuwen's (1996, 2006) approach to multimodal studies has "moved towards a more flexible notion of grammar, with a focus on people's situated choices of resources rather than emphasizing the system of available resources" (Jewitt

2009: 29). It indicates that systemic functional approach and its network systems, though relevant in various aspects for social semiotic multimodal analysis, have lost part of grammatical influence on the social semiotic framework to multimodality (Kress & van Leeuwen 1996, 2006; Kress 2010). In the exploration of visual features of a multimodal ensemble, the attention is not only placed to the pre-defined system networks for semiotic resources, but also to the communicative resources which are available to people in a particular social-cultural context. Shaped by the context of communication and their specific use, the modal systems are not conceived of as entirely fixed or perspective elements, but as components in constant change. In the view of social semiotic multimodality, semiotics can not only be treated as the study of language but refers to the "study of sign systems—in other words . . . the study of meaning in its most general sense" (Halliday 1985a: 4). As the guiding principle of SFL, social accountability is mainly concerned with "linguistic theory as a resource for solving problem . . . [such as] . . . education, culture, health and safety" (Huang 2006: 5). In this sense, the concept of metafunction is not only applied to language, but also serves to explain the kinds of meanings that are made by other semiotic systems besides language. Matthiessen(2007: 21) provides a justification for applying the concept of metafunction to other semiotic resources as follows:

> The potential for "translating" linguistic models into other semiotic systems . . . is of course built into our linguistic resources for construing them within the content plane by means of the linguistic metaphors of wave, prosody, and configuration. That is, the ideational resources of language provide us with arange of strategies for modelling ("conceptualising") all modes and media of expression; and we can then use non-linguistic semiotic systems such as drawing, painting, animation, sculpture, or music for representing these models construed within the content plane of language.
>
> Matthiessen(2007: 21)

Adopting Halliday's SFL and social semiotics as the fundamental basis of their studies, Kress and van Leeuwen provide a full account of grammar to visual language and utilise underlying principles in verbal grammar to explain the grammar of visual. They then posit that language and visual mode play the same important role in realising meaning, and contend that "just as grammar of language describe how words combine in clauses, sentences and texts, so our visual 'grammar' will describe the way in which depicted elements-people, places and things-combine in visual 'statement' of greater or lesser complexity and extension" (Kress & van Leeuwen 1996, 2006: 1). Based on SFL and social semiotic theory, Kress and van Leeuwen attempt to propose an analogy for the construction of visual grammar and to group three kinds of categories which are fundamental to the analysis of image:

> The visual, like all semiotic modes, has to serve several communicational (and representational) requirements, in order to function as a full system of communication. We have adopted the theoretical notion of 'metafunction' from the work of Michael Halliday for the purpose of dealing with this factor. The three metafunctions which he posits are the ideational, the interpersonal, and the textual.
>
> (Kress & van Leeuwen 1996: 40)

Traditionally, the three strands of meanings (ideational, interpersonal, and textual) are intended to be systematically studied through conventional modes of linguistic semiotic (speaking and writing) (e. g. Halliday 1985b). However, both verbal and non-verbal components are regarded as the essential tools for the construction of meaning (Baldry & Thibault 2006; Kress 2010). Kress and van Leeuwen (1996) further explicate that both verbal and visual semiosisare seen to make the same kinds of meanings, but by different methods and from different semiotic systems. In this regard, they rename the three metafunctions of language correspondingly as "representational", "interactive", and "compositional" metafunctions in their visual grammar. They argue that, similar to the verbal text, visual compositions may also serve to convey representational meaning, to establish interaction between the represented participants and the viewer and to form coherent messages.

In summary, social semiotic multimodal analysis gives attention to the rules, regularities and patterns emerging from the modal systems of representation and communication in some specific contexts. It aims to analyses how modal resources available are used by members of a given community to create meanings in social processes. Together with Kress and van Leeuwen (e. g. Kress 2010; van Leeuwen 2005; Kress & van Leeuwen 1996, 2006), the researchers whose work could be identified within the social semiotic approach to multimodality include Machin (2007), Jewitt (2009), Ventola et al. (2004), and Ventola and Moya (2009).

2.2.2   Multimodal discourse analysis

Multimodal discourse analysis (henceforth MDA) as a main perspective to multimodality is "an emerging paradigm indiscourse studies" which extends the exploration of language per se to the examination of the combination of verbal semiotic resources and other non-verbal semiotic resources (e. g. O'Halloran 2008). Halliday's Systemic Functional Grammar (henceforth SFG) (Halliday 1994/2000; Halliday & Matthiessen 2004) provides the main theoretical framework and foundation for MDA (O'Halloran 2004, 2005; O' Tool 1994). The systemic functional approach to MDA contributes to "developing theoretical and practical approaches for analysing written, printed and electronic texts, three-dimensional sites andother realms of activity where semiotic resources (e. g. spoken and written language, visual imagery, mathematical symbolism, sculpture, architecture, gesture and other physiological modes) combine to make meaning" (O'Halloran 2008: 444). The term "discourse" is used in various aspects of people's lives, representing a variety of meanings. Kress and van Leeuwen approach discourse at a macro-textual level and define discourse as "socially constructed knowledge of (some aspect of reality) ⋯ [that is] developed in specific social contexts" (Kress & van Leeuwen 2001: 4). Different from Kress and van Leeuwen who study discourse from a marco-textual perspective, O'Halloran and O'Toole put their analytical focus on the analysis of discourse at a micro-textual level to capture the meaning-making process of texts in both the totality and relations between distinct semiotic systems within multimodal texts.

Influenced by SFG, this perspective to the study of multimodality builds a framework for analysing art images on a constituent structural model with a range of different ranks (O'Toole 1994, 2004). An example is that O'Toole (2004) investigates the Sydney Opera House from a set of hierarchical organisation of elements including differentiated ranks: such as lower ranks (e. g. the element), higher ranks (e. g. floors, and the whole buildings). In hope of building his rank-scale, O'Toole (1994) argues that a large-scale narrative is composed of loosely interrelated episodes which in turn comprise a set of constituent units. He goes on to distinguish different systemic oppositions: narrative scene (+story) against scene (+human) as well as portray (+human) against non-human (O'Toole 1994: 12). Each rank has its own realisations at representational, modal and compositional (textual) level. In this respect, semiotic resources are considered to be organised in metafunctionally orientated systems of meanings.

O'Toole's (1994) approach to the visual analysis of artis then developed by O'Halloran(2004, 2005) to describe the metafunctional-based grammatical systems of semiotic resources as well as their meaning potential. In the exploration of the mechanisms through which different semiotic resources are integrated within a certain multimodal discourse, O'Halloran works on the integration of images, mathematical symbolism and verbal text in mathematic discourses (O'Halloran2005), on visual semiosis in film (2004) and on the use of linguistic semiotic and visual imagery in printed texts (2008). By using the concept rank, Baldry (2004: 84) investigates a piece of car advertisement from an approach termed as "Systemic-functional tradition of multimodality", establishing as well as distinguishing between a set of functional units such as macro-phases, phases, sub-phases, mini-genres, and genres.

While Kress and van Leeuwen's approach to multimodality has placed a particular focus on the social semiotic, MDA approach emphasises the description of metafunctional systems for each semiotic resource and intersemiosis between different semiotic resources (A detailed discussion on intersemiosis will be given in Section 3. 4). The approach of MDA focuses on system choices and system in use. In other words, the description of systems and meaning as choice from systems serve as the basic tenets of MDA approach, indicating that Halliday's theory of social semiotic and SFG provides significant starting points for O'Halloran and other scholars working within the approach of MDA.

The primary objective of the MDA approach is to identify different semiotic resources that are available to the user to make meaning in a specific sociocultural context, and their functions and meaning potential, as well as the integration or combination of them in multimodal discourses (or artefacts). As Jewitt (2009: 33) elaborates, the emphasis of MDA " is placed on understanding and describing semiotic resources and principles of their systems of meaning in order to understand how people use these resources in social contexts for specific purposes". Together with O'Halloran (2004, 2005, 2008) and O'Toole (1994, 2011), some other researchers such as Baldry (2004), Unsworth (2008), Unsworth and Cleirigh (2009), Baldry and Thibault (2006), Stenglin (2009) and so on contribute to the development of this approach to multimodal studies.

2. 2. 3   Multimodal interactionanalysis

The multimodal interactional analysis (e. g. Norris, 2004a; Jones, 2005; Norris & Jones, 2005) as another approach to multimodality gives enormous importance to the notions of action and interaction in use. Interactional sociolinguistics (e. g. Goffman 1963; Gumperz 1982; Gumperz & Hymes 1972), particularly Scollon and Scollon's (2004) work on mediated discourse provide the fundamental theoretical foundations for the development of this approach to the studies on multimodality. The main concern of the study on mediated discourse is the social action, and the aim of discourse analysis from this perspective is " to engage in social action" (Scollon & Scollon 2004: 7). Focusing on the concept of social action, Scollon and Scollon (2003) in their book *Discourses in Place* explore the material characteristics of language-

and "in place meaning" of signs, with a particular emphasis on the meanings of people's actions among these discourses in place. In addition to the interactional sociolinguistics, the other influences towards the approach are brought by Kress and van Leeuwen's (2001, 2006) work on multimodality. Adopting the multimodal interactional analysis, Norris (2004, 2009) investigates how the actions are performed by a social actor to interactively make meaning, and how messages are expressed by the users of language in a specific context of situation as well as how other's individuals' reactions are given to those messages.

Given these historical influences, it is not surprising that the unit of multimodal interactional analysis is the action performed by a certain individual in social interactions with one another. As the basic concept of multimodal interactional analysis, the type of action can be further categorised into higher level and lower level actions. The lower level actions serve as the smallest meaningful units in social interaction, while the higher one is composed of a chain of lower level actions. For instance, an interaction among several individuals is viewed as a higher level action comprising a number of lower level actions. Within the interaction, there are chains of lower level actions carried out by the participants such as the intonation units of individuals, the bodily postures or gestures of them, or shifts in eye contact, bodily stance, etc. (Norris 2004: 13).

In his framework of multimodal interactional analysis, Norris (2004, 2009) distinguishes two concepts which are related to the actions carried out by social actors in a particular context of situation: modal density and modal configuration. The former is determined by the modal intensity and modal complexity through which a higher level action is constructed in a specific interaction. The modal complexity or multiplicity of modes in interaction relies upon the participants' lower level actions which play a part in constituting the higher-level actions. Moreover, any higher level action "is constructed through interplay among a multiplicity of communicative modes" (Norris 2004: 80). Through the notion of modal configuration, Norris (2009) accounts for the hierarchical position of all the modes which are in play at a specific moment of a certain higher level action and the way in which they are organised in relation to one another. Basically speaking, the concept of modal configuration is built on the basis of the meaning that is constructed in various actions.

Unlike O'Halloran (e. g. 2005, 2008) and O'Toole's (e. g. 1994) approach to multimodality which places its primary research space and interest to semiotic system, multimodal interactional analysis (Norris 2004, 2009) pays great attention to the rules and regularities governing the social actors' use of systems of representation. In Kress and van Leeuwen's (1996, 2006) approach, and that of other researchers related to the social semiotic multimodality, the emphasis is placed on the paradigmatic oppositions emerging from modal systems of communication in use. Within O'Halloran's (2005, 2008) framework of MDA, the interest is primary on the social semiotic systems of representation and the way in which different semiotic systems interact with one another. Multimodal interactional analysis as a distinctive perspective to multimodal studies "shifts attention from representation and communication (the focus of Kress, van Leeuwen and O'Halloran) to interaction" (Jewitt 2009: 34). Regarded as a key component within this framework, communication is essentially concerned with the on-going interaction between different participants and the multimodal process in which various communicative modes are at play to convey meaning (e. g. postures, gaze, movement, gesture, material objects, etc.) (Norris 2004, 2009). Some representative researchers whose work focus on the multimodal interactional analysis include Norris (2004, 2009) and Jones (e. g. Jones 2005; Norris & Jones 2005); and those associated with this perspective to multimodality include Scollon and Scollon (2003, 2009).

2.3   Studies on the genre of story

In exploring the narratives of personal experience, Labov and Waletzky (1967) initiate a comprehensive analytical framework with a sociolinguistic orientation. Later, this initiative model is further developed by Labov in his quantitative sociolinguistic studies (e. g. Labov 1972a, 1972b). As a useful and powerful analytical tool, their framework has been applied in a wide range of linguistic studies on narratives. In their framework, Labov and Waletzky (1967/1997: 12) attempt to define narrative informally as "as one method of recapitulating past experience by matching a verbal sequence of clauses to the sequence of events that actually occurred". With the definition as the starting point, they further introduce the concepts of "narrative unit", "restricted clause", "free clause" and "narrative clause" (Labov & Waletzky 1967/ 1997: 13 – 26). Based on these concepts, Labov and Waletzky deal with a wide range of tape-recorded narratives derived from two distinct social contexts. One of such two social contexts is the situation in which the narrator is speaking only to the interviewer (the one who does not belong to the narrator's primary group) in a face-to-face interview. In the second context, the narrator is recorded in talking to other members of the primary group, and even sometimes to a relative outsider on the margins of the primary group (the one who would provide only a part of the stimulus for the narrative). In the analysis of the clause types in a great number of narratives of personal experience, Labov and Waletzky (1967/1997: 27 – 37) attempt to map the overall structure of narratives. The overall structure of narratives in respect to personal experience has been summarised in Table 2 – 1.

Table 2 – 1 The structure of narratives in relation to personal experience
(reproduced from Labov & Waletzky 1967/1997: 27 – 37)

Orientation	It serves the function of orienting the listener in respect to person, place, time and behavioural situation.
Complication	It is viewed as the main body of narrative clauses which comprises a series of events that may be termed the complication or complicating action.
Evaluation	The evaluation is defined as part of the narrative that reveals the attitude of the narrator towards the narrative by emphasising the relative importance of some narrative units as compared to others.
Resolution	The resolution of the narrative is that portion of the narrative sequence that follows the evaluation. If the evaluation is the last element, then the resolution section coincides with the evaluation.
Coda	The coda is a functional device for returning the verbal perspective to the present moment.

In examining the overall structure, Labov and Waletzky have found that there is a generalised structure with which those narratives of personal experience may unfold. Generally speaking, the narratives would progress alongside the stages of Orientation, Complication, Evaluation, Resolution and Coda. Among the different stages in a narrative, the stage of Evaluation is seen as a fundamental component constituting the overall structure of a narrative, without which the narrative is not complete (Labov & Waletzky1967/1997). The importance of the stage of Evaluation lies in its function as a useful interlude linking the stage of Complication and the stage of Resolution. According to Labov and Waletzky (1967/1997: 32), it is important and necessary for the narrator "to delineate the structure of the narrative by emphasizing the point where the complication has reached a maximum: the break between the complication and the result…[and thus]…most narratives contain an evaluation section that carries out this function". It is revealed from the overall structure of the narratives proposed by them that the stage of Evaluation is highlighted with great emphasis put on its significance. However, sometimes it would be problematic in the restriction of the Evaluation stage as being a discrete one that is different from other stages. According to Labov,

A complete narrative begins with an orientation, proceeds to the complicating action, is suspended at the focus of evaluation before the resolution, concludes with the resolution, and returns the listener to the present time with the coda. The evaluation forms a secondary structure which is concentrated in the evaluation section but may be found in various forms throughout the narrative.

Labov (1972a: 369)

Therefore, Labov (e. g. Labov1972a) in his later research of narrative modifies the earlier scheme (Labov & Waletzky1967/1997) of narrative by indicating evaluation as the focus of waves since evaluative devices are distributed throughout the narrative. The prosodic dispersal of evaluative meaning proposed by Labov (1972a) is illustrated in Figure 2 – 1.

By the modifying paradigm, Labov (1972a) explores how the penetration

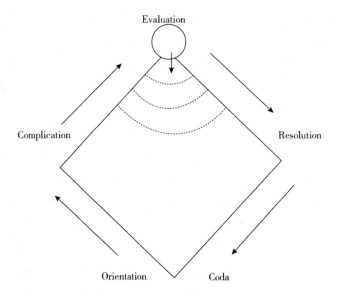

Figure 2 – 1   Dispersed evaluation in narrative (Labov 1972a: 369)

of evaluative meanings is accomplished through the whole internal structure of narratives. However, this paradigm impairs the measuring function of Evaluation in distinguishing the stage of Complication from Resolution, because the evaluative meanings are regarded as distributed throughout the narrative (Labov 1972a: 369). With regard to the distinction of evaluation, Plum (e. g. Plum 1988, Martin & Plum 1997) brings forth a theoretical framework for analysing a set of different genres of story. The data collected from a sociolinguistic interview is "designed to 'elicit' particular genres, including narratives' (Martin & Plum 1997: 299). " Besides the type of recount in relation to story initiated by Martin (1981), Plum (1988) puts forwards several distinct types of narrative texts, namely, anecdote, exemplum and observation. Although there are a number of differences between those types of narrative, all of them place an emphasis on the significant role of evaluation in demarcating types of story genre.

Drawing upon Labov and Waletzky's (1967/1997) research on the narratives of personal experience and Plum's (1988) work on the types of narrative texts, Martin and Rose (2008) develop the concept of "story family" to explore the typology of texts related to the genre of story. According to Martin and Rose (2008) , the differentiated types of stories can be basically distinguished into five categories: recount, anecdote, exemplum, observation and narrative:

Recounts: record a sequence of events without significant disruption. Rather than a distinct evaluation stage, the events are typically appraised prosodically as the recount unfolds.

Anecdotes: involve some remarkable disruption to usuality, which is not resolved, but simply reacted to. There markable event may be tragic or comic, engaging or revolting, so the ensuing reaction may beeither positive or negative affect.

Exemplums: also involve a disruption, but this is interpreted rather than reacted to, and the type of attitude expressed in the interpretation tends to be judgment of people's character or behaviour. Again the incident may involve behaviour that is either admirable or damnable, so the ensuing judgment may either admire or criticise, praise or condemn.

Observations: involve a description of a significant event, followed by a personal appreciating an aspect of it.

Narratives: specifically for the generic pattern that resolves a complication. Evaluation of narrative complications can vary between affect, judgement of people, or appreciation of things and events. The evaluation is often deployed to suspend theaction, increasing the narrative tension, and so intensifying the release when tension resolved.

Martin & Rose (2008: 51 – 52)

Apart from the type of recounts, other members included in the story family, such as anecdote, exemplum, observation and narrative, share some similarities in that they involve a disruption. The narrative is different from the anecdote, exemplum and observation in that it places a particular focus on the action carried out by the protagonist to look for a solution to bring equilibrium back to the story when the story is confronted with disruption. However, among the other three types, events are merely evaluated without action taken to bring back the equilibrium.

In examining the structural potential for the nursery tales, Hasan (1984/ 1996) proposes the notion of the Generic Structure Potential (SP or GSP for short, thus GSP henceforth) to discuss the semiotic structure of the genre of nursery tales. As an essential concept in SFL, genre is regarded as an aspect of mode (Halliday 1978/2001), and a certain genre may serve as "the specific semiotic functions of text that have social value in the culture" (Halliday 1978/2001: 145). Regarded as a useful analytical tool, the GSP model deals mainly with the total potential textual structures within a specified genre, and "enables us to analyse any passage and relate it to its context in discourse, and also for the general background of the text: who it is written for, what is its angle onthe subject matter and so on" (Halliday 1990: 34). In SFL, genre is closely related with the semiotic structure of the context of situation, which can be understood as a short form for the more elaborate phrase "genre-specific semantic potential", bearing a logic relation to contextual configuration (Hasan 1985: 108). In this respect, the textual potential of a particular text belonging to a specified genre includes a repertoire of a wide range of optional or obligatory elements which are organised in a linear order.

Therefore, the main objective that GSP model seeks to achieve is to explore both the representations of the obligatory and optional elements in a certain genre of texts and also to discuss the structural order in which these elements (obligatory or optional) may occur in a given type of genre. To this end, Hasan (1996: 53) demonstrates the capacities of GSP in respect to three aspects of text structure: (ⅰ) it must specify all those elements of structure whose presence is obligatory, if the text is to be regarded as a complete instance of a given genre by the members of some sub-community; (ⅱ) it must enumerate all those elements whose presence is optional so that the fact of their presence or absence, while affecting the actual structural shape of aparticular text, does not affect that text's generic status; and (ⅲ) the GSP must also specify the obligatory and optional ordering of the elements vis-a-vis each other, including the possibility of interaction. A GSP meeting all these conditions would depict the total potential of the texture structures of a given genre, while the actual structure of an instance of the specific genre would perform a particular schematic configuration permitted by the GSP. The three aspects of text structure are concerned with different elements involved in a given genre. Taking into account all these aspects, Hasan (1984/1996) illustrates the structural potential of the genre of nursery tales on the basis of a wide range of data:

[(<Placement>^)Initiating Event^] Sequent Event^Final Event[^(Finale)*(Moral)]

Figure 2 –2   GSP of the nursery tale (Hasan 1984/1996: 54)

As demonstrated in Figure 2 – 2, the elements framed in round brackets are optional elements, including Placement, Finale and Moral. Except from these elements, the other elements (e. g. Initiating Event, Sequence Event and Final event) are labeled as obligatory elements. In other words, a nursery tale without these obligatory elements is not regarded as a complete and generic one. Moreover, Placement and Initiating Event are enclosed in a square bracket and the same as that of Finale and Moral. And the angled brackets which enclose Placement can be interpreted in a way that the lexico-grammatical realisations of Placement are likely to be included or interspersed withthe realisations of Initiating Event. The carat sign ^ accounts for the irreversible order of the elements. That is to say, the left element of the carat sign ^ cannot be preceded by the element on the left side of the sign. On the contrary, the raised dot used between Finale and Moral refers to the reversibility of the order of the two elements.

2.3.1   A review of studies on picture books

Children's picture books often serve as a foundational part in the lives of young children. The most evident function that children picture books can serve is to bring the young into the literary world. The factor for picture books as a favourite reading material of children is that "usually the first contact a child has with books is with picture books, which remain the principle literary form up to and beyond the age at which children master literacy for themselves" (Stephens 1992: 158). Children are introduced into the literary world by a set of complex strategies such as interacting with texts, apprenticing them to appreciate those texts. From this point of view, children's picture books can be recognised as "an especially effective way to introduce readers to more complex strategies for interacting with texts, such as point of view, thematic structure, or considerations of irony" (Nodelman & Reimer 2003: 299).

Another function of picture books for children, especially those in narrative forms, is that they can be viewed as a key means for socialisation. This function is achieved via telling stories which touch upon a wide range of themes and providing the young readers with guiding principles, for instance, to train them to know how to facilitate engagement and interaction with others, how to resolve different problems and difficulties, and how to recognise the external world. In light of the socialising function of children's picture book, a number of researches shed lights on this apprenticeship into literary and social values, such as Nikolajeva and Scott(2000, 2001), Sarland (2005), Spitz (1998) and Stephens (1992). Although the texts within the genre of children's picture books are commonly assumed to be somewhat simple in organisational structure or naive in linguistic description, they apply a series of different kinds of strategies to express and strengthen the social and ideological values which naturalise the social-cultural system. Stephens (1992) elaborates the importance of stories in the process of socialisation:

> The use of story as an agent of socialization is a conscious and deliberate process. In practice itranges from the didactic extremes of 'bibliotherapy', books which purport to help children confrontand deal with specific problems in their lives (death of a close relative; parental separation; starting at school, etc.), to books with no obvious intent to be exemplary. Every book has an implicitideology, nevertheless, usually in the form of assumed social structures and habits of thought. The second kind of book can be the more powerful vehicle for an ideology because implicit, and therefore invisible, ideological positions are invested with legitimacy through the implication thatthings are simply 'so'.
>
> Stephens (1992: 9)

In recent years, there is a wide range of approaches to the study of picture books. Among these existing works on children's literacy, there are a number of studies on picture books analysis with different research focus, such as cultural studies (e. g. Bradford, 1998; Dong 2006); developmental psychology (e. g. Schwarcz, 1982; Nikolajeva and Scott2001); literature and education of children (e. g. Hunt 1994, 1999; Lewis 2001; Stephens 1992); ethnography(e. g. Nichols 2002); stylistic diversity (Feaver, 1977); psychoanalysis (Bosmajian 1999; Crago 1999; Spitz 1999); their therapeutic effects on children (e. g. Spitz, 1999); and pedagogy (e. g. Demers & Moyles 1982). The visual aspects of children's picture books and their relationship to the verbal semiotic has not been attached great attention to in most studies of children's literacy. However, in the past two decades, there is an increasing consensus that the ways in which these two forms of communication (the visual and verbal) work together to create meaning should be emphasised (Moebius 1986; Nodelman1988; Nikolajeva & Scott 2000). The possible relationships between visual and verbal components range from those in which images simply support or even translate what is related in the verbiage, to the more sophisticated forms of interplay and interaction.

The common concerns of the issues considered in these studies which explore the interrelation between verbal and visual components are to explore how children's picture books explicate the underlying themes and messages through the interplay of word and image.

2.3.2 Relation between word and image in children's picture books

Contemporary picture books as a genre which strongly relies on the interdependence of visual and verbal texts can be seen as an essential medium for the research on multimodality. In most of studies on children's literary (e. g. Schwarcz 1982; Nikolajeva & Scott 2001), the visual components within picture books are assumed to be secondary, and relationship between visual elements and verbal texts has been practically ignored. Because of the popular reading literature, it is easy to assume that visual aspect of picture books mainly serves to provide support in the identification of the meanings of verbal text, or to make reading more congenial to the children. However, motivated by the fact that most of space in children's picture book is overtly taken up by visual components, it is reasonable to stress that visual elements also play a crucial role in the apprenticeship for the young. Therefore, increasing attention has been paid to the children's picture book to examine the image-word relationship within it (e. g. Hunt 2001; Nodelman 1988). In the analysis of relationship between pictures and words in story, as Nodelman (1988) explicates, the different affordance of both visual and verbal modes and their cooperation in creating the text as a whole:

> Because they communicate different kinds of information, and because they work together by limiting each other's meanings, words and pictures necessarily have a combative relationship; their complementarity is a matter of opposites completing each other by virtue of their differences. As a result the relationship between pictures and texts in picture books tend to be ironic: each speaks about matters on which the other is silent.
>
> (Nodelman 1988: 221)

With the increasing attention to the word-image relationship in picture books, a good number of works explore how the two modalities of communication (the verbal and the visual text) work together to make meanings in picture books (Moebius, 1986; Nodelman, 1988; Nikolajeva & Scott, 2000; Lewis, 2006). Most of their studies agree that the possible relationship between visual and verbal text in picture books are not limited to one in which pictures simply elaborate on the words, but shift to a more complex and sophisticated form of interaction between the two modalities.

As the present research focuses on the intersemiotic complementarity between the visual and verbal texts, Royce's (1999, 2007) framework of intersemiotic complementarity is employed to examine the interaction of the two modalities for synergistically creating meaningsin children's picture books. A detailed discussion of the relationship between different semiotic resources, especially between visual and verbal semiosis, will be conducted in Section 3. 4.

2. 4 Summary

Since the book aims to examine the interplay of verbal and visual components within Chinese children's picture books, this chapter has reviewed some of relevant studies on approaches to multimodality as well as on children's picture books. It reviews the concept of multimodality and three main lines of research that explore the process of making meaning by various semiotic resources within various multimodal ensembles. Some of the major literature which examines the different studies on children's picture books is then reviewed with a particular focus on the interplay of verbal and visual components within children's picture books. In addition, the concept of "narrative" and "story family", as well as the GSP analysis to nursery tales are also introduced to facilitate the analysis of Chinese children's picture books.

These relevant studies from the perspectives of multimodality studies and picture book studies provide useful insights for the present study. On the one hand, different perspectives of multimodal analytical approaches provide theoretical framework for the analysis of cooperation between different semiotic systems within picture books. On the other hand, the studies on the concept of story and children's picture books shed lights into the reading of contemporary picture books as a special bimodal text in which visual text is not simply regarded as the repetition or supplement of the verbal text.

Chapter Three   Theoretical Foundations

3.1   Introduction

In this chapter, the SFL theory that underpins the theoretical construct of the research is introduced. Although there are some other theories applied for multimodal studies (e. g. multimodal interactional analysis, see Norris 2004 for example), systemic functional approach has proved to be the powerful and effective tool for accounting for both meanings construed by linguistic semiotic resources and non-verbal semiotic resources. In the past three decades, SFL has been widely applied to the multimodal studies and provides a robust tool for investigating multimodal texts (e. g. Kress & van Leeuwen 1996, 2006; O'Halloran 2005, 2008).

In discussing the theoretical construct of the present research, the chapter first introduces some basic tenets of SFL, including the explication of the cline of instantiation and the metafunctional diversification. Each of them is introduced and immediately followed by the correlation of the relevant studies to multimodal texts informed by this particular aspect. It then explicates some relevant studies on visual semiotic resources inspired by the metafunctional diversity (Kress & van Leeuwen 2006; Painter et al. 2013) which are discussed in detail for providing an analytical tool to analyse visual semiotics within Chinese children's picture books. This chapter concludes with an exploration of the theoretical construct of interrelations between verbal and visual semiotic systems.

3.2   Some basic tenets of SFL

The present section is mainly concerned with some basic and fundamental theoretical rationales and preliminaries of SFL. Dimensions in this theoretical rationale of SFL include the cline of instantiation and the metafunctional diversification.

3.2.1   The cline of instantiation

In the past years, the paradigmatic focus from a systemic functional perspective has been on the inter-strata relationship and most attention in SFL research has been placed on the development of two hierarchies (realisation and rank) (e. g. Halliday 1994/2000; Halliday & Matthiessen 2004; Martin 1992). There is another kind of relationship deserving our attention in the architecture of SFL theory. It is the concept of "instantiation" which theorises the relationship between the reservoir of systems to text as the generalised potential to the instance (which is enacted from the potential and manifested in text). As an important concept in systemic functional theory, the cline of instantiation is manifest as potential (the system) and instance (the text) , situated at the two ends. Different from the "realisation" accounting for a scale of abstraction, the notion of "instantiation" is mainly concerned with a scale of generalisation, aggregating the meaning potential of a culture across instances of use. Halliday (1999) holds that:

> Instantiation is a cline, modeling the shift in the standpoint of the observer: what we call the "system" is language seen from a distance, as semiotic potential, while what we call "text" is language seen from close up, as instances derived from that potential. In other words, there is only one phenomenon here, not two; langue and parole are simply different observational positions.

(Halliday 2007: 248)

As for the linguistic semiotic, meaning potential refers to what a speaker can mean on the basis of meaning repertoire, whereas instance accounts for what he/she actually means at that time. In other words, any text can be perceived as an instance of the language system which is enacted from the generalised potential. On many occasions, Halliday (eg. Halliday 1992, 1995, 2004, 2008; Halliday & Matthiessen 1999, 2009) uses the classic metaphor of climate and weather to refer to the relation between system and instance (analogising them as two perspectives on the same phenomenon):

> Climate and weather are not two different things; they are the same thing that we call weather when we are looking at it close up, and climate when we are looking at it from a distance. The weather goes on around us all the time; it is the actual instances of temperature and precipitation and air movement that you can see and hear and feel. The climate is the potential that lies behind all these things; it is the weather seen from a distance by an observer standing some way off in time.
>
> (Halliday 2008: 79)

Since the climate is the potential that lies behind the weather, generalising the trends in the daily weather which we experience, it can be inferred from the metaphor that the system accounts for the potential that lies behind all text instances. To be specific, the essential notion of system is valid only when "it is instantiated in text; each instance keeps alive the potential, on the one hand reinforcing it and on the other hand challenging and changing it" (Halliday & Matthiessen 2009: 80). From SFL perspective, instantiation can be intersected with stratification, and such intersection is illustrated by Halliday's (2007) instantiation/ stratification matrix in Table 3 − 1.

Table 3 − 1   Instantiation/stratification matrix (Halliday 2007: 254)

STRATI-FICATION \ INSTANTIATION	System	sub−system / instance type	instance
context	culture	institution / situation type	situations
semantics	semantic system	register / text type	[text as] meanings
lexical−grammar	grammatical system	register / text type	[text as] wordings

According to Halliday, language and cultural systems (generalising long term patterns) are situated at one end of the cline of instantiation, and texts actualised in particular context are situated at the other, specifying actual instances of language uses. In between the two ends of the instantiation cline, Halliday places the notions of register/text type for language and institution/situation type for context. The instantiation/stratification matrix is of great value in the architecture of language from SFL perspective since "the intersection of the cline of instantiation with the hierarchy of stratification opens up new possibilities of modeling language in context" (Matthiessen 2007: 505 – 561).

In order to clearly illustrate the cline of instantiation, Martin (e. g. Martin & White 2005; Martin 2008) presents an outline of the instantiation hierarchy (Figure 3 – 1), moving from the system to its generic and registerial sub-potentials, adding the notion of reading:

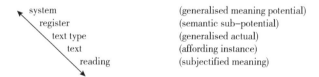

Figure 3 – 1   Cline of instantiation (Martin & White 2005: 25)

As illustrated in the interpretation of the instantiation cline above, the basic idea of this scale, according to Martin (2008), is that "the meaning potential of the culture, as consolidated along the hierarchy of realisation, is progressively narrowed until we arrive at the reading of particular text." The reason for adding the notion of "reading" is that "texts themselves have more than enough meaning potential to be read in different ways, depending on the social subjectivity of readers (Martin & White 2005: 25). Along this instantiation cline, we may conceive of language as a generalised system at one end of the cline, and identify the actual reading at the other end (e. g. the act of reader/listener interpretation).

➢ **Coupling**

In discovering the relatively under-developed research area of instantiation, Martin (2008) proposes two main factors of the analysis on which we should focus: coupling and commitment. The notion of coupling refers to the ways in which meanings combine as any number of (e. g. as pairs, triplets, quadruplets) coordinated choices from system networks. Some pioneering studies on this orientation are proposed by Nesbitt and Plum (1988) in their study of clause complexing, with their particular interests in the interaction of taxis (parataxis and hypotaxis) and logico-semantic relations (projection and expansion). With regard to this orientation to instantiation, Martin (2008) confirms that the study of coupling can be pursued from the perspective of the discourse semantics of APPRAISAL (Martin & White 2005). From a systemic perspective, the options from the simultaneous sub-systems within the APPRAISAL systems (e. g. ATTITUDE, ENGAGEMENT and GRADUATION) can be coupled, and "the logic of system networks allow us to state the relevant coupling at any point in delicacy" (Martin 2008). For instance, the options from two sub-systems ATTITUDE and FORCE are being combined, to be more specific, the options from [raise] couple with [social esteem] in Figure 3 – 2.

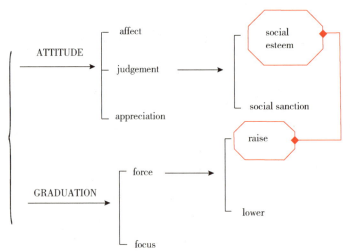

Figure 3 – 2   Coupling across simultaneous APPRAISAL systems
(Reproduced from Martin 2008)

As a notion that addresses issues in the repeated co-patterning from two or more systems/sub-systems, coupling within a text of realisations (either a mono-modal text or across two or more different semiotic modalities) can be within or across metafunctions. Intramodally, we can find in Figure 3 – 2 that a coupling of linguistic choices from two interpersonal systems — Graduation: Force (e. g. intensifying) and Attitude: Judgement (e. g. social esteem/positive), evidenced by a great number of group structures such as *very lucky*, *most powerful*, *highly appreciated*, *extremely brave*, *such a clever* and so on. In the same vein, we may find a consistent coupling across metafunctions, and an example of such kind would be a coupling of semiotic choices of interpersonal meaning (e. g. interpersonal affect) with ideational meaning (e. g. a particular depicted character). With respect to a bimodal text, a hypothetical example of a coupling might be a co-patterning of choices of interpersonal meaning in the visual such as focalisation (e. g. whether the readers make the eye contact with the character or not) with the complementary choices of first or third person narrative (e. g. appreciative stance the readers are invited to take) in the verbal text. Examples of interpersonal coupling within Chinese children's picture book will be provided in Chapter 4.

➢ **Commitment**

Another orientation to the study of instantiation is commitment which refers to "the amount of meaning potential activated or manifested in a particular process of instantiation" (Martin 2008). In other words, commitment has to do with the degree to which meanings in optional systems are taken up and the degree of delicacy selected (Martin 2008). With a particular focus on the ideational meanings, Hood (2008) in her recent work on summary text, reveals that a number of relations (including de/classification, de/composition, de/specification, metaphor/congruence and so on) would offer space for committing different degrees of meaning potential; and exemplifies how meaning is implicated and committed in the process of re-instantiation of original texts to notes and to summary text. By adopting and analysing three texts from Alexander McCall Smith's *The No. 1 Ladies Detective Agency* series, Martin (2008) aims to explore the semantic weight and relative commitment in the different versions of the story. With reference to interpersonal semantics, especially the

APPRAISAL system, the notion of commitment can be employed to re-interpret the various degrees of explicitness in encoding attitudinal meanings (e. g. the cline from "inscription" to "flagging" and "affording") (Martin & White 2005). According to Martin (2008), in terms of commitment, overt inscription is more attitudinally committed than covert flagging, which in turn is more committed than affording.

In China, Chang (2011) focuses on commitment in parallel texts, aiming to explore commitment as manifested in the novel *Pride and Prejudice* and its adapted versions. The three texts that are adopted for analysis include (a) the novel *Pride and Prejudice* by Jane Austen in the original, (b) its simplified version by Clare West which is reproduced as a bilingual edition implemented by Chinese translation and (c) the original version in English with Chinese introduction at the beginning of each chapter. Having renamed the parallel texts in terms of Text 1, Text 2 and Text 3, he further compares how meanings in the systems are taken up and the degree of delicacy is selected within systems. And he points out that the original novel is differently instantiated in the processes of adaptation and the different choices made by the authors and translators are constrained by the different purposes that they set out to achieve.

Martin (2008) further adds that this is perhaps the easiest to illustrate in multimodal texts, where the visual images and the verbal text may co-instantiate meaning, but with different degrees of commitment. For instance, the left image of Illustration 3 – 1 adopted from *Lord Rabbit* (Xiong 2012) includes an image of a Lord Rabbit (a toy for children to celebrate the mid-Autumn Festival) and an osmanthus tree; the verbal text in the below mentions both of them, so the instance is equally committed ideationally (我是住在月亮上的兔儿爷，那儿有一颗美丽的桂花树。I am the Lord Rabbit living on the Moon, and there is a beautiful osmanthus tree.). Similarly, the right image in Illustration 3 – 1 is drawn from *Paper Horse* (Xiong 2008) including a picture of the snow and a coach (filled with a number of passengers who are willing to return home to spend Spring Festival). The verbal text just mentions the heavy snow, whereas the coach is not verbalised and thus is less committed ideationally (那一年，下了很大的雪。It snowed heavily that year.). More detailed discussions on different commitment of ideational meaning across the two modalities (verbal and visual semiotics) within Chinese children's picture books are provided in Chapter 5.

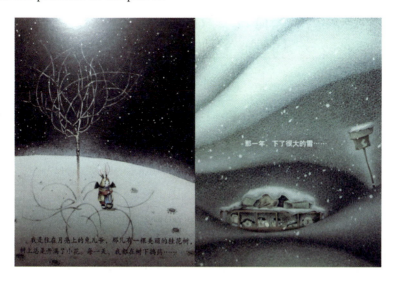

Illustration 3 – 1　from *Lord Rabbit*(2012) and from *Paper Horse*(2008)

> ### System networks

Perceived as a powerful principle of organisation, the concept of delicacy "orders systems on a cline from the most general systems of options to the most specific ones…[and] it orders realisations of these options according to their systemic environment" (Halliday & Matthiessen 2009: 75). Delicacy within SFL is primarily represented by systems as well as system networks. As a general kind of linguistic description, systems and system networks refer to "a kind of cartography, a mapping of the 'meaning potential' in the dynamic, open-ended spiral of community and personal experience" (Butt 2001: 1819). Following a SFL point of view, a semiotic system can be viewed as a resource of meaning which is organised into a range of choices from different systems within three metafunctions. To put it more simply, a system is concerned with a variety of meaning choices through which expressive realisations can be specified. A system consists of (ⅰ) a statement of an option between two or more terms, distinguished by features and (ⅱ) an entry condition, which specifies when the choice is available (Halliday & Matthiessen 2009: 97). Table 3 – 2 represents some major types of system networks on which linguistic descriptions are built.

Table 3 – 2　　　　　**Major types of system network**

(Halliday & Matthiessen 2009: 98)

a→ [x y	system: if 'a', then 'x' or 'y' —abbreviated as 'a: x/y'
a] → [x b] y	disjunction in entry condition: if 'a/b', then 'x/y'
a – }→ [x b – y	conjunction in entry condition: if 'a' and 'b' (abbreviated as 'a & b'), then 'x/y'

a { → [x
        y
    → [m
        n
	simutaneity:
	if 'a', then simultaneously 'x/y' and 'm/n'

a→ [x→ [m
           n
      y
	delicacy ordering:
	if 'a', then 'x/y'; if 'x', then 'm/n'

a { → [x * –>
        y
    → [m –> *
        n
	conditional marking:
	if 'x', then also 'm'

a ⊢ → [x
          y
     → [ll
          'go on'
	recursive system(logical):
	if 'a', then 'x/y' and simultaneously option of entering and selecting from the same system again

Each choice in a system may be represented by some certain expressions or realisations in form. As exemplified in Figure 3 – 3, a system network is developed for mapping out some basic options of the interpersonal meanings within visual semiotic system (Painter et al. 2013: 30). These options constitute the system of visual FOCALISATION. Looking from the left to the right, the system network has more than one meaning system in play. The curly brace is adopted in this case to explicate that choices from the two systems are taking place simultaneously. In the upper meaning system, there are choices of [con-tact] against [observe] and, if [contact], there is a subsystem choice of [direct] and [invited]. The term in square brackets refers to an option or fea-ture within a system (Painter et al. 2013: 8). And the use of downward slop-ing arrow indicates the realisaton of the feature or option within the system. Thus in this case, the option of [contact] is realised by the presence of gaze contact between the represented participants and the reader/viewer. On the contrary, the option of [observe] is realised by the absence of such gaze con-tact between them. It is obvious that the system network would develop more delicacy from the left to the right. If the choice of [mediated] is made, there is a subsystem choice of [inscribed] against [inferred], and the subsystem of [inscribed] has two more delicate choices which are differentiated as [along with character] and [as character].

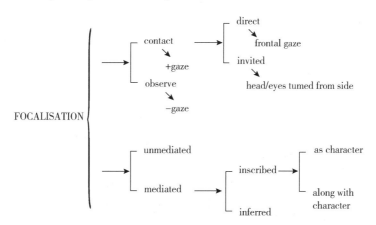

Figure 3 – 3   The system network for FOCALISATION
(Painter et al. 2013: 30).

System networks contribute to providing a powerful descriptive tool for language and other non-verbal semiotic resources. On the one hand, the system networks developed for a particular modality of communication (in-cluding both verbal and non-verbal modality) constitute that semiotic as system. On the other hand, the system networks applied in multimodal texts would help track the meaningful choices which are made in the process of making meaning by different semiotic systems within the whole text. With regard to the analysis of Chinese picture books in the present research, system networks are employed as the primary descriptive form of representing visual features of images within each of the three metafunctions (see Section 3.2.2).

3.2.2 Metafunctional diversification

Drawing upon Firth's ideas about treating meaning of language as function in context, Halliday proposes the functional view of language to delve into "the way language is learnt and, through that, into the internal organization of language, why language is as it is" (Halliday 1973/2003: 315). In SFL, there are two different but ultimately related sense of "function", including both extrinsic functionality (extrinsic uses of language) and intrinsic functionality (internal organisation of language) (see Figure 3 − 4). As an essential-property of language as a whole, the term "function" in the field of systemic functional studies is "used in the sense of intrinsic functionality", which is primarily concerned with "principle of organization manifested throughout the system" (Matthiessen et al. 2010: 101). This general property of human language is distinct in the sense that language has evolved within its own eco-social environment. Within the framework of SFL, there are three kinds of functions which are microfunction, macrofunction, and metafunction. Each of them is correspondently related with three developmental phases in the learning process of language.

During a man's process of language development, his language has to experience a constant change from the protolanguage to adult language through three developmental phases. Phase I of such process is organised into a narrow range of microfunctions so that infants can use their language protofunctionally to perform some basic functions such as regulatory, instrumental, interactional, heuristic functions which are closely linked to context of language use. At this stage, functions of language in fact equal toits extrinsic use. Nevertheless, these microfunctions performed by infants are further generalised into two

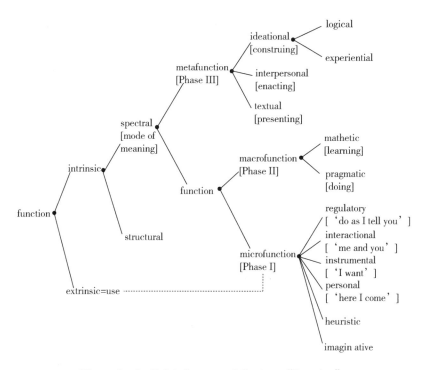

Figure 3 – 4   Related senses of the term "function";
different kinds of "function" (Matthiessen *et al.* 2010: 103)

types of macrofunctions when Phase I moves into Phase II: *mathetic macro-function (one function for learning) , and mathetic macrofunction* (the one for doing). These two macrofunctions are mutually exclusive that represent alternative modes of meaning within the system and that are never instantiated together. As Phase II turns into Phase III (post-infancy adult language) , these macrofunctions are gradually developed into three abstract and complementary modes of meaning: ideational, interpersonal and textual. The three metafunctions" allow the matching of particular types of functions/meanings with particular types of wordings to an extent that other categorizations generally do not" (Thompson 1996/2000: 28). In other words, these strands of meaning can be thus instantiated together and simultaneously realised via different modes of expression.

3.2.2.1   The Ideational Metafunction

As a core concept in SFL, the metafunction embodies "different types of structures" and meanwhile represent "different kinds of meanings" (Halliday 1985a: 8). Among them, the ideational metafunction refers to the linguistic resources used for constructing and organising experiences of the world (including the internal world and the material world) into "particulate forms of representation" (Halliday 1985a: 8). Taking Whorf's ideas upon how grammar models reality, Halliday (e. g. Halliday 1994/2000; Halliday & Matthiessen 2008) explicates the ideational metafunction as the representation and construction of human experience through the use of language because there is "no facet of human experience which cannot be transformed into meaning" and language can be perceived as "a theory of human experience, and certain of resources of the lexicogrammar of every language are dedicated to that function" (Halliday & Matthiessen 2008: 29). The ideational metafunction is primarily realised through the TRANSITIVITY system which is concerned with the lexico-grammatical resources for representing the worldly experience and consists of a range of processes. To use functional labels, the transitivity system can be categorised into a manageable set of process types that can be further divided into six distinct types of process. Each type of process is responsible for construing a particular domain of experience with its own analytical schema (see Figure 3–5).

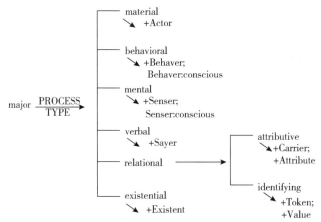

Figure 3–5 Transitivity represented as system network
(Halliday & Matthiessen 2008: 173)

3.2.2.2 The Interpersonal Metafunction

Apart from the ideational metafunction representing worldly experience, language also can be used to enact personal and social relationships with other people around us. This metafunction is defined as interpersonal metafunction which is related with the use of language to exchange information with others, to express our own personal attitudes/emotions, to influence others' opinions/behaviours, and to maintain personal/social relationship with others. Within SFL, the interpersonal meanings are prosodically adopted to enact social relationsand clauses in this sense are viewed as exchanges. The interpersonal metafunction "represents the speaker's meaning potential as an intruder", and serves as the "participatory function of language" (Halliday 1978/2001: 112). It is related to the construction of social relationships between one and another. There are two basic roles in an exchange: giving and demanding. And the commodities that are exchanged in our daily conversations can befurther classified into two categories: information and goods & services. Therefore, interpersonal semantic system within SFL framework initiated with the move as its starting point may serve as "the resource for giving or demanding information or goods & services in an exchange" (Matthiessen *et al.* 2010: 202) (details are illustrated in Figure 3 – 6).

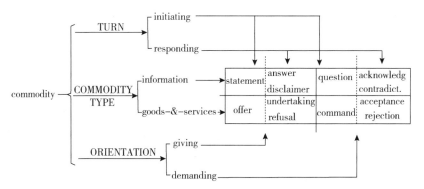

Figure 3 – 6   The semantic systems of SPEECH FUNCTION
(Matthiessen et al. 2010: 41)

The system of speech function is composed of three simultaneous systems: TURN (MOVE): initiating/responding; ORIENTATION (INITIATING ROLE): giving/demanding; and COMMODITY: information/goods &

services. In "initiating" moves, the options within the COMMODITY system and ORIENTATION system intersect to define the fundamental speech functions of statement, question, offer and command. In "responding" moves, all of these options have their own set of feedbacks which are polarised into either "expected" or "discretionary" (See for example Matthiessen *et al.* 2010: 203). Furthermore, the system of speech function operates in the context of the differentiated tenor variables. To be more specific, there is a wide range of more delicate speech functions in conversations which enable speakers to employ various lexicogrammatical resources to negotiate and construe the tenor of the relationship between them and their addressees, such as power and familiarity.

In order to gain a better understanding on the language of evaluation, a group of systemic functional linguists in Sydney have proposed and developed the Appraisal theory (Martin 2003; Martin & White 2005, Martin & Rose 2007) which provides a useful tool for analysing evaluation in different types of discourse. The pioneer work for developing Appraisal framework can be traced back to the project of "Write it Right". The project was undertaken by the Sydney group led by J. R. Martin, with its initial concern on the language of evaluation in the genre of narration (Martin & Plum 1997). And the function linguists in the project attempt to "what contexts, by what linguistic means, and to what rhetorical ends writers pass value judgements, attribute their propositions to outside source or modalise their utterance" (White 1998: 3). In the innovative research, Martin (1992: 336) describes and explains a range of gradable systems in which meanings "enter into oppositions concerned with the evaluation of experience". The past four decades have witnessed a fast growth in the theoretical construct of the Appraisal theory at the discourse semantic level (Martin & White 2005; Martin & Rose 2007).

In recent years, the APPRAISAL framework as an effective tool has been applied to a wide range of different genres of discourse. For example, it has been used to the analysis of media texts (e. g. White 1997), in the discussion of casual conversation (e. g. Eggins & Slade 1997), in the exploration of the ontogenetic development of children (Painter 2003). It also has been extended to the analysis of the genre of writing, with a focus on children's writing in secondary school (e. g. Rothery & Stenglin 1997) , and on the evaluation of language in academic writing (e. g. Hood 2008).

In systemic functional framework, APPRAISAL theory is concerned with the evaluative resources in diverse types of discourse, aiming to explore "the kinds of attitudes that are negotiated in a text, the strength of the feelings involved and the ways in which values are sourced and readers aligned" (Martin & Rose 2007: 25). In other words, the theory is applied to examine the linguistic resources in a number of texts which express (both explicitly and implicitly) a text/speaker/writer's social stance, attitudes and feelings. Regarded as a discourse semantic resource which construes interpersonal meanings, APPRAISAL is constituted by some interacting domains of realisations, namely, ATTITUDE, ENGAGEMENT, and GRADUATION. In discussing the three important domains of evaluation, Martin and White point out that

> Attitude is concerned with our feelings, including emotional reactions, judgments of behaviour and evaluation of things. Engagement deals with sourcing attitudes and the play of voices around opinions in discourse. Graduation attends to grading phenomena whereby feelings are amplified and categories blurred.
>
> Martin & White (2005: 35)

The system of ATTITUDE accounts for "evaluating things, people's character and their feelings" (Martin & Rose 2007: 26). It can be further classified into three subsystems in terms of Affect (related to peoples' feelings), Judgement (in respect to people's character) as well as Appreciation (related to the value of things). A detailed discussion on the attitudinal meanings encoded in children's picture books will be conducted in Section 4. 3.

Another domain of the evaluation resources is Engagement which deals with the meanings "in various ways construe for the text a heteroglossic backdrop of prior utterances, alternative viewpoints and anticipated responses" (Martin & White 2005: 97). To put it simply, the system of Engagement is related to a set of sources of attitudes, comments and commitments. It can be also further subdivided into two subsystems in terms of Heteroglossic engagement and Monoglossic engagement.

As for the third important system of evaluative meanings, Graduation deals with the degree of evaluation evoked by both the system of ATTITUDE andENGAGEMENT. Martin and White (2005: 137) contend that, "graduation operates across two axes of scalability: grading according to intensity or amount, and grading according to prototypical and preciseness by which category boundaries are drawn". In technical terms, the former is defined as Force accounting for the strength or weakness of evaluative resources; while the latter is in terms of Focus, dealing with the non-gradable evaluative resources. In the context of picture books, the Appraisal framework provides a powerful tool for both linguistic and visual analysis of attitudinal meanings. And the present research would focus on ATTITUDE and GRADUATION in Chinese picture books (see Chapter 4).

3.2.2.3 The textual metafunctions

In comparison to the ideational and interpersonal metafunctions, the textual metafunction enables ideational and interpersonal meanings to be organised as a meaningful whole and thus creates "periodic, wave-like patterns of discourse" (Halliday 1985a: 8). According to Halliday (1994/2000: 334), the following features make up the textual component in the grammar of English:

(A) structural

    (1) thematic structure: Theme and Rheme

    (2)information structure and focus: Given and New

(B) cohesive

    (1) reference.

    (2) ellipsis and substitution

    (3) conjunction

    (4) lexical cohesion

The textual metafunction is the enabling metafunction that provides the resources for presenting ideational and interpersonal meanings as a flow of information in a particular text, and gives texture to a piece of discourse. Hence clauses in this sense can be perceived as messages. From the perspective of structural texture, Theme usually refers to the starting point of a clause which "locates and orients the clause within its context", whereas the remainder of that clause consists of the Rheme (Halliday & Matthiessen 2004: 64). There is a direct semantic relationship between thematic structure (Theme + Rheme) and information structure(Given + New). Although they are closely related, Theme + Rhemeand Given + New should not be seen as the same thing. The Theme is what I (the speaker) determine to take as the point of departure and thus the Theme + Rheme structure is governed by the clause order. Whereas the Given is what you (as the listener) "already know about or have accessible to you" (Halliday 1994/2000: 299). Compared with the Theme + Rheme representing speaker-oriented structure, Given + New is listener-oriented structure.

Both theme and information are realised as structural configurations of textual functions, though they are different in some domains. Theme is a system of clauses that is realised by the sequence in which the elements within that clause are placed. Information is not equal to Theme, and it is not a system of clauses, but has its own realisation in the form of tonic prominence. Although with differences between them, Theme and Information "operate at the level of the clause and are parallel and interrelated systems", and therefore constitute the internal resources for texturing the clause as a message (Chang 2004: 115). Besides the internal relationship, it is necessary to take into account the external relationship between one clause or clause complex and another. Cohesion as non-structural resources for discourse "occurs where the INTERPRETATION of some element in the discourse is dependent on that of another. The one PRESUPPOSES the other, in the sense that it cannot be effectively decoded except by recourse to it" (Halliday & Hasan 1976: 4). Cohesion in English, according to Halliday and Hasan (1976), can be categorised into two major types: grammatical cohesion, including reference, ellipsis, conjunction, and lexical organisation; and lexical cohesion including repetition, synonymy/antonymy, hyponymy/meronymy and collocation.

3.3 Metafunctional framework for analysing visual semiotic resources

3.3.1 The framework of visual grammar

In the previous sections, the social semiotic essence of SFL has been introduced with a particular focus on metafuntional perspective on language. However, the study of semiotics can not be limited to the examination of linguistic semiotic resources only. Recent developments in multimodal discourse analysis have applied the concept of metafunction to other semiotic systems(such as images, actions, mathematical symbols, etc.). In examining the grammar of visual semiotic, Kress and van Leeuwen (1996, 2006) propose a metafunctional framework to interpret visual meaning in multimodal discourse which is regarded as a pioneer work in the field of multimodal discourse analysis.

3.3.1.1 Representational meaning in visual grammar

When considering representational structures in the visual transitivity system, Kressand van Leeuwen (1996, 2006) categorise two major types of processes: narrative processes and conceptual processes. Narrative processes "serve to present unfolding actions and events, processes of change, transitory spatial arrangements" (Kress & van Leeuwen 2006: 59). In general, participants in the narrative processes are connected by means of vectors representing the direction of action (one participant doing something to another). Depending on the vectors and depicted participants (or depicted actions, events etc.) involved in an image, they further distinguish four specific processes with respect to narrative patterns: action, reaction, speech, mental, and conversion processes.

Visual representations discussed under the heading of "conceptual" are mainly concerned with the images that do not contain vectors. Unlike the narrative processes, the conceptual processes do not connect participants by vectors of motion, but present entities "in terms of their generalised and more or less stable and timeless essence" (Kress & van Leeuwen 2006: 59). Participants depicted in conceptual images are represented in terms of their class, structure and meaning (Kress & van Leeuwen 2006: 79). Unlike narrative processes focusing on dynamic "doing", conceptual processes have the sense of static "being" or "meaning" which are characterised by constancy. Within the conceptual processes, Kress and van Leeuwen distinguish three kinds of sub-categories: "classificational", "analytical" and "symbolical" processes.

3.3.1.2   Interactive meanings in visual grammar

Despite the resources for representing participants and depicted world, there are also resources for establishing and maintaining the interaction between the reader and represented participants within the visual composition. Kressand van Leeuwen (1996, 2006) suggest that the interactive meaning should focus both on the interrelations among represented participants in visual compositions, and on the interaction between the reader and depicted participant. In their framework of visual grammar, Kress and van Leeuwen (2006) explicitly distinguish three types of interpersonal systems in examining the interactive meanings that are realised in a visual composition: *contact*, *social distance*, *and attitude*. Each of them are made up of options that specify various subtle relations between the reader and the depicted participants such as the visual system of *contact* consisting of "demand" and "offer" subsystem; and the visual system of *attitude* categorised into "subjective attitude" (to express socially determined attitudes) and "objective attitude" (see details in Figure 3 −7).

In the visual system of *contact* illustrated in Figure 3 −7, a major distinction is made between two types of images: those in which the represented participants express a straight look at and establish a kind of gaze contact with the reader; and those in which there is no such gaze contact between the represented participants and the reader. *Social distance* as the second dimension of visual interaction refers to the distance (e. g. Is that close to or far away from) between the readers and the represented participants. Such distance construed between the readers and the represented participants in turn are realised through the "size of frame" in the field of photographic technology. As the third

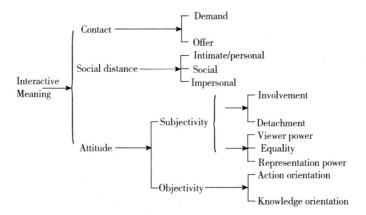

Figure 3 – 7　Interactive meaning in images
(Kress & van Leeuwen 2006: 149)

factor of the visual interaction, *attitude* accounts for the selections made from
the dimension of perspective which aims to express a certain point of view.
Kress and van Leeuwen (1996, 2006) distinguish subjective features of images
and further classify them into horizontal angles and vertical angles: the former
is concerned with the symbolic relations of detachment and involvement; while
the latter with different power relations such as superiority or inferiority.

3.3.1.3　Compositional meaning in visual grammar

Similar to the textual meaning of language, compositional meaning is concerned with "the way in which the representational and interactive elements are
made to relate to each other, the way they are integrated into a meaningful
whole" (Kress & van Leeuwen 2006: 176). Kress and van Leeuwen distinguish
three different systems in relation to the compositional meaning, namely, *infor-*
mation value, *framing* and *salience*. The placement of elements within a visual
composition evidently represents some kinds of specific information value. In
this sense, different zones within a visual composition are endowed with various
information values. The variables such as top/down, centre/margin and left/
right placements may reflect some differences in meaning potential.

Salience as the second factor in composition is mainly concerned with how
some visual elements can be highlighted, or given more eye-catching status

within an image. *Salience* is identified and affected by a number off actors such as the relative size of visual elements, their placement in the foreground/background, the differences in colour and sharpness, tonal contrast, and the use of colour contrast (Kress & van Leeuwen 2006: 202).

The third dimension in composition is termed as *framing* which refers to "the presence or absence of framing devices (realised by elements which create dividing lines, or by actual frame lines) disconnects or connects elements of an image, signifying that they belong to or do not belong together in some sense" (Kress & van Leeuwen 2006: 177). In other words, the framing deals with the connection or disconnection of visual elements. On the one hand, disconnection of elements is primarily realised through a set of framing devices, such as framing lines, pictorial framing devices, empty space between elements, and discontinuity of colour. On the other hand, connection can be created through a wide range of ways, for instance, it can be highlighted by the absence of framing devices, the similarities of colour, and the vectors of depicted elements within an image, etc.

3.3.2 Visual narrative framework

In order to comprehensively explore the meaning making of visual semiotic in picture books, Painter et al. (2013) propose the visual narrative framework which draws upon and develops Kress and van Leeuwen's (1996, 2006) visual grammar. Based on SFL and its metafunctional framework, Painter et al. (2013) examine picture book narratives by extending the social semiotic account to the visual semiotic resources, in particular, to the visual narratives. In comparison to Kress and van Leeuwen's visual grammar, Painter et al.'s visual narrative framework is more suitable for the present research since it involves developing visual grammar in relation to the data of children's picture books. And it develops the visual grammar in providing a systematic framework to enable the analysts to explore some narrative relations across pages such as inter-events relation and inter-circumstantiation in successive images. They provide an applicable descriptive framework for the visual analysis of picture books. The brief introduction of key systems within each metafunction (including options and sub-categorisations) are outlined, aiming to provide applicable descriptive tool for the analysis of visual semiotic in relation to the data in Chapters 4 to 6.

3.2.3.1 Ideational meaning in visual narrative

In exploring the ideational representation in visual narratives, Painter et al. (2013) have proposed an integrated framework on the basis of the studies on experiential meaning in SFL (e. g. Halliday 1994/2000; Halliday & Matthiessen 2004) and Kress and van Leeuwen's (1996, 2006) analysis of representational meaning. According to them, the framework for analysing visual ideational representation is composed of three categories of meaning: participants, processesand circumstances with a particular emphasis on the representational meanings in a narrative sequence.

The first dimension of the representational meaning in visual images is the participant depicted in the visuals which is further considered in two dimensions: CHARACTER MANIFESTATION and CHARACTER APPEARANCE. The former focuses on the identification and construction of the depicted character in visual images. The latter has mainly to do with the reappearance of a represented participant as the story unfolds. The options of the representational meanings of participants are shown in Figure 3 – 8.

As for the MANIFESTATION features, the [complete] option refers to the visual depiction of character including face or head. Unlike the depiction of a complete character, the [metonymic] option deals with the depiction of part of body, excluding the head of the character. With regard to the APPEARANCE features, the option of [appear] is concerned with the depiction of the character as the first appearance in the story. This option is often used in the introductory images of picture books as a brief introduction of the main protagonist, depending on the metafictive context. However, what often happens in a picture book narrative is the reappearance of some certain depicted participant alongside the narrative sequences. The options of [reappearance] are further subdivided into two types: [unchanged] reappearance and [varied] reap-

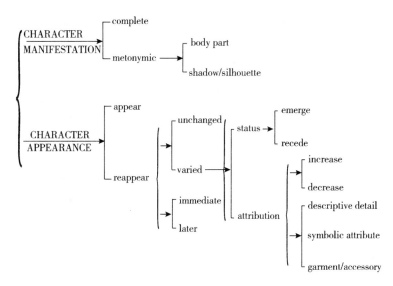

Figure 3 – 8   CHARACTER MANIFESTATION and
APPEARANCE options (Painter et al. 2013: 64)

pearance. When the character is depicted in a particular image as the same in both the participant status and appearance as that of the previous depiction, the image takes the option of [reappearance: unchanged]. However, the character reappears in some given context may change in status or attribution. On the one hand, if the character moves from the background of the image towards the relatively front of the setting (compared with the previous portrayal), it represents a choice of [varied: status: emerge]. On the contrary, a choice of [status: recede] means that the depicted character moves into the background setting of the image when compared to the previous depiction of the character. On the other hand, the choices of [varied: attribution] are realised by the increase or decrease of the depicted character in clothes/accessories, descriptive detail or symbolic attribute with respect to the previous character depiction.

Processes represented in the visual images play another vital part in the construction of visual representational meanings. Different from Kress and van Leeuwen's (2006) framework for analysing visual processes, Painter et al. (2013) shift their emphases to the depicted actions and the relations between actions in the context of a visual narrative. As for them, not only the action represented in a single visual image deserves attention, but also the visual features related to the actions in successive images call for consideration. They further distinguish the notion of sequence. Martin (1992) draws on Barthes' work to elucidate the concept of "activity sequence":

> Barthes's sequence, which is equivalent to the notion of activity sequence used here is defined as follows: "A sequence is a logical succession of nuclei bound together by a relation of solidarity (in the Hjelmslevain sense of double implication: two terms presuppose one another): the sequence opens when one of its term has no solidary antecedent and closes when another of its items has no consequent.
>
> Martin (1992: 537 –538)

Drawing on Halliday's (e. g. Halliday 1994/2000) ideas on the logico-semantic relations between clauses in verbal text, Painter et al. (2013) bring forth the network of INTER-EVENT to explore the relations between different actions depicted in a visual narrative. The visual options of the system are briefly distinguished into two types: [unfolding] options and [projection] options (see Figure 3 –9).

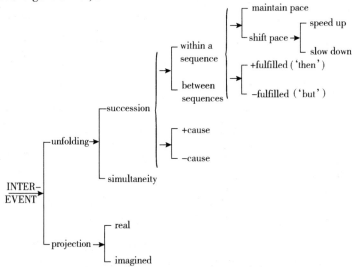

Figure 3 –9　Options for INTER-EVENT relations
(Painter et al. 2013: 71)

The option of [unfolding] is seen as the main possibility for relating two actions in a narrative sequence, which can be classified into two major types: options of [succession] and [simultaneity]. As for [succession], actions of a same participant would be depicted in successive images. If a series of successive events are combined to form part of a single activity sequence, these events are considered to be depicted within a sequence. On the one hand, when each action within the sequence takes up similar number of images, the maintenance of pace is construed within the sequence. On the other hand, the pace shifts in the sequence when the actions are elided, or action illustrated with fewer visual images than usual (termed as "speed up"); and when a certain single action spread over more images than usual (termed as "slow down"). The option of [between sequences] means that different activity sequences are depicted in successive images. If the second image depicts an expected next action/state, it is defined as [+fulfilled] option, whereas [−fulfilled] option is realised via the unexpected next action/state depicted in the second image of the two. Considering the cause relations between different actions, a [−cause] option indicates no casual relation implied between actions in sequence; while when the second image of the two depicts action inferable as the result of the previous action, a [+ cause] option is realised. Aside from the [unfolding] options relevant to the temporal succession between the actions, there is alternative temporal relation between two images, namely, [simultaneity]. The simultaneity relation between two images indicates that both two images show actions of different represented participants. As an analogy of projection relation between clauses in verbal semiotic, the visual projection relations are categorised into [real] and [imagined] options. The former occurs when the first image of the two shows a character looking, and the second one illustrates what is (or can beinferred as) being looked at. Moreover, the latter means that the first image depicts a character who may be thinking, and the second shows what is (or can be inferred as) being thought.

The third essential parameter for visual elements in expressing ideational meaning is the depiction of circumstances. In a visual narrative, it is necessary to consider both the circumstantiation delineated in the single image and the relations of different settings between successive images. Alongside a narrative sequence, a comparison might be drawn on the consistency or change in the degree of the depicted circumstances in successive images. To this end, a network of options relevant to the realistions of INTER-CIRCUMSTANCE is summarised by Painter et al. (2013) to expound both the varying and sustaining degree of detail in the illustration of circumstantial setting related to that of the previous depiction. Figure 3 – 10 demonstrates a detailed discussion of the circumstantial realisations in successive images.

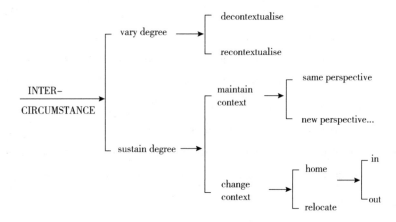

Figure 3 – 10   Options for INTER-CIRCUMSTANCE relations
(Painter et al. 2013: 80)

The principal options of INTER-CIRCUMSTANCE are generally classified into the types of [vary degree] and [sustain degree]. With regard to the options of varying circumstantial setting, degree of detail in circumstantiation differs from that of the previous depiction. An option of [vary degree: decontextualise] means that the circumstance depicted in the following page is removed or reduced from that of previous page. When the circumstantial setting increases when compared to the previous depiction, the option of [vary degree: recontextualise] is realised.

3.3.2.2 Interpersonal meaning in visual narrative

The examination of the interpersonal meaning of a bimodal text (verbal and visual texts) involves a look at the ways in which interpersonal relations are established between the reader and the presented characters and among different represented participants within picture books.

As an important dimension in realising visual interpersonal meaning, the subsystem of AMBIENCE refers to the specific choices in the use of colour which contribute to establishing an instant bonding effect on influencing and provoking emotion, attitude and feeling of the reader. Drawn upon Kress and van Leeuwen's ideas that colour can serve all metafunctions, Painter et al. place a particular focus on its interpersonal role, stressing the great significance of colour in "its emotional effect on the viewer" (Painter et al. 2013: 35). It is safe to say that a visual composition filled with divergent types of colour would bring the readers different kinds of feelings. For instance, a visual in picture book filled with dark sombre tones exerts different influence on readers' feelings from one featuring bright red colours and again from one printed in black or white only. Taking into account the reader's feedback to choices of colours, Painter et al. propose the system of AMBIENCE to refer to "a visual meaning system for creating an emotional mood or atmosphere, principally through the use of colour" (Painter et al. 2013: 36). AMBIENCE system can be further classified into three core subsystems: VIBRANCY, WARMTH, and FAMILIARITY.

As the first dimension of colour choices, the system of VIBRANCY is primarily concerned with the depth of saturation to the colours which are selected and used. The choices from the [vibrancy] network are subdivided into [vibrant] and [muted] colours. As for vibrant colours, high or full saturation may create a sense of vibrant effect or emotional vitality: it may be employed to "generate a sense of excitement and vitality"; whereas lower saturation within [muted] network generates "a gentler more restrained feeling" (Painter et al. 2013: 37).

The second subsystem of AMBIENCE is warmth referring to the depiction of hot and cool physical environments of an image. The choices within WARMTH system are categorised into two general types, that of warm colours such as red and yellow hues and cool colours such as blue and green hues. Apart from the depiction of physical environments of the image, the choices of [warmth] play a vital part in reflecting emotional shades.

The last and also the most important subsystem in creating ambience in picture books is called FAMILIARITY that is distinguished by the total amount of "colour differentiation in the image" (Painter et al. 2013: 38 – 39). According to Painter et al. , the more different colours are used and presented within the image, the greater the sense of familiarity is created. That's because the material world in which we live is filled with a large diversity of colours. By contrast, if the use of colour in an image is restricted to only one or two hues, a sense of being removed from the normal, daily and real world will be generated and the degrees of certainty will definitely be reduced.

➤ **FOCALISATION**

As a reinterpretation and elaboration of Kress and van Leeuwen's idea of "contact", FOCALISATION in Painter, Martin and Unsworth's (2013) framework refers to the opposition between "the presence and absence of gaze" which indicates whether the readers are positioned to engage with the depicted character via their eye contact, or to take an observer's point of view to look on the depicted participants (Painter et al. 2013: 19). In their distinguished visual grammar, Kress and van Leeuwen (2006) attempt to draw a distinction between two types of images: an image in which a depicted character gazes out at the reader to make an eye contact; and an image without such kind of gaze contact. The former is interpreted as a demand that the reader is required to offer some kind of participation. In contrast, the latter without such gaze is interpreted as an offer of information for the reader. The foremost opposition within the system of FOCALISATION is realised by two features: [contact] and [observe]. Picture books often adopt [observe] stance throughout the whole story to prevent the reader from positioning himself/herself into the story world and playing an observer role to learn from what's going on within the story world and what relationship is construed between the depicted participants of the story. However, there are a great number of picture books which do not maintain a consistency in adopting the [observe] stance. An option of [contact] within an image depends on the metafictive nature of children's picture books in their framing part. In addition, the choice of [contact] can be more delicately subdivided as [direct] or [invited]. The former is concerned with an image where the depicted character gaze straight out at the reader; whereas the latter is related to an image where the depicted characters' eyes or heads are turned from the side of the picture to face the reader. Despite its use in the introductory section to present the character, the [contact] option within the system of FOCALISATION is also used to heighten empathy or identification at some essential moments in the story. Within the network, the option of seeing through the eyes of a depicted character is defined as [mediated], as opposed to the visual option of [unmediated] when the reader either observes or makes contact without being positioned in the story world as a character.

➤ GRADUATION

This GRADUATION system focuses on the ways in which visual elements are presented in an image and examines the ways in which visual meanings are grading or scaling for invoking some certain evaluative effect. In linguistic resources, this is described by the system of GRADUATION (Martin & White 2005) which is concerned with linguistic resources for "upscaling" or "downscaling" evaluative meanings (e. g. both attitudinal meaning and engagement). Recent work by Economou (2009) on the studies of evaluative meaning of news photos has built corresponding systems of visual GRADUATION. Economou (2009) explicates that graduation plays a significant role in the expression of visual evaluation in "factual" news photos. Such recognition is supported by Hood's (2006) to claim that graduation serves as a fundamental-evaluative strategy in "objective" and "factual" academic writing. Though Economou's (2009) work establishes the systems of visual graduation (see Figure 3 – 11) on the basis of a quite different kind of visual data (e. g. news photos), Painter et al. (2013) adopt some of key choices identified in her proposed subsystem of Force to analyse picture book illustrations as relevant

and efficient ways of invoking/increasing the evaluative impact of visual elements. Painter et al. focus on the subsystem of "quantification" within the system of Force since quantification choices can serve as a significant part in
"ensuring an attitudinal response in the reader, often working with other interpersonal choices" (Painter et al. 2013: 45).

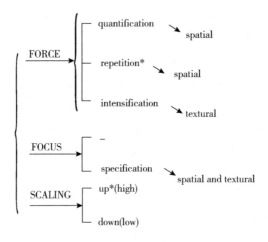

Figure 3 – 11   The graduation system for visual elements
(Economou 2009: 162)

Quantification in visual space can be seen as one of graduation options for
increasing or lowering the interpersonal force of a visual ideational item. To be
more specific, various spatial expression are determined by the different
choices of frame size and visual angles of that image which in turn affect "how
many or how much of a particular material 'item' (such as person, object or
process) is visible in a photo, as well as how much of the photo it covers and
how close it is to the viewer" (Economou 2009: 165). Three types of quantification mapped for language (e. g. Martin & White 2005) are applied to visual items in picture book illustrations by Painter et al. (2013) to analyse the
ideational or attitudinal response provoked by upscaled or downscaled force.

3.3.2.3   Textual meaning in visual narrative

In SFL framework, the textual meaning is concerned with text-forming
function of language (Halliday 1994/2000; Halliday & Matthiessen 2004).

And there are a wide range of ways in which such function may be accomplished in verbal text, such as the choices of "Theme" in a certain clause, and the patterns of unfolding word order etc. Developing Halliday's (1997) idea of "information focus" in verbal text, Painter et al. (2013) propose the concept of "focus group" to refer to the unit of information within a visual image. As a basic unit of visual narratives, the double-page spread is regarded as a kind of macro frame in their framework. In the analysis of visual narratives, they set forth three fundamental dimensions relevant to the textual meanings in visuals, namely, INTERMODAL INTEGRATION, FRAMING and FOCUS (Painter et al. 2013: 92 – 120).

As for the first dimension of textual meanings in visual images, INTERMODAL INTEGRATION deals with the arrangement of a single page (or a double-page) in which the verbal and visual elements are emplaced, which can be further categorised into integrated layout and complementary layout. The INTERMODAL INTEGRATION options for the two types of layout are shown in Figure 3 – 12.

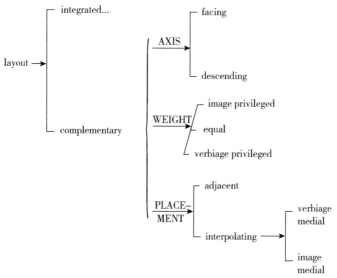

Figure 3 – 12   Options for INTERMODAL INTEGRATION
(Painter et al. 2013: 94)

The integrated layout refers to the visual composition where the verbal text is incorporated as part of visual image, serving as a visual unit. On the contrary, the complementary layout is concerned with the visual composition in which both the verbal semiotic and visual semiotic occupy its own space, each of which plays a distinct role in the synergistic meaning-making of the multisemiotic text. According to the different "weight" of each semiotic, the types of complementary layout might be sub-categoriesed as [equal] layout, [image privileged] layout, and [verbiage privileged] layout. The first option refers to the layout in which each semiotic takes up equal space. The latter two layouts are situated in a contrastive semantic relation. While the option of [verbiage privileged] is concerned with visual composition where the image takes up most of the space; the choice of [verbiage privileged] deals with the visual frame in which the verbiage occupies most of the space.

In considering the alternative aspect of intermodal integration, Painter et al. (2013) further distinguish the integrated layout into two major types: [projected] layout and [expanded] layout. The choice of [integrated: projected] refers to the visual frame where the verbal text is enclosed in a bubble of speech (thus in terms of [locution]), or thought (in terms of [idea]), both comprising a represented projector and a verbal projection. With regard to the second type of integrated frame, the [expand] choice consist of two subtypes, which are in terms of [instated] option and [reinstated] layout. The instating of two different types of semiotic is most common in visual narratives. On the one hand, it may occur when the verbal modality is completely overlaid onto the visual one so that the verbiage is viewed as part of the visual image. On the other hand, the instating often occurs when the represented participants (or actions) are decontextualised (entirely or partly) so that the verbiage and image are framed on the common background (usually white page). Different from the instating layout where the verbiage is subsumed into the image, the [reinstated] option as another subtype of expanded layout accounts for the visual layout where the verbiage appears on a distinct background strip or panel.

Unlike the layout of visual compositions (either page or double page), the options for the system of FRAMING are primarily concerned with whether/

how the image is framed, shifting the focus onto the image itself. According to Painter et al. (2013), the FRAMING options in visual narratives are categorised into [bound] image and [unbound] image, depending on whether there is a margin of visual space enclosing (partly or entirely) the image. The sub-options of FRAMING are presented in the Figure 3 − 13.

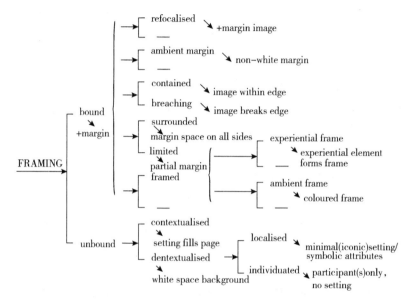

Figure 3 − 13   The realisations of FRAMING (Painter et al. 2013: 103)

As a basic type of FRAMING, the kind of unbound option has to do with the images not enclosed by a margin of space[①]. Bound images, on the contrary, refers to those visuals within a margin of space or border, which separate the depicted world from the reader's world more distinctly than the unbound images. In examining the bound images in visual narratives, there are five simultaneous subsystems meriting great attention. The first aspect relevant to bound images is the colour of the depicted margin. Though the default use of colour for depicting margin is white, a good number of picture books would employ different colours to create a background ambience. This visual feature

---

① According to Painter et al. (2013), while all the instances of complementary layouts are assigned to bound images, the instances of integrated layouts involve unbound images.

of margin in a bound image is thus related to the making of interpersonal meanings. Another potential of margin for affording interpersonal meaning is the use of [bound: refocalised] feature. This kind of bound image contains a depiction of a particular character outside the margin of the main image. As the third important feature of the bound image, the extent of margin concerns either the image entirely enclosed by the margin on all sides—[surrounded] option; or the image that is less bound with partial margin—[litmited] option. Regardless whether the margin surrounds or limits the extent, a [breaching] option occursin a bound image when a depicted character or visual element breaks the margin of the main image, signifying an emergence of confinement. The last dimension of the bound image is the frames of image within the margin or edge, which can be further demarcated by the use ofcolours or by the experiential content within the image.

Having examined the boundaries represented in the visual images such as pages, margins and frames, Painter et al. (2013) come to the analysis of the FOCUS system that accounts for what is contained within those visual boundaries. There are a range of principal choices of the FOCUS system. In the framework of visual narrative, the system of FOCUS is composed of two considerable and contrasting options: the [iterating] option and the [centrifocal] choice. In the former case, a series of same or similar elements are iterated in relatively regular lines (whether vertical, horizontal or diagonal). A choice of [centrifocal], on the contrary, refers to the visual compositions in which different constituent elements are balanced on or around a visual centre. The realisations of centrifocal focus group may take a variety of forms which can be subdivided into the features of [centred] and [polarised]. The most common form that a centred image may take is the choice of [centred: simple], with the centre of the space filled with a focalising character. The alternative option of centred image is the option of [extended] which deals with the visual composition where the visual element taking up the centre of space is ranged around several additional elements in a circular form. An extended centred image corresponds to the "centre-margin" composition in Kress and van Leeuwen's framework (1996, 2006). Another possibility of extended centred image accounts for the visual composition in which the visual element on centre is accompanied by two additional elements on each side, so as to create a "triptych" composition (Kress & van Leeuwen 2006: 197).

With regard to the second type of [centrifocal] compositions, the [polarised] option has to do with the visual layout where various represented elements are opposed or balanced alongside a vertical, horizontal, or diagonal axis. If both the two poles of a balanced composition are filled with visual elements, an option of [balanced] is realised in this visual image. A further option related to the polarised focus group is termed as [mirror], referring to the visual composition where one of the represented elements in polarity mirrors another. The mirror image is widely used when a depicted character looks at his/her reflection.

3.4   Interrelations between verbal and visual semiotic systems

The previous section reviews the basic tenets of SFL theory and the multimodal studies on visual semiotic resources informed by SFL. This section shifts its primary emphasis to the interrelations among different semiotic systems, in particular, relations between verbal and visual semiotics. It first reviews some relevant work which explores the relations and synergy among different semiotic systems. These studies include the image-text relations by Martinec and Salway (2005); the SF-MDA model by O'Halloran (e. g. 2005, 2008), the intersemiotic complementarity by Royce (e. g. 1999, 2007) and the intermodal complementarity by Painter and Martin (e. g. Painter & Martin 2011; Painter et al. 2013). Of all the various studies on interrelations among different semiotics, Royce's intersemiotic complementarity framework is adopted as the analytical model to examine the collaboration of verbal and visual semiotic systems within Chinese children's picture books. And Painter and Martin's framework of intermodal complementarity is also chosen to explore the different affordance for meaning of the verbal and visual semiotics.

3.4.1 The logico-semantic relations on image-text relations

Martinec and Salway (2005) bring forth a detailed explanation of the generalized system of text-image relations based on a variety of different genres of multisemotic discourse in which texts and images co-occur and can be viewed as being related. Their system of image-text relations derives mainly from Barthes' studies (e. g. Barthes 1977) on the relations between text and image (which are in terms of anchorage and relay) and from the SFL architecture of clause relations such as dependency (parataxis or hypotaxis), expansion and projection (e. g Halliday 1994/2000; Halliday & Matthiessen 2004). The system of text-image relations complement those proposed in the semantic model and should be useful for distinguishing various types of relations between text and image in different genres of multimodal discourse, especially in "(genuinely) new and old media" (Martinec & Salway 2005: 337).

The generalised network of the semantics of text-image relations proposed by Martinec and Salway has two primary subsystems: Status and Logico-semantic relations. Similar with the relationship between linguistic clauses in a clause complex, the system of Status is primarily concerned with whether an image can be independent, complementary, or subordinate with the text. Thus the equal and unequal status serve as two basic subsystems within the system of Status. As to the unequal relation between texts and images, one of them modifies the other and hence the modifying element is perceived to be dependent on the modified one. Equal status between texts and images can be further divided into independent relation and complementary relation. On the one hand, a text and an image are considered independent and the relation between them is viewed as equal when "they are joined on an equal footing and there are no signs of one modifying the other" (Martinec and Salway 2005: 343). On the other hand, a text and an image are considered as complementary when they are joined equally and one modifies the other in the process of making meaning.

Drawing on the ideas of Halliday's (e. g. Halliday 1994/2000; Halliday and Matthiessen 2004/2008) grammatical categories of projection and expansion, Martinec and Salway propose the Logico-semantic network in which the relation between text and image may be categorised as elaboration, extension, or enhancement, or locution or idea. Elaboration between images and texts can be further divided into two kinds of relations: exposition and exemplification. Within the system of elaboration, the exposition refers to the relation in which an image and a text are of the same level of generality, whereas the exemplification suggests that the image and the text are of different levels of generality. To be specific, exemplification as a level of delicacy within the system of elaboration serves as the entry point for two more choices: [text more general] or [image more general]. Martinec and Salway identify the circumstantial relations of time, place and reason/purpose and add that for an image to be considered enhancing a text (or vice versa), it should be in relation to its ideational content. Despite expansion subsystem within Logic-semantic system, there is another logic-semantic relation between texts and images: projection. Projection can be subdivided into two particular kinds, depending on whether an exact wording is quoted (adopting Halliday's technical term "locution") or an approximate meaning is represented (adopting Halliday's technical term "idea"). Generally speaking, projection as a logic-semantic relation seems to appear in the co-occurrence of image and text as such: in comic strips that locutions are conventionally enclosed in speech bubbles and ideas in thought bubbles; or in combinations of diagrams and text, for instance, the combinations of diagrams and explanatory text found in textbooks, scientific publications and economic magazines. Martinec and Salway's network for image-text relation is presented in Figure 3 – 14.

Although Martinec and Salway's network provides insightful analytical tool for explaining intermodal relations, there are some inconsistencies in the Status system (see Unsworth & Cleirigh 2009). Since this model places a particular focus on the stratum of lexicogramar, it is not so suitable for the present research to conduct a comprehensive account of meaning making of verbal and visual semiotic resources within Chinese children's picture books.

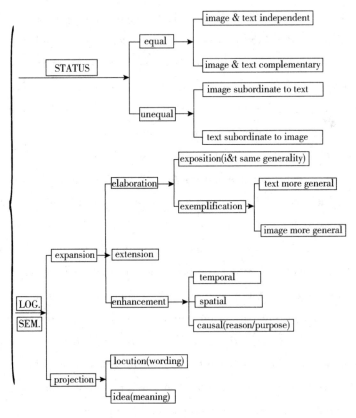

Figure 3 – 14   The network of combined Status and Logico-semantic relations
betweentext and image (Martinec & Salway 2005 : 358)

3.4.2 Intersemiosis among different semiotic systems

O'Halloran (2008 : 452) argues that the theorisation of intersemiosis is essential for the "investigation of the processes which results in a convergence of meaning (co-contextualising relations of parallelism) and/or divergence of meaning (re-contextualising relations of dissonance)" in different types of multimodal texts (see also Royce 1998 , 2002 ; Thibault 2000). As a powerful tool which provides an integrating platform for the theorisation of intersemiosis, Halliday's (e. g. Halliday 1994/2000 ; Halliday 2004) principle of meta-function serves as a basis for exploring the functions of each semiotic within a multimodal text and the ways in which the semiotic choices interact to create integrated meanings. According to O'Halloran (e. g. O'Halloran 2005 , 2008) , multimodal discourses perform four major kinds of functions: the ideational, the logical, the interpersonal, and the textual. The ideational function accounts for the representation of natural reality and subject matter; the interpersonal function construes intersubjective reality and enacts social relations, the textual function is responsible for the organisation of the discourse; and the logical function construes the logico-semantic relations between different semiotic systems within multimodal discourses.

Based on the analysis of page-based discourses, O'Halloran (2005, 2008) proposes an integrated framework for investigating intersemiosis in printed multimodal texts (see Table 3 – 3). Similar to multi-stratal linguistic texts, multimodal texts are categorised into the two strata: the CONTENT stratum and the DISPLAY stratum. As illustrated in Table 3 – 3, there are a set of substrata of Mini-Genres, Items and Components, Discourse Semantics, and Grammar within the stratum of content. As the stratum of expression, the Display stratum is further stratified into the substrata of Materiality and Typography/Graphology and Graphics. O'Halloran goes on to point out that, within and across these substratums, intersemiosis takes place between different semiotic systems (especially between language and images).

Table 3 – 3   SF-MDA framework for printed texts: language and visual imagery (O'Halloran 2008: 456)

IDEOLOGY		
GENERIC MIX		
REGISTERIAL MIX		
CONTENT Stratum	←————————————INTERSEMIOSIS————————————→ Mini-Genres, Items and Components (Linguistic, Visual and/or Other)	
	LANGUAGE	VISUAL IMAGES
	←————————————INTERSEMIOSIS————————————→ Discourse Semantics	
	Discourse	Intervisual Relations Work

Continued

CONTENT Stratum	←——————————INTERSEMIOSIS——————————→ Grammar	
	Clause complex Clause Word Group/Phrase Word	Scene Episode Figure Part
DISPLAY Stratum	←——————————INTERSEMIOSIS——————————→ Materiality	
	Typography/Graphology and Graphics	

Drawing on Royce's (1999) framework of intersemiotic complementarity, O'Halloran (2005, 2008) develops a set of intersemiotic mechanisms "where semantic expansions of co-contextualizing and re-contextualizing relations take place across linguistic, symbolic and visual elements in mathematical discourse" (O'Halloran 2008: 452). There are six kinds of mechanisms that drive the intersemiotic process among different semiotic resources: semiotic cohesion, semiotic adoption, semiotic mixing, juxtaposition and spatiality, semiotic transition, and semiotic metaphor.

➤ Semiotic Cohesion: is concerned with how system choices function to make the text cohesive. (For instance, the verbal item "年兽" coheres the depiction of the monster *Nian* in the cover of a picture book to construe a kind of semiotic cohesive relation).

➤ Semiotic Adoption: accounts for the system choices from one semiotic resource to be incorporated by the choices from another semiotic system (For instance, the same element *x* appears in both linguistic and visual images in mathematics discourse, see O'Halloran, 2007b).

➤ Semiotic Mixing: refers to items in multimodal discourses consisting of system choices from different semiotic resources (For instance, a large number of mathematic formulation are composed of the mathematical symbolic selections as well as linguistic choices).

➤ Juxtaposition and Spatiality: has mainly to do with compositional arrangement of multimodal texts to facilitate intersemiois (For instance, in some introductory pages of picture books, verbal introduction of the main protagonist is placed on the top of the character depiction, forming a cohesive relation of juxtaposition).

> Semiotic Transition: is concerned with the system choices which cause a transition (macro or micro) from one semiotic system to another (For example, in the ninth double-page spread of the picture book *The Adventure of the Postman*, where the postman as the main protagonist receives a mysterious letter. Within this spread, the linguistic expression "上面歪歪扭扭的写着: " (the scrawled writing on [the letter] is:) shifts the discourse from the verbal semioticsystem to the visual semiotic system).

> Semiotic Metaphor (SM): refers to shifts of functions taking place across different sorts of semiotic systems. (O'Halloran provides an example of anti-aids advertisement in which the photograph of a semi-naked person involves a shift to the metaphorical linguistic entity "sexual contact", see O'Halloran 2008).

Halliday's (1994/2000) social systemic functional theory and the concept of intersemiotic mechanisms between verbal and other non-verbal semiotic systems provide the foundation for O'Halloran's theoretical construct of Systemic Functional Multimodal Discourse Analysis (henceforth SF-MDA). SF-MDA takes a systematic focus to various semiotic resources as a large number of metafunctionally orientated systems (following a view of SFG as the ideational, the interpersonal and the textual). As a key aspect of metafunctionally based systems for intersemiosis, the systems choices in respect to ideational meaning are elaborated in Table 3 – 4, expressing intersemiosis across language and visual display.

Table 3 – 4　　**SF-MDA systems: the ideational metafunction**

(O'Halloran 2008: 459)

INTERSEMIOSIS ACROSS LANGUAGE AND VISUAL DISPLAY			
Metafunction	**Discourse**	**Grammar**	**Expression**
Experiental	INTERSEMIOTIC IDEATION Activity sequences and relations which span visual and linguistic elements	TRANSITIVITY RELATIONS Relational processes to set up identifying relations	JUXTAPOSITION Use of space and position to create lexical and visual relations
		LEXICALIZATION & VISUALIZATION Functional elementsare re-representedusing an alternative semiotic resource	FONT Use of font style, size and colour for experiential meaning

Continued

INTERSEMIOSIS ACROSS LANGUAGE AND VISUAL DISPLAY			
			COLOUR Use of colour for experiential meaning
Logical	INTERSEMIOTIC IMPLICA-TION SEQUENCE Cohesive and structural devices	INTERSEMIOTIC LOGICO-SEMANTIC RELATIONS & INTERDEPENDENCY Cohesive and conjunctive devices	SPATIAL POSITION Alignment of items in the text
		INTERPLAY OF SPATIALI-TY & TEMPORALITY Visual transformation of linguistic elements and vice versa	COLOUR Use of colour to direct the sequence for the construction of log-ical relations

Although SF-MDA model is indeed insightful to the exploration of in-tersemiotic relations (especially between verbal and visual semiotics) , it is somewhat problematic in analysing different types of multimodal texts. It is not so suitable for the present research in that the systems within the SF-MDA model as parameters to examine meanings making are not applicable to the vis-ual narratives to explore the inter-event relations across images.

3.4.3 The intermodal complementarity framework

Unlike some other SFL based approaches to the analysis of multisemiotic discourse, which center upon the text-forming relation between different semi-otic resources within a multisemiotic discourse, such as the analysis focusing on intersemitoic cohesion between verbal texts and images (Royce 1999, 2007) , on logico-semantic relations between words and visuals (Martinec & Salway 2008) , on information structure (Kress & van Leeuwen 1996, 2006) , or on intersemiotic mechanisms (O'Halloran 2005, 2008) , Painter and Martin (e. g. Painter 2007; Painter & Martin 2011; Painter et al. 2013) endeavour to propose an integrated framework to explore the intermodal complementarity across image and verbiage within a visual narrative, with great attention to the construction of intermodal relation by examining the various meaning realised by each semiotic within the multisemiotic text. As a cornerstone of the theoreti-

cal construct of their framework, the availability of "descriptions for both linguistic and imagic semiotic systems modelled as sets or 'systems' of meaning
choices with specifiable realisations" is key to the analysis of multisemiotic
texts (Painter & Martin 2011 : 133). For the modelling of linguistic semiotic
systems, they draw upon the insight of metafuncional diversity in SFL (Halliday 1994/2000; Halliday & Matthiessen 2004) and appraisal resources (Martin & White 2005; Martin & Rose 2007); while for building visual semiotic
systems, they develop a systematic framework for analysing visual narrative on the
basis on Kress and van Leeuwen's (1996, 2006) visual grammar (for the details of
the framework of visual narrative, see Section 3. 3). With these choices of semiotic
systems and realisations, Painter et al. conduct a comparative study on visual narratives by checking the diverse affordances for meanings of both verbal and visual
semiotics (e. g. Painter & Martin 2011; Painter et al. 2013). Based on the concept
of "instantiation" (Martin 2008, 2010), Painter and Martin (2011) put forwards
a comprehensive analytical framework of intermodal complementarity to account for
the meaning making between verbal and visual semiotics and the relation between
the totality of meaning choices ofthe multimodal discourse and the specificity of
the instantiated text (both verbal and visual texts) within it. In order to examine
the interplay of verbal text and visual text in a visual narrative, Painter at al. map
out the complementarities between meaning systems across language and image
within three metafunctions (Painter & Martin 2011, Painter et al. 2013). In Table
3 – 5, complementary interpersonal meaning systems across language and image
are illustrated. On the left column, meaning potential of images and its realisations
are mapped out and the right column explicates the meaning potential of language
and its realisations.

The complementary systems of meaning across visual and verbal modalities may serve as a schematic presentation, suggesting the general feature of
linguistic (and visual) meaning potential and the general forms expressed by
the specific realisations. In the table, the meaning systems related to image are
listed first at the left column with different domains of linguistic systems of
meaning as complementarities at the right. Since verbal and visual semiotic

systems may have their own affordances for meaning, there would not be a complete complementarity between the two semiotics in respect to each specific areas of meaning potential. For example, there is no specific verbal system obviously complementing visual pathos.

Table 3 – 5   Complementary interpersonal meaning systems across image and language (Painter et al. 2013: 137)

	Visual meaning Potential	Visual realizations	Verbal meaning potential	Verbal realizations
Affiliation	Visual focalisation	Direction of gaze of character; reader's gaze aligned or not with character's	Verbal focalisation	Sourcing of perceptions as internal or external to story
	Pathos	Drawing style: minimalist, generic, naturalistic	Characterisation	Various descriptive and attitudinal linguistic resources
	Power	Vertical angle of viewing (high, mid or low) by viewer; by depicted characters in relation to another	Power	Reciprocities of linguistic choices between characters
	Social distance/ proximity	Short size; proximity/touch of depicted participants	Social distance	Nature of naming choices, endearments etc.
	Involvement/ orientation	Horizontal angle of viewer; horizontal angle of character to other depiction; + / − mutuality of character gaze	Solidarity	Proliferation of linguistic choice (e. g. in attitude, naming, specialisedlexis); contraction of realisations
Feeling	Ambience	Colour choices in relation to vibrancy, warmth and familiarity	"Tone"	Elaboration of circumstantiation in service of "tone"
	Visual affect	Emotion depicted in facial features and bodily stance	Attitude Verbal affect	Evaluative language Emotion language
	(Judegment)	no system, but meaning may be invoked in the reader	Attitude	Evaluative language
	Graduation: force	"Exaggerated" size, angle, proportion of frame filled, etc. ; repetition of elements⋯	Graduation: force	Intensification, quantification, repetition⋯

To explore the meanings activated and represented by actual instantiated texts, another factor in respect to instantiation should be considered, that is in terms of coupling (Martin 2008, 2010). The notion of coupling is concerned with the ways in which meanings are combined througha number of coordinated choices from different system networks. For instance, we may find a choice of coupling from two interpersonal subsystems in the phrase "very happy", or "extremely sad". There is a choice from the system of FORCE coupled with a choice from ATTITUDE system, intensifying (or downscaling) the attitudes (positive or negative) expressed by the verbal text. With regard to multimodal discourse, coupling concerns "the repeated co-patterning within a text of real-isations from two or more systems" which can be realised within a metafunc-tion or across different metafunctions (Painter & Martin 2011: 144).

Although coupling in multisemotic discourse involves co-patterning of choices from two semiotic systems, it does not mean that the choices within the two semiotics have to amplify each other, making corresponding kinds of meanings to reinforce the convergence of different semiotic choices. Obviously, there are plenty of couplings between choices from two different semiotic sys-tems in children's picture books showing some kind of sharp differences. For ex-ample, a choice of third person pronoun in the verbal text may be coupled with a focalising choice of [contact] within the image. The former choice is used to create a relatively objective and neutral voice of the narrator and to avoid an en-gagement between the depicted participants and the reader, while the latter contributes to establishing some kinds of affiliation between them as well as in-viting the reader to get involved in the story world. A divergent coupling is re-alised in such a case, adding to the meaning potential which is beyond the scope of either one sole semiotic system. In terms of converging couplings in vis-ual narratives, Painter and Martin distinguish a set of intermodal complementar-ities between verbal and visual semiotic systems: "concurrence" (converging ideational coupling), "resonance" (converging interpersonal coupling), and "synchrony" (converging textual coupling) (Painter & Martin 2011).

3.4.4 The intersemiotic complementarity framework

With its primary focus on the page-based multimodal texts (e. g. economical magazine articles), Royce's framework of intersemiotic complementartity targets to the nature of the intersemiotic semantic relations between different modes (specifically between verbal and visual semiotics), elucidating the intersemiotic features within the multimodal text which enable a "verbally-visually coherent"text (Royce 1999, 2007). The concept of intersemiotic complementarity is mainly concerned with "the ability of elements, in the act of combining, to produce a total effect that is greater than the sum of individual elements or contributions" (Royce 2007: 103).

Like other researches adopting a metafunctional hypothesis to analyse visual images (e. g. Kress & van Leeuwen 1996, 2006; O'Toole 1994), the intersemiotic complementarity framework also follows a metafunctionally oriented approach which keeps the ideational and interpersonal metafunction, while substitutes the compositional for the textual metafunction. Like the stratification model for linguistic texts, the principle of stratal organisation is applied to the multimodal texts. As shown in Figure 3 – 15, the intersemiotic complementarity framework is demonstrated in realisation relations between a set of meaning systems across verbal and visual semiotics within page-based multimodal texts.

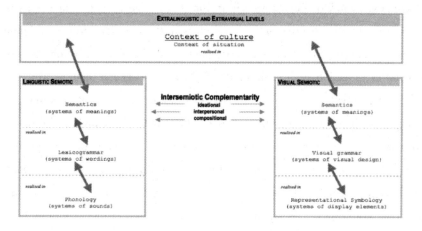

Figure 3 – 15   The framework for visual-verbal intersemioticcomplementarity in page-based multimodal texts (Royce 1999: 127)

The context of culture suited at the extralinguistic and extravisual levels can be instantiated by a context of situation which is further realised by the verbal and visual semiotics within a page-based text. In the left column within the table, the level of verbal semantics is realised by lexicogrammar level which is then realised by the expression level (phonology, the system of sounds and graphology, the system of writing). In the right column, the level of visual semantics is realised by the level of visual grammar which is further realised by the representational symbology, the systems of displayed elements. In a particular multimodal text consisting of verbal and visual semiotics, both two modes are correlated by a series of intersemiotic complementary relations in relation to ideational, interpersonal and compositional meanings.

3.4.4.1 Ideational intersemiotic complementarity

With regard to intersemiotic ideational complementarity, Royce (1999) draws upon Halliday's (1994/2000) ideas of functional categories and the TRANSITIVITY system for analysing verbal semiotic system. In SFL (e. g. Halliday 1994/2000, 2004), there are a set of fundamental categories that should be taken into consideration in respect to the ideational analysis of language: participants, processes, circumstances, and attributes. At the level of lexicogrammar in SFL, the ideational meanings are primarily realised by the units of clauses as representations, and the linguistic choices in this regard can be made through the TRANSITIVITY system. The system of TRANSITIVITY is mainly concerned with the types of process, and the participants represented in the process, the attributes of the participants, and the circumstances of such process (Halliday 1978/2001: 101).

Compared with the verbal semiotic system, Royce (1999, 2007) puts forward the concept of Visual Message Elements (hereafter VME or VMEs) to classify the visual features of elements that carry semantic properties. Visual images, like verbal text, are also representations of reality (or of experience of human beings), that can serve as the realisation of ideational meanings. Royce goes on to explicate that the VMEs are briefly categorised into the following types: Identification(the represented participants), Activity/RelationalActivity(the represented processes), Attributes(the qualities or characteristics of the participants), and Circumstances(the represented context). Based on the concept of VMEs, Bowcher (2012: 225) proposes the concept of verbal-pictorial message element (V-PME) to highlight the visual features that "bear a visual (pictorial)-verbal overlap that is intermediate to typically verbal or typically visual forms". As for the current multimodal discourse studies, the concept of VMEs is significant for the interpretation of the semantic relations between verbal elements and visual elements in a multimodal text.

In order to investigate the ideational intersemiotic meanings construed in both verbal semiotic system and visual semiotic system, Royce introduces the theory of cohesion proposed by Halliday and Hasan (1976). According to Halliday and Hasan, the general cohesive devices in language are categorised into the following types as such: repetition, hyponymy, antonymy, meronymy, synonymy and collocation. Royce then extends those cohesive devices to the analysis of the cohesion across visual semiotic system and verbal semiotic system in a multimodal text.

In Royce's framework of ideational complementarity, the intersemioticrepetition indicates a repetition of a lexical item that may represent the same meaning expressed in the VME within the visual composition. The intersemiotic synonymy occurs when the same or similar experiential meaning is expressed by the VME in the visual text and the lexical items in the verbal, and the two are used interchangeably. Antonymy refers to the opposite experiential meaning represented by a lexical item and a VME in a multimodal text. The intersemiotic hyponymy refers to the classification of the cohesive relations between a general class (in terms of Super-ordinate) and its sub-classes (in terms of the Hyponyms and Co-hyponyms). As for the intersemiotic meronymy, it accounts for the sense relations between the whole of something (termed as the superordinate) and its constituent parts (termed as the meronyms and co-meronyms). The collocation as the final type of intersemiotic cohesive relations is different from other types of semantic relations (e. g. hyponymy, meronymy), and it means that some linguistic items and visual elements have the tendency to co-occur as collocates in a multimodal text. Based on the analysis of lexical items and VMEs and the cohesive relations between them, Royce endeavours to explain how ideational intersemiotic complementarity works in different types of multimodal texts.

3.4.4.2   Interpersonal intersemiotic complementarity

The interpretation of visual interpersonal features within the framework of intersemiotic complementarity are primarily based on Kress and van Leeuwen's (1996, 2006) layout of visual grammar. In the lexciogrammatical system of language, the interpersonal meaning is mainly realised by the subsystems of Mood and Modality. In the similar vein to language, Royce (1999) adopts Kress and van Leeuwen's categorisation of Visual Mood and Visual Modality to interpret the non-verbal semiosis in the multimodal texts, especially the visual interpersonal meanings construed by the multimodal texts.

From a systemic functional perspective, the systems of Mood and Modality in language basically account for the speech function of language, and the speaker's feelings, attitudes, and comments being exchanged via the use of language. To be specific, the Mood system of language mainly deals with both the exchange of goods and services (through offer and command) and that of information (via statement and question) (Halliday 1978/2001, 1994/2000) (A detailed discussion of interpersonal meaning encoded in language has been conducted in Section 3.2.2) In language the speech roles in a communicative exchange are combined into four primary types which can be realised by a range of particular lexico-grammatical structures, for instance, commands realised by declarative clauses, statements realised by declarative and questions realised by interrogative clauses. Similar to the speech roles of language, the visual systems also perform certain interpersonal functions which engage the viewer of the image interactively as well as establishing intimacy between the viewer and the represented participants. Nevertheless, it is important to note that the system of Visual Mood is not easily analysed within visual compositions and it differs from that of language in various aspects.

First of all, the categories within the system of Visual Mood are not as clear-cut as that of the linguistic Mood system. In other words, the categories which are demarcated in images always need the support of verbal text to "make the nature of speech function clear" (Royce 1999: 149). For instance, a questioning facial expression of the depicted participant in an image often needs to be reinforced and complemented by a printed question. Compared with the goods and service exchanged in the verbal texts, what visual images offer most to the viewer is typically exchanges of information. It is motivated by the fact that the images (especially page-based images) may serve as only semiotic representations which offer some particular kinds of information rather than providing them with service. The offer of information via visual techniques goes to the heart of the nature of one pictorial genre, mathematic form. It is safe to say that the mathematical visuals simply offer information to the viewer by the display of represented participants (actually graphic lines and numbers) than establishing other relationship with them. The viewer of such kinds of images is supplied with information that could only be agreed or disagreed with. Secondly, the most essential visual feature to determine the speech role of a certain image is the presence or absence of *visual address*. As clearly demarcated into two main types of images, the kind of "command" images and "offer" images are determined via the presence and absence of gaze with the viewer (Kress & van Leeuwen 1996, 2006). For example, the depicted participant in an image gazing directly at the viewer might indicate a command from the viewer or invite him/she to enter into a particular kind of "imaginary relationship" with the represented participants. On the contrary, if there is no direct gaze between the represented participant and the viewer in an image, it is likely to provide with some kind of information to the viewer. For instance, if there is no eye contact between the represented participants within an image of picture book, then the child reader is not required to be engaged in the ways of rejecting or accepting the information offered by the author/illustrator.

Aside from the visual techniques of *visual address*, the system of Visual Mood can be examined from other perspectives such as *involvement*, *power relations*, *and social distance*. The degrees of involvement realised in the image are determined by a horizontal angle (whether the frontal or oblique angle is adopted). In their visual grammar, Kress and van Leeuwen (2006) elucidate that diverse angles utilised in a certain picture realise different degrees of involvement:

> The horizontal angle encodes whether the image-producer (and hence, willy-nilly, the viewer) is "involved" with the represented participants or not. The frontal anglesays, as it were, "What you see here is part of our world, something we are involved with". The oblique angle says, "What you see here is not part of our world; it is their world, something we are not involved with".
>
> Kress and van Leeuwen (2006: 136)

In comparison to involvement that is manifested via horizontal angle, the power relations between the represented participants and the viewers are encoded along the vertical axis. In a similar vein to cinematography, the viewers are likely to be required to give feedbacks to the represented participants in a visual image, depending on whether the viewers are looking up to the represented participants, or up to, or at eye-level with them. Thus there are three possibilities encoding power relations: a high angle, an eye-level angle, and a low one. In a visual image, if the viewer is looking down upon the represented participants, an imbalance of power relation is construed, in other words, a superiority of the viewer over the represented participants. The low angle, on the contrary, means that the represented participants within the visual composition are looking down upon the viewer, suggestive of an inferior stance to the viewer. Apart from the high and low angle, there are also images where the viewer cast the attention at the eye-level angle upon the represented participants, suggestive of a sense of equality in power relations between the viewer and the represented participants in that visual image.

The degree of social distance between the represented participants and the viewer is mainly realised through the size of frame. In our daily conversations, varying distance between people are generally categorised as being friendly and intimate (such as with a couple or friend), social (such as with a colleague) or unknown (such as with a stranger). Though social distances are culturally-based and context-determined, there are commonly accepted associations of the degrees of distance between the viewer and the represented participants: close shot, the medium shot, and the long shot. Royce (1999) accepts the general categories of social distance in visuals where a close-up shot demonstratesthe represented participant's head and shoulder, depicting the intimate social relations between the represented participant and the viewer; a medium close shot shows approximately from the waist of the represented participant; a medium shot shows approximately at the knees of the represented participant; and a long shot demonstrates the human figures occupying about half the height of the frame. (The discussion of social distance in Kress and van Leeuwen's framework for analysing interpersonal meaning is conducted in Section 3.3).

Apart from Visual Mood, the system of Modality is equally significant in accounts of visual communications and interactive meanings expressed by visual images. On the basis of the framework within SFL, the system of Modality in language is concerned with "the speaker's judgement of the probabilities, or the obligations" (Halliday 1994/2000: 75). By the same token, the system of Modality in visual compositions accounts for the viewer's acceptance of the credibility/truth of the represented participants. Unlike the modal adjuncts (e. g. *certainly* and *probably*) expressing Modality in language, the system of Modality in visual images is realised by the use of a wide range of Modality markers such as contextualisation, the degree of representing, illumination, depth, brightness, colour saturation, colour differentiation and colour modulation. The Modality markers in visual images are explained in detail as follows: (see Kress & van Leeuwen 2006: 160 – 163)

> ➤ Colour saturation: a scale running from fully saturated colour (high modality) to the absence of colour (low modality);
> ➤ Colour differentiation: a scale running from a maximally diversified range of colours (high modality) to monochrome (low modality)
> ➤ Colour modulation: a scale running from fully modulated colour (high modality)

to plain, unmodulated colour (low modality).

➤ Contextualisation: a scale running from the absence of background (low modality) to the most fully articulated and detailed background (high modality).

➤ Representation: a scale running from maximum abstraction to maximum representation of pictorial detail.

➤ Depth: a scale running from the absence of depth (low modality) to maximally deep perspective (high modality).

➤ Illumination: a scale running from the utmost play of light (high modality) and shade to its absence (low modality).

➤ Brightness: a scale running from a maximum number of different degrees of brightness (high modality) to just two degrees (low modality).

In a similar vein to Modality in language, the configurations of these Modality markers in different types of visual images can be expressed via the use of options made from a continum of possible choices ranging from high modality to low modality. Royce (1999: 155) proposes a continuum with such scales for analysing the visuals portraying naturalistic scenes and visuals derived from mathematical source in *The Economist* magazine. He also provides an outline of different scales of visual modality in the naturalistic visuals as demonstrated in Figure 3 – 16. As shown in the figure, the highest modality in the naturalistic visual continuum is the colour photography with high degree of adopting different kinds of colours, playing with brightness and light and depicting context in detail. Very close to colour photograph, black and white photograph represents a relatively high modality in the visual continuum. Although sketch drawing may be represented as realistic, it is not depicted as real as the black/white photograph and thus represents a median modality in the visual continuum. In the last two types of naturalistic images in the continuum, sketch caricature with a twist to reality has a relatively low modality whereas the line sketch demonstrates the lowest modality in such visual continuum. Among those forms of visuals, Royce finds that the type of sketch caricature is the mostly used form of naturalistic visual in *The Economist* magazine.

With regard to the interpersonal intersemiotic complementartity, Royce

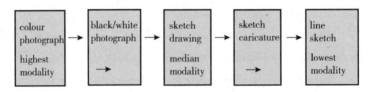

Figure 3 – 16 The naturalistic visual continuum (Royce 1999: 195)

points out that it can be realised via the intersemiotic interpersonal relations of *reinforcement of address*, *attitudinal congruence*, as well as *attitudinal dissonance* (Royce 1999: 165 – 166).

> *Reinforcement of address*: an identical form of address, where the visual and the verbal modes, utilising the methods inherent in their modes, both ask questions or make statements in the exchange of information.
> *Attitudinal congruence*: the same or a similar kind of attitude, where the proposition presented by both modes are treated in the same or similar attitudinal fashion
> *Attitudinal dissonance*: an opposite or ironic attitude, where the propositions presented by both modes are treated in different ways attitudinally.

Reinforcement of address indicates that both verbal and visual mode address the reader/viewers in the same or similar way to create a coherent multimodal text. The intersemiotic complementarity in respect to the domain of attitudinal congruence can be realised via the visual Modality Markers and the Modality features of the clauses expressing the same or similar attitudinal meanings. As for attitudinal dissonance, the attitude presented in the visual can be one which is opposite or ironic to the attitude expressed in the verbal mode of a multimodal text. Attitudinal dissonance is an effective rhetorical device often used in literature, where the irony is adopted to achieve some kinds of dramatic effect.

3.4.4.3 The compositional intersemiotic complementarity

In Royce's (1999, 2007) framework of intersemiotic complementarity, the study on the intersemiotic compositional features of a particular multimodal text serves to facilitate the intersemiotic complementarity between the verbal and visual modes, and to create a coherent message. As mentioned in the beginning of the present section, the textual metafunction (e. g. Halliday 1978/2001, 1994/2000) of language is renamed compositional meanings in visual images by Royce. On the one hand, that is motivated by the fact that the term compositional "captures more fully the sense of two modes within one page interacting within one page interaction with each other to form a coherent page-based text" (Royce 2007: 67). On the other hand, the concept "refers not only to systems of layout, but also to a text's positioning within a whole magazine or book, as well as a particular section or department" (Royce 1999: 168). In other words, both verbal and visual features are taken consideration in respect to the page's layout in the multimodal text.

In examining the visual compositional meanings, Royce conflates three structuring principles which are emphasised by Kress and van Leeuwen (1996, 2006).

The first one of the compositional structuring principles is termed as *information value* which refers to "the placement of the elements (participants and syntagms that relate them to each other and to the viewer) endows them with specific informational values attached to the various ' zones' of the image". The left-right placement indicates the "Given and New" information; while the top-down placement indicates the "Ideal and Real" information; and the center-margin placement means the comparison between the nucleus of the information on the center and ancillary elements in the margins. The second important principle is termed as *salience* referring to the represented participants in the visual images that may attract the viewers' attention by assigning different "visual weight". It can be realised by factors as such: (i) the placement in the foreground or background; (ii) the placement in the visual field (e. g. the more close to the top, objects are "heavier") ; (iii) the relative size (e. g. object in larger size is more easily noticed than that in small size) ; (iv) contrasts in tonal value (v) colour contrastsand (vi) differences in sharpness. As for the third essential structuring principle, *framing* deals with the presence or absence of framing devices which connects or disconnects elements in an image, indicating whether they belong together or not. It can also be realised by a set of elements:

(i) frame lines and border; (ii) variations in visual shape; (iii) discontinuities of color saturation; (iv) empty space; (v) vectors formed by the arrangement of abstract graphic elements and (vi) vectors formed by the differences in size or volume (Royce 1999: 169).

As for the verbal compositional features in multimodal texts, Royce proposes that the verbal element might be referred to as the "body copy", or be treated as an orthographic visual whole that is organised by the same structuring principles as that for the analysis of visual compositional features. To put it more simply, the verbal element is also organised through the principles of *information value*, *salience* and *framing*.

Information value relevant to the verbal composition features has mainly to do with the diverse placement of typographic elements which endows those elements with specific information values. In this regard, the relative placement involves the pictorial layout of different elements attached to various "zones" of the body copy. For instance, the element placed on the left zone is regarded as the Given information, while element on the right zone of the body copy is the New one. Besides, the importance of placement in terms of bottom-top of the body copy lies in the contrast between the Ideal and Real information: the top of page represents the Ideal information whereas the top refers to the Real.

In terms of *salience*, different typographic elements are placed to attract the attention of the viewer to various degrees and to assign "visual weight". It is a relative concept which indicates the different degrees of importance among the represented elements within the image. In respect to the verbal aspects in a certain multimodal text, the letters and characters in larger size can be easier to recognise. The features of salience relevant to verbal element can also be generated by the varieties of boldness, where extra-bold may be used for a "low voice" while light face used for a "high voice" (Royce 1999: 73).

Framing deals with the various compositional elements that are ulitised to connect or demarcate the parts of the body copy to show whether they belong in one multimodal text or not. The use of frame lines (e. g. above, under and between the typography) as well as borders (e. g. around the typography) are the most obvious devices of framing in a multimodal text to set the typographical elements apart from any other visual elements. Despite the framing devices of frame lines and borders, another significant device is the use of empty space around the typography which plays the role of marking it off from the space of gutters and margins. Depending on different typographical tonal values, framing via the use of borders and frame lines can be strong or weak. A salient example is that "the framing values of black in white spaces are of course higher than in that of grey-shaded, less distinct borders and frame lines" (Royce 1999: 175).

After examining the compositional features of both verbal and visual texts, Royce(1999: 178 – 192) points out that an intersemiotically coherent multimodal text is potentially achieved via the compositional relations as follows:

  · *Information valuation on the page*: an examination of the relative placement of the visual and verbal modes in terms of their vertical or top/bottom placement on the page, their horizontal or left/right placement on the page, and their relative placement on the page in relation to the centre and margin.
  · *Salience on the page*: an examination in terms of the relative sizes of the visual vis-a-vis the verbal aspect of the text, and perhaps vice versa.
  · *Degrees of framing of elements on the page*: the ways that the visual and verbal elements are divided between themselves and the remaining empty space on the page.
  · *Inter-visual synonymy*: the degrees of semblance in form across visual modes which can work to present a kind of inter-visual harmony, realising an inter-visual intersemiotic complementarity.
  · *The importance of potential reading path*: the hypothetical viewer's eye movement from the most salient points in the composition to the next or less salient points.

3.5　Summary

In this chapter, some basic tenets of SFL that inform the present study have been examined in order to gain a better understanding of language as social semiotic. Each of them is outlined and followed by the correlation of the relevant studies to multimodal texts informed by this particular aspect. It then moves to the introduction of two different approaches to study visual semiotic which are informed by SFL theoretical concept and its metafunctional diversification. In comparison to Kress and van Leeuwen's (1996, 2006) visual grammar, Painter et al. 's (2013) visual narrative framework is more suitable for the present research to examine visual semiotic resources since it involves developing visual grammar in relation to the data of children's picture books. By outlining the key systems within the framework of visual narrative, it provides applicable descriptive tool for the analysis of visual semiotic in relation to the data in ensuing chapters. This chapter concludes with an introduction of some relevant studies on interrelations among different semiotic systems. Among them, Royce's (e. g. 1999, 2007) intersemiotic complementarity framework is adopted as the analytical model to explain the synergistic cooperation between visual and verbal semiotic systems, while Painter and Martin's (e. g. Painter & Martin 2011; Painter et al. 2013) framework of intermodal complementarity is chosen as analytical tool to explore the different degrees of meaning construed by the verbal and visual semiotics.

Chapter Four   The Synergy of Visual and Verbal Semiotics in Creating Engagement

4. 1   Introduction

The previous chapter is mainly concerned with the theoretical construct underlying the present research and the interrelations between different semiotic systems (especially between verbal and visual). This chapter primarily deals with the interpersonal meanings encoded and expressed by the two semiotics (image and verbiage) within the Chinese picture books. It aims to analyse the visual and verbal choices available for writers (and illustrators) to establish engagement between various participants in the database of Chinese picture books, including both the interactions between different depicted characters and the alignments between represented characters and the child reader. The chapter firstly identifies the interpersonal features of visual components throughout the data of Chinese picture books which are in relation to the visual semiotic examined through the parameters of FOCALISATION, AFFECT, AMBIENCE, and GRADUATION. It then examines the attitudinal meanings inscribed or invoked in picture books, exploring the ways in which visual and verbal resources are deployed to encode attitudinal meanings. Moreover, this chapter selects the picture book *The Monster Nian* as the main object and extends Royce's (1999, 2007) intersemiotic complementary framework to investigate the interpersonal intersemiotic complementarity between verbal and visual semiotic systems to establish engagement and affinity. The last part of the chapter delves into the different affordance for meaning of verbal and visual texts in relation to interpersonal meaning and their relative contribution to the whole meaning when they are co-instantiated in the picture books.

4.2　Interpersonal features of images in Chinese children's picture ·books

4.2.1　Involving FOCALISATION

This section deals with the interpersonal meanings or "interactive engagement" (O'Toole 1994) encoded in children's picture books, which is primarily reflected in theway verbal texts and images attract the reader's attention and is concerned with the type of social relationship established between the participants involved in the process of story narration. Kress and van Leeuwen (2006) have distinguished three types of participants related to images: (i) the creators or producers of the image, e. g. the designers and illustrators; (ii) the viewers of the image, e. g. the young children of the special reading material; and (iii) the represented participants that are depicted in the visual compositions, correlated to one another via vectors or eye lines. [1]

As one of the most salient ways to enact social interaction between different types of participants, focalisation or eye contact enables viewers to be situated in diverse reading positions (i. e. involved as an identification of the depicted characters or just treated as an outside observer). Within the framework of their visual grammar, Kress and van Leeuwen (2006) basically differentiate between images in which engagement and some kinds of demands are enacted through visual contact and those where there is no such visual contact. In their terms, the former refers to "demand" images, requiring viewer's participation in the depicted world and engagement with the focalising character; the latter are defined as "offer" images which simply provide viewers with information instead of demanding from them certain reactions and feedback (For a detailed discussion on "demand" and "offer" images, see Section 3.3). As

---

[1] As a special reading material, children's picture books may include a range of stories devoted to the very young readers with problems of literacy. Therefore, there is another type of participant involved in the reading process, who (usually parents or teachers) intend to mediate and tell the story to the children.

was discussed in the previous chapter, the distinction between demand and offer images might be perceived as an analogy with Halliday's (Halliday 1994; Halliday & Matthiessen, 2004) linguistic analysis of dialogue. However, Painter et al. (2013) point out that such basic distinction is somewhat problematic. They argue that the nature of "demand" images should not depend on the depicted character's facial expressions and bodily postures since facial and bodily stances may function mainly in conveying character's affect and emotion rather than realising dialogic negotiation as demanding something. Hence, Painter et al. (2013) propose the system of FOCALISATION to draw a fundamental distinction between two general types of visual opposition via the presence or absence of visual gaze, namely "contact" and "observe" images. The images with contact features indicate that the viewer would be engaged with the depicted character through eye contact. On the contrary, the depicted participants in observe images do not gaze at the viewer and thus the viewer would be positioned to take detached observation of the depicted participants and the world. This section will take a focalisation analysis of our samples on the basis of Painter et al. 's system network of FOCALISATION.

Throughout the database, there are a great number of images depicting human-beings, animals, and anthropomorphized characters. However, most of the represented animate participants in the visual frame do not gaze out at the reader. That is to say, the majority of the represented participants within the visual compositions provide the reader with a kind of observing stance, and thus, these visuals are "observe" images. Since the main topic of the children's picture books are closely related to the Spring Festival, some of those depicted participants are characters ofthe story-world relevant to the origin of the Spring Festival, while some others offer information about the folktale and the Chinese customs displayed on such traditional festivals. Through observe images, the depicted characters are presented as some particular items of information for the reader (especially for children), rather than creating an affinity with them.

It is evident that picture books for children tend to avoid contact images, especially those that offer "straightforward stories" (Lewis 2006) to the childreader, enabling him/her to keep a suitable distance from the story world to enjoy the well-designed narrative process. Nevertheless, when contact options are employed in pictorial frame, they are meaningful in construing a range of key points in the narrative structure. As is shown in the example(see Illustration 4 – 1), a focalising choice of contact is taken in the image within which a ferocious monster gazes out directly at the reader. This image is the opening page of the picture book which serves as an introduction of the monster Nian accompanied with an instruction from verbal narration. Therefore, the choice of contact within the pictorial composition overtly presents an invitation for the reader to participate in the imaginary world. The reader is then engaged with the focalising participant via eye contact and shares the extreme emotion with the other depicted participants in the imaginary world who are afraid of being attacked and eaten by it. In addition, this image adopts a very close-up shot to vividly depict the full figure of the monster, enhancing the engagement between the reader and the represented participants. In a nutshell, such focalisation option of contact in this case achieves a strong interaction between the monster and the reader as well as highlighting the "metafictive nature" (Painter et al. 2013) of the story framing in children's picture books.

Illustration 4 – 1   from _Nian_ (2013)

Apart from contact images that establish engagement between participants, the visual option of seeing through the eyes of a particular character has the function of enacting social relationship between the depicted character and the reader. The type of image with such visual feature is termed as a mediated image.

One notable example is drawn from the book *The Adventure of the Postman* (Zheng & Zhao 2014). The book tells a story about the adventure of a postman whose name is Da Guan on the day of the Spring Festival. After a hard-working day, Da Guan returns home when he suddenly finds a letter put in his bicycle basket. In this example (see Illustration 4 − 2), the writer uses the visual technique of inferred character focalisation. It is a visual frame of a double page spread with a two-picture narrative sequence. The verso image of the spread shows a front view of the depicted character staring at an unknown letter in his hand with a puzzled facial expression. In the following image, in this case on the recto, the reader sees the letter is unfolded and the content of it is clearly depicted. The recto image presents the reader with a close shot of what is written in the letter, offering information about where the letter is from and what the purpose of the letter is. As for this visual composition, the reader is positioned to be Da Guan and thus aligned to see with Da Guan's eyes. Unlike maintaining a perspective from observing outside, we are involved in the imaginary story world to make a strong connection with the depicted character. The interpretation of vicarious focalisation in this second case is facilitated by the extreme emotion by positioning the reader as character.

Illustration 4 − 2　from *The Adventure of the Postman* (2014)

4.2.2 Representing AFFECT

The previous section has discussed the visual options of focalisation embodied in the picture books, which establishes engagement between different types of participants through eye contact. This section discusses the way characters are framed and shaped in children's picture stories, with a particular emphasis on the styles of depicted characters in terms of their significance for the diverse sorts of identification and alignment that are construed between different participants, especially between the child-reader and the represented character.

Picture books for children are not only perceived as a reading material for entertainment and joyfulness, but also as a significant means for the reader to learn knowledge and define the material world. To this end, the authors of well-designed picture books also attempt to employ the appropriate pictorial styles of depicted characters to establish social interaction, apart from situating the reader in the distant stance by the proper choice from focalisation.

For example, in *The Monster Nian* (Xiong 2007), the author uses a third person narrative technique in the verbal text and the characters in the picture book are not highly individuated. Along withthe verbal narration are a great number of observe images through which an appropriate distant reader stance is achieved so that the reader merely observes the story events and learns some lessons from the book. For this reason, the readers are not expected to forge identification with those depicted characters to share with them some particular personal affect. Besides the combination of oblique angles and observe stance, the style of character depiction plays an essential role in the construction of such detached narrative orientation, and in this case, the depiction style of character adopted is "minimalist" style (A categorisation of differentiated styles which will be further elaborated in the following discussion).

Drawing upon Welch's (2005) ideas of categorisation of character depiction, Painter et al. (2013) suggest that the ways in which characters are represented in the context of picture book can be primarily classified into three types: minimalist style, generic style, and naturalistic style. The classification of these three styles is based on the degree of drawing detail, depiction of facial affect and realism of the character depiction. As Welch (2005) states that:

> Eye Detail is one of the most effective indexes of realism in texts⋯The Minimalist category tends to draw a pupil and an eyebrow. Occasionally pupils are given more volume through the suggestion of an eye-socket. . . The Generic category gains an iris, as well as the potential for wrinkles around the eyes, and bags under the eyes to indicate fatigue. In the Naturalistic system individuated eyebrow hairs and eye-lashes appear, top and bottom lids appear and eyes can water.
>
> (Welch 2005: 3 –4)

It is evident from the sample texts that the minimalist style is the most commonly used way of character depiction in picture books. That is motivated by the fact that the author is not restricted by the equivalent physiognomy of actual human facial details, and that the depicted characters created in picture books are always portrayed in cartoons with certain degrees of distortion. These characters are depicted in a non-realistic way and the depictions of their emotion are highly schematic so as to vividly represent happiness/unhappiness. Welch (2005) points out that the utilisation of minimalist style can afford a wide range of emotional repertoire and most strongly express the different degrees of character's sadness or happiness.

Illustration 4 –3　from *Nian* (2015); from *Reunion*(2008);
from *The Spring Festival in Beijing* (2014)

In Illustration 4 – 3, the first image (the sequence is from left to right) is adopted form *The Monster Nian* (Xiong 2007) and the character within which is portrayed in minimalist style. As was discussed earlier, lots of picture books adopting this style intend to require the reader to take a relatively detached stance to observe the depicted participants and story events rather than to invite them to participate in the imaginary world and remember these characters. This is a story of a Chinese traditional folktale about the Spring Festival and monster Nian. According to the story narration, there was a monster called Nian in ancient China, who was likely to hunt human beings for food. A boy as the protagonist lived in the village nearby whose family members were threatened by the monster. Finally, the boy found the effective method to defeat the monster with the help of a god. The minimalist style deployed in the depiction of character is supported with the verbal text in terms of third person narration as well as form of address. The protagonist in the depicted storyworld even does not have a name, instead, the author employs "a boy" and "the boy" throughout the story to refer to the protagonist. In conclusion, the minimalist style in this picture book offers to the reader a great deal of knowledge about the traditional folktale and teaches the reader a lesson, hence it suits a "social commentary" (Painter et al. 2013).

In comparison with the first image with minimalist style, the second image (in the middle) representing a generic style is taken from *Reunion* (Yu & Zhu 2008). The book narrates a story of a reunion of family members (father, mother, and their daughter). After one year's hard work, the father returns home to spend the Spring Festival with his wife and daughter. During the holiday, he takes part in a number of social activities with his lovely daughter, cherishing the valuable annual reunion. By employing the generic style of character depiction, the author is likely to forge the identification between the reader and the depicted participants, implicitly expecting the reader to participate in the story world and align with the protagonist (here the daughter) to view the story events in her stance. In other words, such generic style invites the child reader to take an empathetic stance rather than an observe stance.

Complemented with use of first person address "I" (referring to the daughter) in verbal narration, the reader will be expected to feel the protagonist's complex emotion of seeing her father and learn from the story the importance of family as well as cherishing the time with their family and friends.

Unlike the other two types of depiction style, the naturalistic style represented in the last image from *The Spring Festival in Beijing* (Yu 2014) is considered to be the most restrained and nuanced one. The facial expression of the represented character within the visual composition is expected to be read as authentic as real people. *The Spring Festival in Beijing* conveys to us some key information about how people in Beijing spend their holidays as well as what the custom for Beijing inhabitants to prepare the Spring Festivalis. Throughout the story, the author uses the naturalistic style to portray a range of characters. Therefore, their emotional repertoire might be extended to the impressionistic and nuanced expression, and the complexity of face is subtly depicted. Such feature of depiction contributes to provide the reader with inferences on the depicted character's emotion. Generally speaking, the texts related to the naturalistic style are designed for older reader, some of which are essential for "leading children towards the kind of literate reading called for in secondary and higher education" (Painter et al. 2013: 33). Obviously, this example with naturalist style falls into this type of social function. The verbal text in this book is selected from Laoshe's[①] essay, and hence the child reader is required to have a certain degree of ability to read and write.

4.2.3　Construing AMBIENCE

Although the style of depiction is an important method for indexing the way the reader may be encouraged to engage with the story book, the use of colour can be conceived as the most instant and effective visual resource which influences the reader's emotion as soon as he/she looks at the image. For example, it is commonly acknowledged that an image filled with dark tones

---

① Laoshe was a famous Chinese novelist, writer and dramatist. He was one of the most remarkable figures of 20th century Chinese literature, whose best known novel was *Teahouse*《茶馆》.

would differ from another (e. g. filled with bright colours) in providing the reader with differentiated effect on his/her emotion. In Kress and van Leeuwen's (2006) visual grammar, the use of colour variation functions as a means for expressing visual modality. The choices of the colour variation within a visual composition exhibits different degrees of modality, that is, the lower the modality is, the more that colour is reduced. Kress and van Leeuwen also contend that colour saturation serving as a continuum of visual modality is closely related to the common standard of pictorial naturalism which ranges from a complete absence to a full saturation of colour. In terms of the absence of colour, images referring to merely black and white have only one colour variation, that is, the variation of brightness. Another parameter of visual modality defined by them is colour differentiation, which runs from monochrome in the visual composition to a "reduced palette", and finally to full colour differentiation (Kress & van Leeuwen 1996: 165). Instead of conceiving of the use of colour as a method of expressing visual modality, Painter et al. (2013) proposes the system of Ambience to refer to the use of colour in picture books which is developed on the basis of Kress and van Leeuwen's framework of visual modality, with particular regard to their concepts of colour saturation, temperature, and colour differentiation. Painter et al. (2013: 35) propose that the Ambience in picture books should be seen as "a visual meaning system" that is mainly composed of three core subsystems named Vibrancy, Warmth, and Familiarity.

Firstly, the choices of the use of colour are available simultaneously in these core subsystems when " activated ambience " is adopted. When the choice of colour within the image is black only, it falls into the category of "denied ambience". It is found from our sample texts that all picture books adopt activated ambience in the story narration. That is motivated by the fact that the special genre of picture books facilitates the use of colour saturation and colour differentiation to please the child reader. It is also important to note that the main topic of the sample texts is closely related to the Spring Festival, strengthening the use of colour in the visual depiction of the bustling setting in which the represented characters are placed. Thus the considerations of the use of colour will be placed on the activated ambience in picture books which are realised via three dimensions.

Secondly, in considering choices made through the system of VIBRANCY in picture books, analysis is mainly conducted on the depth of colour saturation. The choice of a high or full saturation in a picture means that a "vibrant" effect is generated. In general, the vibrant option is often used to create a sense of vitality, joyfulness and excitement. While a "muted" option made up of lower saturated colour expresses a gentler, restrained and relatively depressive feeling.

An example is selected from *Reunion* (Yu & Zhu 2008) where the daughter is waiting her father for family reunion and watching her father walking towards their house (see Illustration 5 − 4). The colours used in this image are bolder and highly saturated, combined with the use of bright red hues, encouraging the reader to stand in the protagonist's shoes to share the excitement and touching atmosphere. The verbal text suggests that the father is returning home, complementing the image in foregrounding the depicted character's joyousness of the annual family reunion. The highly saturated colours deployed in the depiction of the immediate context demonstrate a warm, fragrant and comfortable setting, involving the reader in a touched and delightful moment.

Illustration 4 − 4   from *Reunion* (2008)

With regard to the second ambience subsystem, the choices of Warmth can be primarily classified into warm colours (e. g. red, yellow, and orange hues) and cool colours (e. g. green and blue hues). Choices made in this subcategory not only contribute to the construction of hot or cool physical environment in which the represented characters are suited, but also to the conveyance of attitudinal as well as emotional affect to the reader. In the context of picture books for child reader, such variation in the use of colour contrast is significant at a range of moments for influencing the reader's personal affect, and for enhancing the positive/negative effect built by other visual strategies within the image such as visual choice of full saturated colour or a contact option from focalisation system. Contrasts in the options of Warmth play a vital part in creating two totally different types of mood.

The example (Illustration 4 – 5) consisting of a double spread composition is adopted from *The Monster Nian*. As is seen from the figure, the verso page within the composition is filled with the choices of the warm option that are realised by bright sunny yellow hues. The warm ambience used here signals a comforting, light-hearted and positive mood. Whereas the recto image is filled with choices of cool option, showcasing the gloomy, lonely and depressing environment in which the boy is placed. The image demonstrates that a boy sitting glumly beside a window and a kind of desperate mood is evoked by the restrained dark hues of the background window. Therefore a vivid comparison between two types of mood (hopeful versus hopeless) is construed by the different choices of warmth, and such comparison is complemented with the verbal literary strategy.

The author adopts verbal description of the immediate context of the moment to reference the depicted characters' emotion. By adopting the visual ambience, the author facilitates our reading and understanding of the diverse emotional mood of the story characters.

Lastly, the third important subsystem of Ambience in picture books is Familiarity, depending on the amount of the use of colour differentiation within images. In other words, the more different colours are used in the visual com-

Illustration 4 – 5   from *The Monster Nian*(2007)

position, "the greater the sense of the familiar" (Painter et al. 2013: 38). It is testified by our daily experience that we recognise the world not only in one or two restrained hues, but in a full range of diverse colours. In the similar vein, if the use of colours in an image is restricted to one or few colours, the image probably creates the meaning of removed from the actual material world that we are experiencing. In Kress and van Leeuwen's (2006) terms, the colour differentiation as a dimension of realising visual modality also indicates that the reduced certainty in the depiction will be achieved by the lack of differentiation of colour. An example is presented in Illustration 4 – 6 with a range of different colours.

The image depicts a scene in the celebration on the day of Spring Festival. As a Chinese traditional ceremony, the dragon dance is highly favored and valued which expresses the wish for a prosperous and lucky year. Within the image, different colours are adopted to decorate the circumstances and the depicted characters, such as the bright-coloured clothes of sightseers, the dark-gray roof of houses, earthy yellow hues of bridges, etc. Through the use of the differentiated colours, the image provides the reader a sense of familiar to the actual situations in which he/she has witnessed and experienced. Thus the child reader is more involved in the story to participate in the joyful moment, and the certainty of the image is enhanced by the presentation of a coloured

Illustration 4 – 6   from *Reunion* (2008)

and familiar world.

In the present study, the analysis of Familiarity in children's picture books suggests that there is always more colour differentiation presented in the story world. A possible reason for why picture books are likely to choose the options of more differentiation rather than that of less colour differentiation might be genre related. Based on the genre conventions of picture books, fictional characters portrayed in the story world are expected to be interpreted as real beings and the fictional world as real in all its variety of colour by children readers.

4.2.4   Visual GRADUATION

In this section, we take into account the final visual technique for enacting social relation between the reader and the represented character. As mentioned earlier, the system of GRADUATION is concerned with the linguistic resources used for "upscaling" or "downscaling" evaluative meanings (Martin & White 2005). For instance, in the expressions *slightly foolish*, *millions of ideas*, *a very distant mountain*, the evaluative meanings are upscaled or downscaled over qualities, the measuring of number, and distribution.

Based on Martin and White's (2005) APPRAISAL theory, Economou (2009) proposes a set of corresponding systems of visual GRADUATION for analysing the evaluative meaning encoded in news photographs. According to Economou (2009), visual GRADUATION can be further classified into the system of visual FORCE and visual FOCUS. The force of a visual ideational element can be upscaled or downscaled by its intensification (e. g. brighter or duller), and by its quantification (e. g. smaller or bigger), and also by repetition (the presence of two or more similar ideational items in the image, and hence always raising the force). As for visual FOCUS, it has mainly to do with the visual identification of a vector, or with the shape as a specified ideational element. When a high focus option is adopted in an image, the ideational item is highly specified and more visual information are represented within that image. Although the visual data of Economou is different from that of Painter et al. 's (2013) studies, they adopt some of the key choices in the subsystems of visual FORCE to probe into the ways in which the attitudinal impact of visual elements can be increased.

Drawing upon the ideas of visual FORCE (e. g. Painter et al. 2013: 44 –46; Economou 2009: 169 – 178), this section deals mainly with the choices of the subsystem of "quantification" exemplified in the data of Chinese picture books which upscale or downscale the attitudinal meanings committed in visual images. The use of quantification choices in picture books can play an essential part in "ensuring an attitudinal response in the reader" (Painter et al. 2013: 45).

An example (see Illustration 4 –7) is derived from the book *Nian* (Zhu 2015). The image chooses a [cool] ambience to create a depressed and fearful mood to the reader. The reader is thus involved in a horrific story world in which people are ruthlessly hunted and eaten by a huge monster. Furthermore, the direct focalisation used here would establish a strong engagement with the child reader, as well as encouraging the reader to react emotionally to the frightened scene of story world. Combined with these visual interpersonal choices, the reader is likely to be involved in the negative visual affect even if there is only one character depicted in the image. However, the negative feeling of and negative reaction made by the reader will be more strongly invoked by the use of upscaled quantification.

Illustration 4 – 7　from *Nian*（2015）

4.3　Inscribed and invoked ATTITUDE in images

Within the framework of systemic functional grammar, the appraisal-framework provides a powerful analytical tool to examine interpersonal meaning. The appraisal system proposed by Martin and his colleagues (e. g. Martin 2000; Martin & White 2005; Martin & Rose 2007) is perceived as an integral model that attempts to achieve a full understanding of "how interlocutors are feeling, the judgements they make and the value they place on various phenomena of their experience" (Martin 2000: 144). As one of the most fundamental dimension in their theoretical construct (Martin & White 2005), attitudinal meanings are concerned with "evaluating things, people's character and their feelings" (Maritin & Rose 2007: 26).

The attitudinal meanings are firstly examined in verbal texts. For example, in the expressions *a very significant work* and *the nation is more progressive*, the intensifier *very* and *more* serve to amplify the attitudinal meaning invoked by the use of the lexis *significant* and *progressive* in the attribute of a relational process. As mentioned in Section 3. 2. 2, ATTITUDE is sub-categorised into three domains, namely, affect, judgement and appreciation. A further explanation of these three sub-categories is proposed by Martin and White (2005) as follows:

> Affect is concerned with registering positive and negative feelings: do we feel happy or sad, confident or anxious, interested or bored?... Judgement deals with attitudes towards behaviour, which we admire or criticise, praise or condemn... Appreciation involves evaluations of semioticand natural phenomena, according to the ways in which they are valued or not in a given field.
>
> Martin & White (2005: 42 –43)

According to Martin and White (2005), the coding of attitudinal meanings in different discourses involves three fundamental domains. First of all, affect related to positive or negative feelings is classified into three main sets: un/happiness, in/security and dis/satisfaction. The variations of un/happiness cover emotions concerned with "affairs of the heart" such as hate, sadness, happiness and love; the in/s ecurity variable covers emotions concerned with ecosocial well-being such as anxiety, fear, confidence and trust; and the dis/satisfaction variable covers emotions concerned with telos (the pursuit of goals) such as ennui, displeasure, curiosity, respect (Martin & White 2005: 49). Secondly, the variables of encoding judgement are mainly categorised "social esteem" and "social sanction" which are sub-divided into normality (how unusual someone is), capacity (how capable they are), tenacity (how dependable they are), veracity (how honest someone is) and propriety (how ethicalthey are). As the third fundamental dimension of the Attitude system, appreciation concerning our feelings and evaluations of things can be primarily sub-categorised into reaction (focusing on impact, e. g. "did it grab me?" / "did I like it?"), composition (focusing on quality, e. g. "did it hang together?" /and balance, e. g. "was it hard to follow?") and valuation (focusing on valuation, e. g. "was it worthwhile?").

Apart from the overt realisations via the use of evaluative lexis, attitudinal meanings can also be triggered and invoked by adopting a number of strategies such as the use of experiential lexis and lexical metaphor. Instead of being inscribed explicitly in the language, attitudinal meanings invoked are triggered and realised by the selection of ideational meaning that "is enough to invoke evaluation, even in the absence of attitudinal lexis that tells us directly how to feel" (Martin & White 2005: 62).

In examining the attitudinal meanings encoded in verbal texts, Martin and White (2005) propose an outline of the different strategies for triggering ATTITUDE (e. g. inscription and invocation) that is represented in Figure 4 – 1 with examples.

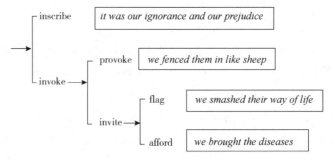

Figure 4 – 1   Strategies for inscribing and invoking attitude
(Martin & White 2005: 67)

The APPRAISAL framework has also been extended to the analysis of visual images, providing an effective and comprehensive tool for analysing how attitudes, feeling, values are encoded and expressed in different types of images. The pioneering studies on the appraisal analysis of visual mode indicate the attitudinal repertoire embedded in images and the important role that images play in construing evaluative stance in a multimodal discourse (e. g. Economou 2009; Tian 2011).

This section is mainly concerned with the attitudinal meanings that are encoded in Chinese children's books. An analysis of attitudinal meaning in visuals is exemplified in Illustration 4 – 8. The example is excerpted from *The Spring Festival* (Hua 2013) which is a typical use of cartoons in picture books for narrating story events. As illustrated in the image, there are a number of depicted characters sitting in a table. Besides a female character with ambiguous affect on her face, each of the depicted characters in the image represents an expressive feeling of delight and happiness, which can be shown by their facial expression of laughing (with eyes closed and mouth open) and their bodily behaviour. As shown in the image, the depicted participants are sitting together around a table to make Chinese dumplings, and one participant (the boy) is feeding his mother a dumpling. It is important to note that both human faces and bodily behaviour may serve as the part of visual ideation (or visual experience) and can be most easily recognised by the viewers. Therefore, some kinds of depicted facial expressions and gestures can be viewed as the types of universally shared visual lexicon of emotions, or as the values of "primary affect" (Lewis & Haviland-Jones 2000). For instance, sensations and feelings of the depicted participants expressed by facial emotions such as a smile or frown, or via depicted bodily behaviours like weeping or laughing can be unambiguously visually represented as " visual affect inscriptions " (Econoumou 2009: 111). On the one hand, the depicted character of a particular kind of emotion (expressed by the facial depicted expressions and bodily behaviours) is identified as the "Emoter". On the other, the identified or implied cause of the depicted emotion is termed as the "Trigger" that may be represented in the image or not (see Martin & White 2005: 46; and Economou 2009: 111). Therefore, in this example a positive affect meaning is unambiguously and directly inscribed in the image with the depicted characters (exactly three women characters and a little boy) as Emoters and the family activities (making Chinese dumplings together) as the Trigger.

In order to achieve a nuanced examination of the attitudinal meanings (in this case AFFECT) encoded in Chinese picture books, we would draw on Martin and White's (2005: 46 – 52) categorisations of AFFECT in terms of six parameters. These six factors are explicated as follows: (i) whether the feelings are construed by the culture as positive or negative; (ii) whether the feelings are realised as a surge of emotion involving some kind of behavioural manifestations, or as an internal state and mental process; (iii) whether the emotions are construed as reactions to a specific emotional Trigger, or as a general ongoing mood; (iv) how the feelings are graded along the scale of in-

为了比比来年谁的运气好，妈妈、大娘和姑姑分别在饺子里包了一枚干净的硬币。

Illustration 4 – 8　from *On the Spring Festival* (2012)

tensity ranging from higher value to lower value; (ⅴ) whether the emotions involve an intension with respect to a stimulus that is irrealis (e. g. *the captain
feared leaving*), or involve a reaction to a certain stimulus that is realis (e. g.
the captain disliked leaving); and (ⅵ) whether the emotions are concerned
with "affairs of the heart" (un/happiness), or the "ecosocial well-being"
(in/security), or the "pursuit of goals" (dis/satisfaction).

　　Based on Martin and White's basic categorisation, different types of AF-
FECT are analysed and explicated in Table 4 – 1 below, with the corresponding visual patterns also demonstrated. At the first glance, the reader of this image is easier to be attracted by the use of red and pinkish-orange colours. A
comforting and joyful mood is created via the option of [warm] and [vibrant]
through the system of AMBIENCE. It is not difficult to understand that the use
of warm colours can facilitate the reading of the emotions of the depicted characters who are spending New Year with other family members. Another important part in creating social interaction is the differentiation of the use of colours
in the image, such as red, pale yellow and pinkish-orange hues adopted in the

depiction. Such visual technique provides an engagement between the depicted characters and the child reader. Moreover, the generic style of the depiction of characters used in this example is likely to expect the child readers to be involved in the story world and stand in the character's shoes to perceive themselves as the protagonist. Hence, the generic style of depiction invites the reader to take an empathetic stance to share the comforting and cheerful emotion with the depicted characters and experience the love between the family members. To complement with those visual techniques employed in the image, a kind of positive AFFECT is represented in the image which can be inferred from a set of apparent visual realisations such as the facial expressions of and bodily manifestations of the depicted characters in this image.

Table 4 - 1   Types of AFFECT in relation to Illustration 4 - 8

Type of AFFECT	Corresponding visual patterns
positive AFFECT	the facial expression of delight representing a warm and comforting atmosphere
surge of emotion	the extralinguistic manifestation of ebullient gestures showing an strong engagement in the family activity
reaction to Trigger	the feelings expressed towards the ongoing family activity and interactions to other depicted participants
high value	the strong emotions directly inscribed, and the dramatic joyfulness expressed
realis AFFECT	the emotions of the depicted characters involvingthe reaction to the stimulus of family activity and social interaction between them
happiness security satisfaction	joyfulness and excitement expressed on their faces comfortable in the conducting interaction involved and satisfied in the family activity

It is clear that the image illustrates a moment (on the Spring Festival) where four depicted characters sitting on a table to participate in family activities (making Chinese dumplings). And the verbal text in this image is depicted on the top of the page is "为了比比谁的运气好，妈妈、大娘和姑姑分别在饺子里包了一枚干净的硬币。" Obviously, the verbal text is primarily concerned with the narration of the story events, including the introduction of the depicted character (exactly by the personal address) and the family activities which they are taking part in (making jiaozi as well as randomly putting a coin into the jiaozi). However, as for the interactive meanings expressed at the lexico-grammatical level, there are no attitudinal meanings inscribed or invoked in the verbal texts. It is difficult for the reader to determine what kinds of attitudes are construed and encoded (e. g. whether the depicted participants are happy or somber, excited or depressed) by merely reading the verbal text. In a nutshell, the verbal text in this example shows no "commitment" (Martin2008; Martin & White, 2005) of attitudinal meanings. Compared with the verbal text, the visual image commits more affectual meaning, and thus it is through the visual text that attitudinal meanings are conveyed to the reader. The different degrees of meanings committed in the verbal text and visual image are closely related to Painter and Martin's (2011) framework of "intermodal complementarity". As Painter and Martin (2011) explicates, the model of intermodal complementarity focuses on "the question of how choices combine across modalities, and how they complement one another" (Painter & Martin 2011: 133) in multimodal texts, and in the current research, in bimodal texts. In examining the different degrees of meaning committed in the process of instantiation, Painter and Martin (2011: 132) focus on "the degree to which each [semiotic] 'commits' meaning in a particular instance and the extent to which—for each metafunction—that commitment converges with or diverges from that of the other modality". In other words, when the same meanings are committed both in the verbal text and visual image, an "intersemiotic convergence" is established; on the contrary, the "intersemiotic divergence" occurs when the verbal mode and visual mode commit different meanings of the same semantic domain. The present section adopts Painter and Martin's (2011) concept of intersemiotic convergence as well as intersemiotic to analyse the attitudinal meanings encoded in Chinese picture books, with a particular interest in the inscribed affect in the visual image and the verbal text.

The interaction between the affectctual meaning encoded in verbal and visual system is also examined by Tian (2011), focusing on the interaction between visual AFFECT and verbal AFFECT. She proposes a model (see Table 4－2) for the analysis of the convergence and divergence in intersemiotic affectual meanings. If a certain kind of affectual meaning is committed via the visual display of a depicted character's facial expression without a corresponding commitment in the verbal text, it is regarded as intersemiotic divergence. And when the affectual meanings are committed in the verbal text and visual image realised in a contradictory direction (e. g. positive versus negative) , it is seen as intersemiotic divergence. However, if both visual and verbal models realise the same kind, or neither of them commit any kind of meaning, it is defined as intersemiotic convergence.

Table 4 – 2①　　　**Intersemiotic convergence and divergence**

in affectual meaning (represented from Tian 2011: 62)

Verbal	Visual	Intersemiotic relation
affect	██████████	divergence
██████████	affect	divergence
positive affect	negative affect	divergence
positive affect	positive affect	convergence
████████████████████		convergence

Therefore, Illustration 4 – 8 can be considered as an instance of intersemiotic divergence, where positive facial affect is committed in the depiction of several characters and no affect committed in the verbal. An example of intersemiotic convergence is presented in the first spread of *The Monster Nian* (see Illustration 4 – 9). As illustrated in this image, it is an introduction to the main protagonist of the story, with a depiction of a monster Nian. The face of the depicted character is illustrated with four eyes (the lower two of them are directed downward) , and the bodily gesture illustrated as squatting on a mountain and curling up with his claws hidden. Thus a negative affect is inscribed in this illustration, though it is not specified what kind of the negative affect is. The monster Nian depicted with a dark background may be depressed, lonely, or fearful. The verbal text written at the bottom specifies the exact negative affect encoded in the visual image. The verbal text is demonstra-

---

①　Dark shading in the cells signals that no such meaning is realised.

ted as follows:

很久很久以前，有一个很<u>孤独</u>的怪物，他的名字叫做"年"。
他住在高高的山上，从来没有人和他玩。
Once upon a time, there is a lonely monster whose name is 'Nian'.
He lives on a high mountain and nobody ever played with him before.

Illustration 4 – 9   from *The Monster Nian* (2007)

Aside from the facial expression and bodily gesture, there are other visual techniques used here to reinforce the loneliness of the depicted character in this image. The use of colour in this story-page is represented via the [muted] and [cool] option which creates a depressed and distressed mood, showing a lonely and desolate story world to the reader. In addition, the depicted character is gazing out directly at the reader, aiming to strongly invite the reader to be engaged in the imaginary world to play with him since he has always been alone in the story world. In a nutshell, the intersemiotic convergence of attitudinal meaning is construed in this case with the verbiage amplifying the particular negative affectual meaning, and thus shaping intermodally a lonely character and enhancing reader's impression of him.

4.4   The interplay of verbal and visual semiotics in creating engagement

Having identified the interpersonal features of visual components, this section shifts its focus on the collaboration between words and images to synergistically create interpersonal meanings. To facilitate the analysis, this section selects the picture book *The Monster Nian* (Xiong 2007) as the main objective to explore the interpersonal cohesive relations between the two modalities within the book. It first explores the interpersonal aspect of language via the analysis of Mood structures of the clauses within the book (Halliday 1994/2000; Halliday & Matthiessen 2004), and then comes to the account of the interpersonal features of visual images on the basis of Painter et al. 's (2013) analytical framework.

4.4.1   Interpersonal meanings in verbal text

Among three metafunctions distinguished in SFL, the one that primarily deals with enacting social relations between the speaker and the listener in a particular context of social interaction is referred to the interpersonal (Halliday 1994/2000; Halliday & Matthiessen 2004). The discussion of the interpersonal features of a multimodal text involves a look at "the ways that both modes *address* the viewer/readers" (Royce 2007: 70). With regard to the linguistic system in SFL, the interpersonal meanings are lexicogrammatically realised by the clause of exchange and the ordering of Mood structure in relation to that clause. The Mood structure mainly comprises the ordering of Subject, the Finite and the Predicator, revealing some specific speech functions of the clauses (Halliday1994/2000). To explore the interpersonal meanings encoded in the verbal text of *The Monster Nian*, the Mood structure of the whole text is analysed clause by clause with corresponding speech functions realised by them. A schematic representation of the Mood structure in verbiage and the demonstration of the choices of focalisation in images within the picture book are outlined in Table 4 – 3.

Table 4 – 3   **Mood structure and focalisationin the bimodal**

text of *The Monster Nian*

Page	Subject/Finite/Predicator Positioning (verbal text)	Mood	Speech Act	Eye Contact (visual text)	Type of Eye Contact
1	你们/知道 you/know 他/是 he/is	Int.[①] Dec.	Com. Stat.		observe
2	(elliptical subject)/有 ("have") 他/叫 he/names 他/住在 he/lives 没有人/玩 nobody/plays	Dec. Dec. Dec. Dec.	Stat. Stat. Stat. Stat.		contact
3	他/会/感到 he/would/feel (elliptical subject)/不/知道 don't/know 他/会/感到 he/would/feel 他/冲下 he/rushes (elliptical subject)/吓唬 scares	Dec. Dec. Dec. Dec. Dec.	Stat. Stat. Stat. Stat. Stat.		observe
4	(elliptical subject)/救命 help	Imp.	Com.		observe
5	大家/聚, 挂, 做, 穿, 过 people/gather, hang, do, wear, celebrate 年/不/出现 Nian/doesn't/appear	Dec. Dec.	Stat. Stat.		contact
6	人们/会/过年 people/would/celebrate 许多人/忘记 lots people/forget	Dec. Dec.	Stat. Stat.		contact
7	(elliptical subject)/是 is (elliptical subject)/有 have	Dec. Dec.	Stat. Stat.		contact
8	年/会/抓住 Nian/would/capture	Dec.	Stat.		observe
9	年/会/跳出 Nian/would/jump 年/钻到 Nian/jumps into	Dec. Dec.	Stat. Stat.		observe
10	年/会/笼罩 Nian/would/envelop (elliptical subject)/使 make	Dec. Dec.	Stat. Stat.		contact

① Int. = interrogative; Dec. = declarative; Imp. = imperative; Stat. = statement; Com. = command.

— 114 —

Continued

Page	Subject/Finite/Predicator Positioning (verbal text)	Mood	Speech Act	Eye Contact (visual text)	Type of Eye Contact
11	(elliptical subject)/让 let	Dec.	Stat.		contact
12	人/被/吞掉 people/are/swallowed	Dec.	Stat.		contact
13	(elliptical subject)/不能 can't 结果/是 result/is 谁/不/愿意 anyone/doesn't/like 我们/重新来 we/restart	Imp. Dec. Imp. Imp.	Com. Stat. Com. Com.		contact
14	(elliptical subject)/逃脱 escape (elliptical subject)/是 is	Imp. Imp.	Com. Com.		contact
15	你/要/有 you/should/have	Imp.	Com.		contact
16	你/要/忘记 you/should/forget 你/要/打电话 you/should/telephone 你/要/说 you/should/say (elliptical subject)/要/说 should/say	Imp. Imp. Imp. Imp.	Com. Com. Com. Com.		contact
17	(elliptical subject)/别/漏下 don't/miss (elliptical subject)/别/忘 don't/forget	Imp. Imp.	Com. Com.		contact
18	年/有 Nian/has 年/变 Nian/changes	Dec. Dec.	Stat. Stat.		contact
19	新年快乐 Happy New Year	Imp.	Com.		contact

As shown in the table above, with few exceptions the clauses employed within the picture books take the form of declarative, contributing to the continuity of the picture book narrative. Generally speaking, the structure of declarative tends not to encourage much engagement between the reader and the story. When compared with declarative structure, the form of interrogative and imperative involve more interaction and engagement. The significance of declarative clauses in the story lies in that while the interrogative and imperative clauses may interrupt the guiding thread of the story narrative, declaratives serve to keep the continuity of the narrative without an excess of interruptions. This strategy has been wildly applied in the initial and intermediate stages of the story, which offer information of the main protagonist and several characteristics attributed to him. In the beginning part of the story, the reader is told by a continuous number of declaratives that Nian is a monster derived from loneliness and desolateness and he is easily to be exasperated by the people who have the same sense of loneliness. The reader in this stage is required to be relatively detached observers who are likely to receive the pulse of information rather than actively taking part in the story. As the story unfolds, the reader is told that the monster intends to hunt for the people who are lonely and unhappy during the Spring Festival. By utilising a series of declarative clauses, the story activates introductory stage and leads the reader to know the default situations in which people would be attacked by the monster Nian. By the same token, the declarative mood structures employed in this stage do not encourage the reader to engage with the story and to see themselves in the protagonist role to feel the mood of painfulness and pressure.

The exceptions in this story appear in the very opening and final stage of the book. At the beginning part of the story, the writer adopts an interrogative clause to ask the reader a question on what constitutes the monster Nian. The interrogative clause serves as a kind of command which requires the reader to be immediately involved in the story to give some certain feedbacks to it, and to make enough imaginations on the theme of the story (such as what is the monster, what he looks like, is he ferocious or dangerous, etc.). However, a following clause in the form of declarative gives the answer to the reader, describing the monster Nian as the main protagonist of the story and opening the story narrative. Obviously, the purpose of the interrogative clause in this case is not really asking the reader for an answer; but it is a rhetorical question to create an interactive relationship between the reader and the main protagonist, inviting the reader to participate in the unfolding story events. In addition to the interrogative clause, commands are also realised through imperative clauses which have been found in a swift succession (in double spreads 13, 14, 15, 16 and 17). Theses imperatives play a vital part in informing the reader a range of measures to escape from the monster Nian such as to wear red clothes on the Spring Festival, to make a phone call to greet friends, and so on. In this stage, the imperative clauses make ordersto the reader, expecting him/her to enter into the story world to stand in the protagonist role and to do like the protagonist via taking these suggested instructions. Followed the instructions expressed through these imperatives, the reader would achieve a full understanding of the essence of the story, as well as being taught from the story some lessons about the customs of Chinese New Year.

So far, it seems that an objective and distant narrative voice has been construed via the relatively high occurrences of declarative clauses, and scarce uses of interrogative clauses and imperative clauses.

4.4.2   Interpersonal meanings in images

This section mainly deals with the interpersonal meaning realised by visual components within the picture book. The analysis of some basic choices of visual systems is first illustrated in Table 4 − 4.

Table 4 − 4   **Visual features in *The Monster Nian***

Categories		Number
FOCALISATION	contact	14
	observe	5
AFFECT	appreciative	16
	alienating	2
	emphatic	1
AMBIENCE	warm	6
	cool	13
FORCE	upscaling	5
	downscaling	6

Concerning the options from the system of FOCALISATION, the analysis in picture books shows that there is predominance of [contact] focalisation (13 instances) over [observe] ones, which count for six of the cases identified. By using the observe options, the illustrator could keep the child reader outside the story world, and the represented participants in the image are offered to the reader as items of information. In this regard, the children can take an observing stance, rather than participating in the story activity, and hence they may learn from what is going on in the narrative context. The first observe option appears in double spread 3, where the monster Nian is chasing after a single man without companion, only with a livestock besides him. The facial expression of the monster Nian is represented as murderous with the exaggeratedly open mouth and sharp claws. While the chased man is depicted as extremely frightened and deeply scared. The options of the colours used in this spread are muted and cool colours, which provide the reader with a sense of depression and flurry. In this case, there is no eye contact with the reader and, consequently, the reader is not required to take part in the story world but only accept or reject the information offered by the visual images. Complemented with the verbal text, the reader easily understands the offers of information that "compared with men with companion, Nian is more likely to hunt for the lonely man". In the similar vein, the observe options in double spread 8 and 9 inform the reader about the sequence of story events and actions without involving the reader and establishing engagement with the depicted characters and the reader. In these images, the represented characters have no eye contact with us, reminding us to keep the distance with the story world, and just to observe what happens within it and learn from the offers of information. The choices of observe focalisation in the picture book are always combined with use of long shots which establishes a far social distance between the depicted characters and the child reader, reinforcing the role of the reader as an observer.

In contrast with observe images, the contact options are preferred by the illustrator of the picture book. One of the primary functions that the focalising-choices of contact may serve is the opening introduction of the main protagonist of the story. As discussed earlier, the opening spread of the book adopts a choice of contact where Nian is gazing out directly at the child reader, with the supplement of verbal text by introducing the origin of Nian. This function of contact image is depending on the "metafictive context" (Painter et al. 2013) of the narrative framing, which brief introduces the main protagonist of the story (often with the depicted immediate context of the character) and facilitates the reading of the narrative. However, the use of eye contact is not restricted to this kind of metafictive nature, such as in the double spreads 5, 7, 10, and 11. In the 5th spread, the recto image depicts an occasion of celebration for Chinese New Year where a number of people assemble to conduct a series of activities to celebrate the coming New Year. While in the right bottom of the recto, the monster Nian is depicted in a very small size. The characters depicted in both left and right side of the spread are staring at the reader, inviting him/her to the depicted context to interact with them, as well as encouraging him/her to empathise with them. The child reader is thus involved in the story world to share a joyful and positive mood with the depicted characters in the context of New Year celebration. In addition, the monster Nian looking at us is depicted in a comparable small size which creates a sense of irony and humour, offering a light-hearted emotion to the child reader. In the double spread 7, although there is a contrast between the recto and verso in the narrative setting, all of the depicted characters are gazing out at us. Thus a strong engagement is established between the represented characters and us, and we are then invited to be involved in the story scene to feel the strongly contrastive emotion (the happy and enjoyful emotion in the recto while the sad and depressive feeling in the verso). The options of eye contact between the characters and the child reader are also employed in the spreads 10, 11, 12, and 13. These four spreads illustrate a series of painful situations in which a lonely man is captured by the monster Nian. The illustrations clearly convey the information that the lonely man, by gazing at the child reader, is looking for support from him/her as well as imploring him/her to rescue the lonely man from the control of Nian. The contact options in the 12th and 13th spreads are supported by the use of close shots which create a very close social distance between the reader and depicted characters, reinforcing the social engagement between them. Therefore, these images with the contact options achieve a forceful engagement between the child and the depicted characters, and forge a strong identification of the child with the suffering man in the images.

With regard to second visual features of interactive meaning, the [cool] options dominate in the use of AMBIENCE in the picture book. It is apparent that the use of colours would offer to the child reader the most instant bonding effect. The choices of different ambience certainly create diverse kinds of mood and evoke in the reader differentiated emotion. In this picture book, two different styles are construed by the choices of different ambience. The [warm] options adopted in the 5th and 6th spreads in which people are cele- brating the New Year create a sense of enjoyment and happiness with the use of warmer colours such as red and orange hues. The reader at first glance of the images is attracted by the positive and harmonious ambience and shares the joy and happiness felt by the depicted people in the celebration. Further- more, the relatively richness of colour differentiation in the spread enables the reader to achieve a sense of familiarity with the reality that he/she experi- ences, and thus a correlation of a happy mood to the Spring Festival is well established in the reader's mind. Another example appears in double spread 15, where the depicted characters (the monster Nian in the verso; while the man in the recto) are situated in a warm ambience by the use of a complete set of red hues. The facial expression of Nian is clearly recognised as scare and anxiousness, whereas the expression on the man's face is represented as comfortable and delighted. According to the story narrative, the use of red colours is supposed to be one of the solutions to escape from Nian's control. And thus the warm options used here build a positive and encouraging mood, enabling the child reader to associate the red colour with the Spring Festival and to learn the sprite of not being discouraged while being confronted with difficulties.

In comparison to the [warm] colours employed in the picture book, the images filled with [cool] colours attempt to construe an opposite style of am- bience. The [cool] options of ambience in the picture book are mostly used to demonstrate three kinds of visual environments of the story events. Firstly, it is used in the depictions of being alone during the Spring Festival. Instances of this kind are found in double spreads 3, 11. In these cases, the choices of colours create a negative, lonely and even hopeless mood with a combination of blue and dark hues. Secondly, it is employed in the depictions of the monster Nian such as in the double spreads 2, 4, and 14. Through the choices of cool colours, the illustrator aims to portray an image of ferocious and cruel monster of which the child reader is afraid. Moreover, the cool colours are adopted in the situations of being captured by the monster Nian, contributing to the construction of a sort of despair and struggling emotion, such as in double spreads 10, 12, and 13. Through different ambience options, the illustrator attempts to facilitate the reading of the disparate emotions of the depicted characters as the story unfolds. A salient example is in double spread 7 (see Illustration 4 – 5), where the background of the verso is filled with bright yellow hues while the depiction of the recto is decorated with dark and blue hues. Corresponding to the verbal text, the left side of the visual composition can be interpreted as a scene of family reunion, creating a positive and light-hearted emotion. On the contrary, the left one represents a scene of being alone, evoking in the child reader the sadness and loneliness felt by the depicted character.

The third important visual feature the present analysis takes into account is AFFECT. The analysis relevant to this dimension shows that there is a predominance of the minimalist style and only two instances of generic style are adopted in the picture book. As mentioned before, the system AFFECT is mainly concerned with the depiction style of characters. The most often used option in the picture book is the minimalist style which primarily contributes to the function of social commentary. The minimalist style would provide the child reader with a relatively long distance as the story unfolds, and consequently, to reinforce the role of the observer and learn lessons from the story. For example, the 5th double spread represents a wide range of different characters in the New Year's celebration, and all of them are not highly individuated. It can be inferred from the style of character depiction used here that the reader is not expected to establish personal affinity with any one of them as a specified individual as in our daily life, such as parents, classmates, colleagues and so on. Instead of that, the illustrator offer a relatively detached reading stance to the reader, requiring them not to recognise them as highly individuated characters but as a symbolic collective group which function in pushing the story forward as well as offering information of the narrative events and narrative world. Another important factor motivate the options of minimalist style in this book is that the minimalist style is more "iconic and stylised" (Welch 2005), with a particular focus on the expression of un/happiness. In the context of this book, the contrastive representations of happiness and unhappiness serve as the narrative tones of the story. By applying the minimalist style to the character depiction, the reader is expected to easily recognise the happiness (e. g. the people smiling in the 6th double spread) or sadness (e. g. the lonely man sobbing in the 7th double spread).

As for the visual GRADUATION, the options of upscaled graduation and downscaled graduation have taken almost the same proportion; there are five instances of upscaled graduation and six instances of downscaled graduation within the picture book. Graduation in visual images is conceived of as significant in expressing attitudinal meanings and provoking the reader's emotional response. For instance, the choice [quantification: number: up] in the verso of the 7th double spread intensifies the positive attitude inscribed in the image. Even if there is one depicted character in this image, other interpersonal choices applied here (such as the choices of [focalisation: direct] and the warm colours) would also express the positive attitude. But the positive attitude is strengthened by the use of upscaled quantification (a crowd of people invoke more positive attitudinal meanings). On the contrary, in the double spreads 15, 16 and 17, there are two depicted characters involved in the story event, a single man and the monster Nian. The ideational content of these images seem to be relatively neutral since the monster and the single man get along quite well without any apparent facial expression on their face. However, it is noteworthy that the monster is depicted in a small size and occupies tiny amount of the image space. Consequently, the option of [quantification: extent: down] in the image contributes to reducing the danger of the monster and invoking the feeling of security. The interpersonal analysis of *The Monster Nian* in relation to the visual semiotic resources is provided in detail in the Table 4 − 5 below.

Table 4 – 5   Visual analysis of *the Monster Nianat* interpersonal level

Page	Ideation	Focalisation	Ambience	Affect	Pathos	Social distance	Graduation	Power relation
1	Nian	contact	muted: dark, cool, removed		appreciative	far		equality
2	Nian	contact	muted: dark, cool, removed	lonely	appreciative	far		Nian power
3	Nian hunting	observe	muted: dark, cool, removed	angry, aggressive (Nian), scared (people)	appreciative	far		Nian power
4	Nian catching	contact	muted: dark, cool, removed		appreciative	far		equality
5	people celebrating	contact	vibrant, warm, less familiar	happy, positive, encouraging (people)	appreciative	medium	quantification: number, up mass: down	equality
6	New Year landscape	observe	less vibrant warm, removed		appreciative	far	quantification: number, up	equality
7	People on the Spring Festival	contact	vibrant, warm, removed; and muted: dark, cool, removed	positive, happy, encouraging (verso); and negative, somber, lonely (recto)	emphatic	close	quantification: number, up quantification: number, down	equality
8	Nian	observe	muted: dark, cool, removed		alienating	medium		equality
9	Nian jumping	observe	muted: dark, cool, removed	negative, scared	appreciative	far	quantification: mass/amount, down	equality

Continued

Page	Ideation	Focalisation	Ambience	Affect	Pathos	Social distance	Graduation	Power relation
10	Nian	contact	muted: dark, cool, removed	negative, suffering (the lonely people)	appreciative	far	quantification: extent, up	Nian power
11	Lonely man	contact	muted: dark, cool, removed	negative, angry, mad	alienating	medium		equality
12	Lonely man	contact	muted: dark, cool, removed	sad	appreciative	close		equality
13	Lonely man	contact	muted: dark, cool, removed	unwilling	appreciative	close		equality
14	Nian	observe	muted: dark, cool, removed		appreciative	far		equality
15	the	contact	vibrant, warm, removed	happy (people); unhappy (Nian)	appreciative	medium	quantification: mass/amount, down	equality
16	People telephoning	observe	vibrant, warm, familiar		appreciative	medium	quantification: mass/amount, down	equality
17	People telephoning	contact	vibrant, warm, removed	forgivable	appreciative	medium	quantification: mass/amount, down	equality
18	Nian turning into red	contact	muted: dark cool, removed; vibrant, warm, removed	bashful, positive	appreciative	medium	quantification: number, up	equality
19	Red Nian	contact	vibrant, warm, removed	happy	appreciative	medium		equality

4.4.3   Analysing interpersonal intersemiotic complementarity

The previous sections in the chapter have discussed both the verbal and visual modes of *The Monster Nian* as independent texts, each of which conveys some specific interpersonal meanings to the reader. In this section, a comprehensive analysis will be conducted to explore the ways in which verbal texts and visual images are combined to create interpersonal meaning as a synergy of bimodal text. To this end, Royce's (1999, 2007) framework of intersemiotic complementarity provides a useful analytical tool to probe into the interpersonal meanings which are created by the intersection and synergy of words and images in the picture book. Based on the choices of Mood and Modality in SFL, Royce (2007) distinguishes two basic and distinct interpersonal intersemiotic relations between different semiotic systems within a multimodal text: *attitudinal congruence* and *attitudinal dissonance*. *Attitudinal congruence* takes place in a picture book when both verbal texts and visual images cooperate to present similar interpersonal content and parallel kind of attitude. A congruence of attitudinal meaning is produced, for instance, when the depicted character does not represent any engagement with the reader (e. g. lack of eye contact towards the reader) and the verbal text employs an external voice to merely offer information (e. g. the narrator's voice without showing any intimacy). Whereas the *attitudinal dissonance* in the book is recognised as an interpersonal interaction in which the image and the verbiage construe an opposite or ironic attitudinal meaning. A dissonance of attitude occurs in a picture book, for example, if there are choices of engagement in the visual semiotic system that converge with the options of propositions showing lack of such kind of interpersonal meaning in the verbal semiotic system.

In the examination of the combination of images and words in the book, it can be found that images and verbiages tend to cooperate with each other to express interpersonal meanings, whether in the converging or diverging way. In general, the verbal texts and visual images within the book are organised in a convergent attitudinal fashion, which correspond to each other to synergistically make interpersonal meanings. A striking example is the 10th double spread of the book (see Illustration 4 – 10) , where an interpersonal congruence is realised by the interplay of the visual image and the verbiage within the composition. The verbal text on the left top is composed of several declarative clauses, realising the unmarked speech function of offering a statement to the reader. Meanwhile, the visual mode also addresses the reader from a distance perspective without requiring him/her to react or give a response. A choice of minimal style for character depiction reinforces the observe position for the reader, who is expected to take a relatively detached stance and to perceive the depicted characters as some certain items of information.

Illustration 4 – 10   from *The Monster Nian* (2007)

As for the perspective of proxemics (Hall 1966, Kress & van Leeuwen 1996, 2006) in the image, a long shot is employed in the visual so that the represented participants are positioned in a far social distance to the reader. Moreover, the monster is depicted at a vertical angle from below who looks down on the reader, exerting symbolic power on the reader. According to van Leeuwen (2000: 338) , " to look up at someone signifies that someone has symbolic power over the viewer, whether as an authority, a role-model, or otherwise". Another dimension of visual interpersonal meanings is the use of colours in the image. The visual composition applies a [cool] ambience to evoke a depressed and subdued mood, emphasising that the painful feelings of being captured by the monster Nian. It also adopts a [removed] choice of

FAMILARITY to signal a removal from the material world and thereality via utilising a reduced palette. In sum, the combined verbal and visual modes of the bimodal text construe an interpersonal congruence in a similar attitudinal fashion to create a distant relationship between the depicted characters and the reader so that there is no need for him/her to give a feedback apart from agreeing or disagreeing with the represented information. The synergy of both modes attempts to position the reader in a role of observer, informing him/her the suffering and miserable experience of being hunted by the monster Nian.

Despite a large number of intersemiotic relations of convergences within the book, verbal texts and images would sometimes express different interpersonal meanings. As mentioned before, most of the clauses in verbal semiotic are in forms of declarative, offering some certain pulses of information to child readers without requiring them for any particular engagement. However, there are alternative interpersonal features of the visual images in the book which enact social interactions and engagement between the represented participants and the child reader, symbolising a dissonance in the attitudinal meanings reflected by different semiotics of the picture book. In the 7th double spread of the book, for instance, the declarative clauses in the verbal semiotic system convey information as a statement of fact and underline the different situations on the Spring Festival in a seemingly objective tone with a third person voice of narrative. It contributes to keeping the reader outside the story world to appreciate what is going on within it, and to providing the reader with some items of information about the contrastive situations in which different people are involved. However, the visual mode of the composition expresses the interpersonal meanings in an opposite way. The illustrations of the depicted characters adopt a focalising choice of [contact] to force the reader to engage with the represented participants, and to react or to give some kind of response (positive or negative) to the emotions presented via their facial expressions and bodily gestures (e. g. sobbing or laughing). In terms of proxemics, the visual composition establishes a strong intimacy between the represented participants and the child reader by the use of a close shot and an eye-level angle, all of which working together to present an invitation for the reader to get involved and to share the various feelings of them (either the happiness of the family reunion or the sadness of the lonely man). The contrastive ambience choices for the depiction of two completely different situations, such as the warm bright orange colours for the family reunion and the cool dark hues for the lonely man, are key parameters in representing the circumstantial backgrounds of the story in which various emotions are easy to be invoked in the child reader. In summary, the verbal text contrasts with the visual elements in realising interpersonal meanings with different features on the one hand; and on the other, they collaborate to communicate interpersonal meanings which are beyond the scope of the sole semiotic (verbal or visual).

Another aspect of interpersonal intersemiotic relation proposed by Royce (1999, 2007) is the *reinforcement of address* which refers to the identical form of address in the verbal and visual modes. In this picture book, for instance, most of the declarative clauses in the initial and intermediate stages of the story utilise the third person pronoun or third person plural pronoun which correspond to the use of observe illustrations, working together to construe a seemingly remote and objective voice of the narrator. When it comes to the final stage of the story, a sets of imperative clauses are employed to give explanations of how to escape from the monster, supported by uses of the second person pronoun (你, you) and the inclusive first person pronoun (我们, we). As for the visual mode in these compositions (from the thirteenth double-page spread to the seventh spread), the represented participants are depicted in a short distance between the child readers with their eyes gazing out directly at them. These visual techniques favour the reader's identification with the main depicted characters and invite them to get involved in the story world to follow the instructions as the protagonist does. Thus, a reinforcement of address is achieved through the cooperation of verbal texts and visual texts in creating a strong engagement between the characters and the child reader as well as forging the reader's identification with the represented characters to learn a lesson of Chinese traditional customs.

4.4.4 Analysing the commitment of interpersonal meaning

So far the verbal and visual modalities of *The Monster Nian* are examined as independent texts and the intersemiotic complementary between them is discussed. This section moves to the analysis of the differences between their affordances in terms of interpersonal meaning by each semiotic within the book. To facilitate this comparison, this present section selects the 7th double spread of the book (see Illustration 4 − 5) as the exemplar for the analysis of different commitment of meaning in relation to verbal and visual semiotics.

In considering the commitments of interpersonal meaning for each modality in the composition, the affiliation between the reader and the depicted characters (and between themselves) needs to be taken into account firstly. As for visual focalisation, the depicted characters (whether the represented smiling characters or the crying man) are gazing directly out at the reader, inviting the child reader to get involved in the story world. The represented characters are placed in a quite close social distance to the reader via the use of a close shot (Kress & van Leeuwen 2006). Meanwhile, the reader is kept in a neutral power relation with the reader by adopting an eye-level angel with him/her. All of these visual features contribute to creating a strong engagement with the child reader, in case he/she is detached from the story and not take the represented characters to their hearts. When it comes to the affiliation between the depicted characters themselves, it can be found a vivid contrast in the visual composition that the represented characters in the verso page are situated in a quite close proximity to one another, while the lonely man depicted in the recto is placed in a far distance from them, ensuring no actual physical touch between them. Through the choices of proximity between represented participants within the composition, two differing situations (the family reunion versus the lonely man) on the day of Spring Festival are modelled to train the child reader to keep a closer attention at such visual divergence. In the middle of the visual composition, the monster Nian is depicted as moving across the gutter of the composition, showcasing a horizontal movement from the family reunion to the lonely man. The choices of orientation strengthen this physical movement. In the left part of the image, the monster leaves his back to the family members, precluding any eye contact with them. However, in the recto page, the monster looks straight at the lonely man, providing a strong statement of interpersonal engagement. Thus the child reader is apprenticed to read a visual metaphor that the monster Nian is more likely to hunt for those lonely men on the Spring Festival rather than the family members staying together on that day. By comparison, the linguistic text at the right bottom of the composition is in a much smaller size. In respect to the interpersonal affiliation, there is no similar meaning committed by the verbal text; besides an external focalisation to the story, informing the reader to pay some attention to the lonely man. With regard to the orientation and proximity between the represented participants, there is no verbalisation of any kind of social distance and power relation between them, suggesting a greater distance for us to read the story narration and keeping us outside of the story world.

Turning to the expression of feeling, different meanings are committed in the visual and verbal semiotic systems. At first sight of the visual composition, the emotion and affect of each depicted character is provided via their facial expressions as well as by their bodily gestures. The depicted members in the verso page express a happy and light-hearted emotion by smiling at us and the head-to-head orientation between one another. The lonely man sitting glumly beside a window shows a depressed and lonely emotion, crying painfully with tears dropping on his face. The strong contrast of emotions is reinforced by the choices of ambience within the composition. The characters showing happiness are filled with a warm ambience via the bright sunny yellow hues, creating a comforting and positive feeling so as to keep the reader in an upbeat mood. Nevertheless, the lonely man is represented in a cool ambience with dark hues, signaling a depressed and negative feeling and keeping the reader in a downbeat mood. Notably, the visual attitude of happiness inscribed in the verso page is intensified by the graduation choice of [quantification: number: up]. A quantification of number in effect reinforces the depicted emotion of happiness and meanwhile foregrounds the mood of loneliness inscribed in the face of the single man. The reader is thus encouraged to appreciate the divergent expressions of mood (hopeful versus hopeless) , taught a lesson by the story that do not be along on the Spring Festival. Another important visual feature in the composition is the drawing style of the character depiction. The represented characters within the composition are illustrated in the cartoon-like minimalist style. It is motivated by the fact that choices of minimalist style are more "iconic and stylised" (Welch 2005) , effectively expressing un/happiness of the depicted characters. Therefore, the visual features achieve a deep engagement between the reader and the depicted characters, and forge the identification of the reader with them to share the differing mood of both happiness and sadness. Concerning the linguistic text, the meaning systems in play are those of verbal attitudes and affects, realised by choices of lexical inscriptions within the verbiage. The lexical inscriptions of attitudes in verbiage consist of two different kinds of moods: "热闹的" (jolly) and "孤独的" (lonely) ; while the former provides a positive emotion of happiness and security, the latter choice of verbal expression expounds an opposite affect of sadness and insecurity.

In examining how the visual image and verbal text contribute to the construction of meaning in terms of commitment, it can be summarised that there is more interpersonal meaning committed in the visual text than in the verbal text. Within the whole composition, the visual text is more "eye-catching" to the reader than verbiage, not only in terms of the visual space occupied by each modality, but also in terms of their relative contributions to the whole interpersonal meanings encoded in the double-page spread. While there are some degree of interpersonal meaning committed in the visual systems (such as pathos, social distance, ambience, and visual graduation) , no commitment at all has been found in the complementary meaning system within the verbiage. It is evident that the visual text plays a more fundamental part in building engagement between the child reader and the illustrated characters as well as in establishing identification of the former with the emotional differentiating characters. The differing commitment of the visual and verbal semiotic systems in this visual composition with regard to affiliation and feeling is summarised in Table 4 – 6.

Table 4 – 6①   **Degrees of commitment of interpersonal meaning related in Illustration 4 – 5**

	Image	Commitment	Verbal text	Commitment
Affiliation	Focalisation	Full: (depicted characters) gazing out directly at us	Focalisation	Partial: perceptions as external to story
	Pathos	Full: minimalist style	Charaterisation	
	Social distance	Full: a very close shot; (family members): in close proximity to each other	Social distance	
Feeling	Visual affect	Full: (family members) "happy", "jolly"; (lonely man) "sad", "lonely"	Verbal affect	Partial: 热闹的("jolly"), 孤独的("lonely")
	Ambience	Full: (verso) vibrant, warm, light; (recto) muted, cool, dark	Tone	
	Attitude	(family members) "happy" (lonely man) "sad" inscribed via facial expression	Attitude	Partial: 热闹的("jolly"), 孤独的("lonely")
	Graduation	quantification: number, upscaled	Graduation	

4.5 Summary

This chapter has conducted a systematic analysis of interpersonal meanings encoded and expressed by the two semiotics (image and verbiage) within the Chinese picture books. The chapter firstly identifies the interpersonal features of visual components throughout the data. The interpersonal features in

---

① Shading in the cell is employed to facilitate the analysis of areas of commitment. Dark shading indicates no commitment, while light shading signifies minor degree of commitment.

relation to the visual semiotic are examined through the parameters of FOCAL-ISATION, AFFECT, AMBIENCE, and GRADUATION. It then examines the attitudinal meanings inscribed or invoked in picture books, exploring the ways in which visual and verbal resources are deployed to encode attitudinal meanings. Based on Royce's (1999, 2007) intersemiotic complementarity, it then moves on to an account of interpersonal cohesive relations between verbal and visual texts within the exemplar picture book. The examination reveals that there is a difference between the two modalities in involving the reader. The verbal text intends to maintain a continuity of story narrative via the over-whelming uses of declarative clauses, while the visual text is likely to establish affinity and engagement with the reader by the frequently-adopted type of contact image and other visual strategies (e. g. the widely-used activated ambience). It is found that the cohesive relations between the two modalities are mainly realised through the *attitudinal congruence* and *attitudinal divergence*.

Apart from the cohesive relations between the two semiotic systems within the picture book, the chapter also conducts an account of the difference of the two semiotics in affording interpersonal meaning. A commitment analysis has been carried out to track the way in which each semiotic system is instantiated in the text and to compare their relative contributions to the creation of overall interpersonal meaning. It is observed that the visual text is more responsible for the interpersonal meaning committed in the data and the interaction and identification between the reader and the depicted characters are more subjected to the visual text.

The next chapter is mainly concerned with the ideational meaning construed byvisual and verbal semiotics, aiming to explore the ways in which both semiotics are co-deployed to create representations within Chinese picture books.

Chapter Five   The Interplay of Visual and Verbal Semiotics in Processing Reality

5. 1   Introduction

Because of the more accessible nature of a visual semiotic representation, children intend to choose picture books as their first reading material than a linguistic one. The previous chapter deals with the interpersonal meaning expressed by verbal and visual texts, and the cohesive relations between the two modes as well as different affordance for interpersonal meaning of each modality within the selected picture book. This chapter shifts the focus to the examination of ideational meanings encoded in the verbal and visual components of Chinese picture books. Based on the framework for visual narrative (Painter et al. 2013), the chapter firstly identifies the ideational/representational features of visual components throughout the data of Chinese picture books, in terms of Participants, Processes and Circumstances. Then the chapter selects the picture book *The Adventure of the Postman* as the main object and extends Royce's (1999, 2007) intersemiotic complementary framework to analyse the ideational intersemiotic complementarity between images and verbiages, delving into the way in which each modality complementanother as interdependent components to construct the represented world and to transmit ideational messages to the child writer. The last part of the chapter places a particular emphasis on the different commitment of verbal and visual texts in relation to ideational meaning when they are co-instantiated in the picture book.

5.2   The analysis of representational features of images

Picture books are more accessible for children to understand the representation of the depicted world and characters. This section deals primarily with the depiction of the participants, and the construction of their identities as well as the symbolic expression of their attributes in Chinese picture books. Based on the Painter et al. 's (2013) framework, the section examines the ideational meanings realised in the visual semiotic of picture books and the strategies available to the illustrator to convey the representational meanings to the child reader. The analysis will be conducted in terms of three aspects: participants (how are characters depicted in the images of story book), processes (how are they involved in different types of actions) and circumstances (the represented context and interrelations between different circumstances).

5.2.1   The representation of participants

As we have discussed earlier, Kress and van Leeuwen (2006) distinguish the "narrative processes" from the "conceptual processes" by the existence of vectors through which participants involved in a process are connected. It is not difficult to find that the characters represented in picture books are usually connected in narrative processes. A large number of visual images show that the depicted characters in a visual narrative are engaged in such kind of process, connected by different types of vectors. A salient example is in Illustration 4 – 5, where the monster Nian is creeping furtively towards the lonely man sobbing besides the window. In this case, the two participants (Nian and the man) are engaged in an actional process, and the vector in the process is created by the arms of Nian and also by the eye contact. Nevertheless, the characters may also be represented to the child reader in a more static way. These images with the lack of vectors correspond to the type of conceptual processes (Kress & van Leeuwen 1996, 2006), which are usually deployed in the introductory part of the picture story. At the very beginning of a picture book, the character is more likely to be depicted as static with one or more portraits, illustrating the character as the main protagonist of the picture book story. An example can be found in the first spread of *The Monster Nian is Coming* (Liu 2013). It represents a static image in which a character is represented to the reader without any established vector, only portraying the manifestation and appearance of the represented character. In this example, the static image in the beginning of the story initiates the "Orientation stage" (Martin & Rose 2008). Apart from playing an introductory part in the depiction of character, static images including depicted participants are deployed in picture books to serve another function. They are adopted in a set of moments within a story to indicate "a pause or a reflective moment" (Painter et al. 2013: 56), rather than evoking an action. Take Illustration 5 – 1 as an example, the depicted character within the image is engaged in a conceptual process, referring to a pause on the rhythm of the story narrative.

Illustration 5 – 1   Static representation of the character.
(The recto of double spread 6 from *A Battle with Nian*)

The image following the verbal text on the verso of the spread depicts an old man standing quietly in a snowfield. The verbal text is quoted as follows:

他威风的站在雪地，静静的等候即将出现的年兽。

He is standing on the snowfield, waiting quietly for the Monster Nian.

As indicated in the verbal text, the represented participant is waiting for the monster Nian, expecting to defeat the ogreish monster. An experiential reader will certainly know that the next pages of the picture book are likely to be the climax of the story, concerning with the methods adopted by the represented participant to defeat the monster and of course the result of the drastic fight between them. Before a series of actions being portrayed in the coming pages, this static image offered to the reader meets the requirement of a short pause in the rhythm of the story narrative, serving as a prelude of the climax of the narrative events.

Regardless the sharp difference between the images involving an action and the static images, most of the reader's attention would be firstly placed on the depiction of characters in picture books, including both the manifestation of characters, and character's appearance as well as reappearance. As for the manifestation of the depicted characters in images, a certain character represented in a purely visual narrative can be identified in subsequent pictures by a set of salient depiction features such as the re-depiction of head and facial expression, and the clothes he/she wears in the previous demonstration. As demonstrated in the Illustration 5 − 2, an option of [metonymic: body part] is used to infer the character identity and to enable the reader to stand on the character's shoes. Although the image provides only the portrait of her back, the reader is expected to recognise the identity of the represented participant by a series of salient depiction features similar with the previous depiction, such as the little red coat and black scarf. It is most common in the context of picture books that a complete manifestation (e. g. including the depiction of head) precedes a metonymic option. The reason underlying this option is that a preceding complete manifestation enables the reader to infer the identity of a particular participant and makes the depictions of character in various moments coherent and diversified.

Another important factor in recognising a certain participant as the story

大年初二，天阴沉沉的，要下雪了。一大早，爸爸就忙着
起来，补窗户隙，刷新门漆，换新灯泡……
啊，家里一下子变得亮堂了。
"走，补墙缝去喽！" 爸爸冲我男了男嘴。
太好了，那儿是妈妈从来不愿我一个人上去的地方呢。

Illustration 5 – 2   from *Reunion* (2008)

unfolds is whether the represented participant reappears in the next image or at
some other moments of the story. The difference between the two types of reappearance lies in that a reappearance occurs immediately would reinforce the
identification of the same character, while a reappearance at some later point
relies strongly on the support of the verbal text to infer the same identity within
a visual narrative. When the represented participant reappears in a visual narrative, the depicted circumstance in which the participant is placed would
probably shift. An option of reappearance is termed as [reappear: varied: sta-
tus], dealing with the shift of the status of a depicted character by moving the
character into/out circumstantiation. Take Illustration 5 – 3 for example, in
the first double-paged spread, the depicted participant is shown as an extremely small element in the background at the very bottom of the recto image;
however, when the page turns, the represent participant has moved from the
background to the front and center place of the visual composition. Thus a
choice of [status: emerge] has been employed in the example to move the depicted character from the status of being embedded in the insignificant circumstantiation to being a fully fledged character with distinguishing features. The
reader's attention is consequently attracted by the varied status of the depicted
character in his immediate reappearance in the page-turn, and the character is

foregrounded in the image to show the reader his wondrous adventure on a snowy day.

Illustration 5 – 3   Character reappearance in *The Adventure of the Postman*(2014)

5.2.2   Construing the processes

With regard to the visual processes in picture books, it is safe to say that the majority of processes in their visual images can be defined as narrative processes (Kress & van Leeuwen 2006) containing explicit vectors or oblique lines. According to Painter et al. (2013), the interpretation of ideational meaning in a visual image depends on the real-world knowledge and depicted context rather than merely on the presence or absence of prominent vectors. From this point of view, the man in the 13th spread of *The Monster Nian* is interpreted as speaking to the other participant even thought there is no speech bubble deployed to represent an explicit vector.

Unlike Kress and van Leeuwen's (2006) analytical framework for analysing representational meanings in images (especially the processes), the model proposed by Painter et al. (2013) to explore the ideational meanings in visual narratives focuses on the way "one event relates to another". Compared with the logico-semantic relations between different clauses, a visual text does not have the same potential to specify the relations of various events such as the relations of expansion or projection (e. g. Halliday 1994/2000; Halliday & Matthiessen 2004). Painter et al. (2013) specify a variety of INTER-EVENT options which are based on the analysis of visual narrative corpus to expound the relations between actions represented in successive images and the realisations of the interrelations between these depicted actions. In our corpus of Chinese picture books, it is easy to find a majority of successive images representing the option of temporal [succession]. For instance, Illustration 5 – 4 provides a type of temporal succession of events.

Illustrate 5 – 4   from *Nian* (2015)

The first image (the 13th and 14th spread image) depicts a boy giving some food to an old starving man in front of a house, and the adjacent image illustrates the old man giving a box to the little boy in a background of a mass of houses. Thus it is clear that the relation between the two successive images is interpreted as [succession: between sequences]. According to the verbal narrative, the kind-hearted boy helps an old man by offering all the food he has and thus rescues the old man from starving to death. Having a good rest, the old man gives the boy a box in which a stack of red papers are placed. In these two adjacent images, there are two different actions depicted and certainly two activity sequences are distinguished. However, not all the images in which a certain or some certain characters reappear in successive images (either in single page or across double spread, or cross a page turn) can be interpreted by the reader as temporal relation between the actions. Take Illustration 5 – 5 for example, the double-page spread merely represents the successive moments of a same activity, in this case, different moments of the monster Nian changing his original colour (e. g. dark black) to the bright redness.

Illustration 5 – 5   from *The Monster Nian* (2007)

While the significance of the activity in a picture book narrative lies in the temporal sequence, the reader has to be at risk of encountering counter-expectation of the next action in a sequence. As Barthes (1977) stresses that, the concept of activity sequence includes "expectancy" as well as "risk". In other words, while reading some important moments of activity sequence, the child reader would like to make a guess at the next possible action to come in such sequence, and there are certainly the risks for the expected possibility of not being fulfilled. Illustration 5 – 6 is drawn from *Reunion*. Within the story, the little girl lost her lucky coin when she was playing snowballs with other companions in the outside. Having noticed that the lucky coin has been lost, she returns to the snowfield to search for it attentively. The image depicts the girl rushing to the snowfield, seeking for the lucky coin all around, and the next action followed by the girl heart-broken crying for the failure to seek out her lucky coin. In the images, an option of [reappear: unchanged] has been combined to reinforce the counter-expectation of the coming action, inviting the child reader to engage with the sorrowful girl in the failure of getting her coin back and to feel sympathetic with her sadness.

天快黑的时候，我才回到家里，一摸口袋——啊，不见了！
好运硬币不见了！
我冲到院子里，袜子里全是雪，我的好运硬币在哪儿？

Illustration 5 – 6   from *Reunion* (2008)

Aside from the fulfilled or unfulfilled relation between the activity sequences in successive images, another visual feature of picture book narrative is the representation of a cause relation between the activity sequences of different participants. An example is shown in Illustration 5 – 7 which depicts the protagonist (the boy with red cloak) setting firecrackers, and the following image illustrates the monster Nian running away immediately with a frightened and painful expression on his face. Though there is no explicit relations depicted in two activity sequences (e. g. the boy drives away the monster by his arms or power), the activity sequences of the protagonist is likely to be inferred as causing the monster to retreat from the village in a hurry. Thus a relation of causality is established between the activity sequences of different represented participants. However, it is noticeable that the interpretation of a casual relation between a pair of differentiated activity sequences is always considered to be "a matter of inference" (Painter et al. 2013), relying on the reader's ability to understand how the depicted actions relate to another one and on the understanding of how the reactions of the represented participant can be interpreted.

Illustrate 5 –7   from *Nian* (2015)

5.2.3   Creating circumstances

After examining the ideational representations of participants and processes in Chinese picture books, this section comes to the third parameter in realising visual ideational meanings. Since any image in a picture book story would contain a depiction of background context or not, the circumstantial setting plays an essential role in expressing both visual interpersonal meanings (e. g. the ambience of setting afforded by the use of different colours; or visual attitudes evoked by the fully removed background[1]). However, the visual depiction of

---

[1]   The interpersonal function of circumstantial setting decontextualisation for the inscription or invoking visual attitudinal meanings, see Painter (2008).

the circumstantial context is most relevant to the ideational function which affords the details of physical environment in which the depicted participants act, as well as providing a visual location in which the processes take place.

In considering the genre of picture books, not only the depiction of circumstantiation in a single image needs to be examined, but also the relations of background context in successive images should be taken into account. Based on the analysis of our corpus, a movement of circumstantial depiction from less to more (or vice versa) seldom occurs in the Chinese picture books. An exception is shown in Illustration 5 – 3 where the background setting of the previous image is a snowy world in which a number of houses and tress are depicted, with the participant portrayed in a small size at the right bottom of the recto spread. As the page turns, the successive image offers a shift to recontextualise by removing the background context, and then an option of [INTER-CIRCUM-STANCE: vary degree: decontextualise] is employed in the image to lead the reader to place his/her attention to the depicted participants again. By the change in the depiction of circumstantial context, the image in the following spread brings the main participant (the postman) into focus, highlighting the reappearance of the protagonist. Combined with the interpersonal choices of visual attitudes expressed by his facial expression and bodily postures, an emotion of surprise and gratitude has been then invoked and reinforced. The shift in the circumstantiation attracts the reader's attention and invites him/her to participate in the story world and make a guess at who helps the postman and why.

5.3 The synergy of image and verbiage in representing narrative reality

Having identified the ideational features of visual components, this section shifts its focus on the collaboration between words and images to synergistically create ideational meanings. To these end, this section selects the picture book *The Adventure of the Postman* (Zheng & Zhao 2013) as the main objective to explore the intersemiotic cohesive relations between the two modalities within the book. It first explores the representational aspect of language via a transitivity analysis of the process types within the verbal text (Halliday 1994/2000; Halliday & Matthiessen 2004) , and then comes to the account of the ideational features of visual images on the basis of Painter et al. 's (2013) analytical framework.

To further illustrate the ideational choices in relation to verbal and visual texts, we will present a brief introduction of *The Adventure of the Postman* (Zheng & Zhao 2013). It is a Chinese picture book with thirteen double page spreads. The author[①] is well-know and has garnered extensive readership in China. The main protagonist of the story is Uncle Da Guan, a postman who has tosend letters to the villagers on the eve of Chinese Spring Festival when other people are staying at their homes. As the story develops, the main protagonist experiences a peculiar adventure of meeting a kind-hearted snowman on the special winter day.

5.3.1   Representing the narrative reality through language

In a systemic functional approach, the ideational metafunction of language "enables human beings to build on a mental picture of reality, to make sense of what goes on around them and inside them" (Halliday 1994/2000: 107). To use functional labels, the transitivity system as a significant dimension of ideational metafunction organises human's experience of the world (including both internal and external world) into a manageable range of process types. It is mainly concerned with the function of language as "consisting of 'goings-on' involving things which have attributes and which go on against background details of place, time, manner, etc" (Thompson 1996/2000: 86). The transitivity system can be further classified into six major types of processes. Each of them contributes to signifying a particular domain of experience. Even with a same or similar going-on happening around us, we are able to express it through language in various ways or by using different types of process. In the same vein,

---

① Zheng Chunhua is a famous author of children literature in China. Her representative work *Big Head Son and Small Head Dad* is widely known and favoured by lots of Chinese children.

the verbal texts in the picture book story serve as the key means to represent the reality of the story world, which convey a variety of ideational meanings about what's going on in the represented world. In examining the tale reality represented by the verbal choices, an analysis of the process types of the clauses within the verbal mode has been conducted. The analysis of process types of clauses within the picture book is outlined in the Table 5 − 1.

Table 5 − 1   **Types of processes in verbiage within**
The Adventure of the Postman

Process type	Number	Percentages
Material process	13	17. 1
Relational process	13	17. 1
Mental process	4	5. 3
Verbal process	8	10. 5
Behavioural process	32	42. 1
Existential process	6	7. 9
Total	76	100

As illustrated in table above, material and behavioural processes are the predominant types within the book, accounting for as much as 60% of the clauses counted in the story. It is motivated by the fact that the material and behavioural processes are primarily concerned with actions and movements taken by the represented characters in a depicted circumstance. In this respect, the two types of processes employed by the author to construct the development of plot. For instance, a number of verbs such as "送" (send), "推" (push), "走" (walk), "骑" (ride), "坐" (sit), "拿" (take), "打开" (open), and etc., are adopted by the author to express action and movement taken by the main protagonists of the picture book story. In the beginning of the story, the main protagonist is described as being occupied by the work of sending letters to villagers on the day before Spring Festival. The verbs "工作" (work) and "送" (send) in the clauses "可是邮递员大关叔叔还得工作" (however, the postman Da Guan has to work) and "他必须把今天到达的信件给村民们送去" (he must send the letters that arrived today to the villagers) stress the actions that the protagonist has to take, serving as the "Orientational Stage" of the picture book story. The two material processes used here emphasise the actions of the postman and the narrative identity of him as the protagonist whose adventure on the Spring Festival is going to begin. It seems evident that the utilisation of action processes (including material processes and behavioural processes) is significant for conveying a feeling of activity and movement in the story written for the child reader. As illustrated in these examples given, the processes including both material and behavioural actions are primarily associated with the doers of these actions verbalised in the clauses, essentially Uncle Da Guan and the snowman in such a fantastic adventure. The choices of material processes are adopted to encourage the child reader to keep his/her eyes on the movements and narrative of events, and eventually to get involved in the depicted story world and to give response to the dramatic protagonists represented in the picture book.

Nevertheless, the reality constructed in this picture book is not exclusively based on the processes of action (e. g. doing or happening). By utilising a number of relational processes with an identifying function, the author of the book aims to provide a range of information about the represented participants as well as their attributes. In the opening two clauses within the narrative, two relational processes "今天是大年三十" (today is New Year's Eve) and "明天就是新年了" (tomorrow is the Spring Festival) are deployed via using the verb "是" (be) to fulfill a descriptive function, suggesting the temporal background in which the plot of the story is going to be developed. Another relational process is employed to identify the attributes of material objects. For instance, the relation process in the clause "不过是用冰块做的年糕" (the niangao[①] is made up of ice) functions to describe the attributes of the niangao. Aside from the processes of doing and processes of being, there are also some verbal processes used to represent narrative reality to the child reader. A salient example is found in the final stage of the story where the postman re-

---

① Niangao is a traditional Chinese food made by rice which connotes the meaning of auspicious.

ceived a mysterious letter without any information about where is it from. A verbal clause is used here "信封上写着'邮递员收'" (the cover of the letter reads 'the postman receives') to signal that the letter is to the postman and indicates its function as a gift for the kindness of the postman.

Different types of processes are used in the verbal text with a majority of action processes, providing the child reader a vivid sense of activity and moment, and also with a few relational processes identifying or describing the represented participants and their attributes. A detailed demonstration of processes in verbiage as well as actions represented in visuals is outlined in Table 5 – 2.

Table 5 – 2　　　　**Types of processes in the bimodal text of**
The Adventure of the Postman

Page	Subject/Verbal Phrase/ Process Type (in verbal text)		Process Type of Actions (in images)	
1	今天/是 today is 明天/是 tomorrow/is (elliptical subject)/准备年货 prepare 很多人/不工作 many people/don't work	Relational Relational Material Material		Material action Material action
2	大关叔叔/工作 UDG/works 他/送信 he/sends 大关叔叔/推着 UDG/pushes 天空/下起了雪 it/snows	Material Material Material Material		Material action Mental perception
3	大地/被覆盖 the world/is covered (elliptical subject)/望去 looks 大关叔叔/像 UDG/looks like	Material Behavioural Relational		Material action
4	大关叔叔/骑 UDG/rides (elliptical subject) / 轻松起来 feels relaxed 自行车/好像 bicycle/seems 他/看 he/looks 雪人/在后面 there is a snowman 它/推 he/pushes (elliptical subject)/跑 runs	Material Relational Relational Behavioural Existential Material Material		Material action
5	大关叔叔/送 UDG/sends	Material		Behavioural action Behavioural action

Continued

Page	Subject/Verbal Phrase/ Process Type (in verbal text)		Process Type of Actions (in images)
6	(elliptical subject)/送 sends	Material	 Material action Behavioural action
	大关叔叔/回家 UDG/goes home	Material	
	他/走 he/walks	Material	
	(elliptical subject)/发现 finds	Relational	
	雪人/指 snowman/points to	Behavioural	
	(elliptical subject)/示意 indicates	Behavioural	
	"哇" Wow	Verbal	
	雪人/比 snowman/is	Relational	
	大关叔叔/伸出 UDG/extends	Behavioural	
	(elliptical subject)/抱住 embraces	Material	
	"好冰哟" "So icy"	Verbal	
7	雪人/送 snowman/sends)	Material	Behavioural action
	"谢谢你" thank you	Verbal	
	雪人/笑 snowman/smiles	Behavioural	
	(elliptical subject)/转身 turns around	Behavioural	
	大关叔叔/望着 UDG/looks	Mental	
	雪人/不见了 snowman/disappears	Behavioural	
	(elliptical subject)/走进 walks	Material	
8	屋里/飘出香味 there/emanates delicious smells	Existential	Mental perception
	大关叔叔/推 UDG/pushes	Material	
	(elliptical subject)/低头 yields	Behavioural	
	(elliptical subject)/发现 finds	Relational	
	"怎么回事" what happens	Mental	
	他/拿起 he/picks up	Material	
	信/写着 the letter/writes	Verbal	
	大关叔叔/打开 UDG/opens	Material	
	上面/写着 it/writes	Verbal	
9	大关叔叔/笑 UDG/smiles	Behavioural	Behavioural action Mental perception
	(elliptical subject)/进屋 enters in	Material	
	(elliptical subject)/拿了 picks up	Material	
	(elliptical subject)/装进 packs into	Material	
	(elliptical subject)/跨上 gets on	Material	
	往哪儿送呢" where to deliver	Mental	
10	大关叔叔/下来 UDG/gets down	Material	—
	(elliptical subject)/挂 hangs over	Material	
	自个儿/进屋 he/enters in	Material	

Page	Subject/Verbal Phrase/ Process Type (in verbal text)		Process Type of Actions (in images)	
11	天/黑 it/gets dark	Material		Material action
	雪人/来了 snowman/comes	Material		Mental perception
	(elliptical subject)/跟着 followed	Relational		
	它们/看见 they/see	Behavioural		
	(elliptical subject)/扑 run towards	Material		
	一人/抢 one/grabs	Material		
12	雪人/走 snowmen/walk	Material		—
	大关叔叔/走 UDG/walks	Material		
	自行车/少了 here/are less	Existential		
	(elliptical subject)/多出 there/are more	Existential		
	竹篮/装 basket/is filled by	Material		
	(elliptical subject)/好像是 seems	Relational		
	(elliptical subject)/是 is	Relational		
	上面/压着 it/is covered	Material		
	"年糕生活年年高"	Verbal		
13	大关叔叔/望 UDG/looks	Behavioural		Mental perception
	大关叔叔/想 UDG/thinks	Mental		Material action
	过年啦 Happy New Year	Relational		Material action
				Material action

5.3.2 The representation of characters and reality through images

Based on Painter et al. 's (2013) analytical framework for visual narrative, this section is mainly concerned with the ideational meaning of visual components within the picture book story. It aims to examine the ideational features of the images with respect to the representation of participants, processes and circumstances within the story.

> **Character manifestation and appearance in the story**

With regard to the depiction of character in this picture book narrative, there are two parameters serving as a fundamental role in conveying visual ideational meanings to the reader: the manifestation of the depicted characters and their appearance. Although the picture book narrates a story about the adventure of the postman, Uncle Da Guan, he does not appear in the opening of the story as the reader would expect. Instead, the visual narrative opens initially with a double page spread depicting two houses in the foreground and a number of small houses in the background. In the house of the verso spread, a boy is pasting a character of "FU" upon the window, while two women are depicted as making dumplings beside a table in the recto house. It is well-known that the two social activities are regarded as typical Chinese traditional celebration of the New Year, functioning as the "symbolic attribute" (Kress & van Leeuwen 2006: 105) in evoking the reader's interaction with the story world. Within the image, choices of [CHARACTER MANIFESTATION: complete] have been employed with their facial expressions clearly illustrated to present the reader a sense of happiness and joyfulness at the beginning of the story. This mood is reinforced by the choices of [AMBIENCE: warmth: cool] with the use of red purple hues. However, when the page turns, the protagonist, Uncle Da Guan, is firstly illustrated to the reader with a complete depiction. He is depicted in the image as standing beside a bicycle with a mailbag hanging over its backseat. It can be inferred from the facial expression that a mood of depression and loneliness has been created as a strong contrast with the cheerful ambience construed in the previous images. And thus a contrast opening is initiated to engage the reader in the story world, and to trigger his/her curiosity about the adventure coming soon. Except from the option of [CHARACTER MANIFESTATION: metonymic] used in the third double-paged spread, all of the manifestations of character are realised via complete illustrations. The only use of metonymic manifestation is adopted to offer the reader a back view of the protagonist. Uncle Da Guan reappears immediately in the next image in a negligibly small size which can be identified as an option of [reappear: varied: status: recede]. Through the choice of the varied status of the main protagonist, Uncle Da Guan emplaced on the periphery of the image recedes into the background circumstantiation, symbolising the shift of depicted character's status into the narrative events of the story. Therefore, a visual strategy of receding the status of Uncle Da Guan towards the background circumstantiation shifts the reader's attention back into the story narrative per se and facilitates the narrative thematic process of the story. In comparison to the choices of receding status, the successive image (the 4th double page spread) in which the postman reappears applies an opposite visual strategy of [reappear: varied: status: recede], functioning in bringing our attention back to the depicted character as protagonist, and involving the child reader in his adventure of meeting the snowman. In this respect, a visual strategy shifts the depicted character (Uncle Da Guan) from being embedded in the circumstantial setting to a foreground portrayal, inviting the child reader to share his emotion (may be surprise or gratitude) and affinity with the depicted character. Another noticeable use of variation relevant to the reappearance of the protagonist is shown in the 9th double-paged spread where Uncle Da Guan is portrayed with changes in attribution (see Illustration 5 – 8). To be specific, the depicted character is illustrated without the green cotton-padded cup. On the one hand, the minor variation in his dress does not influence the reader's cognition and identification of the character. On the other, it serves as an important role in the shifts between the stages of working and finishing, thus enabling the reader to distinguish two different segments of the narrative sequences

Illustration 5 – 8   from *The Adventure of the Postman* (2014)

and inducing the reader to experience the changes between two emotional states of the protagonist.

> **Processes in the story**

Concerning with the processes in which the represented participants are involved within the story, the analysis focuses not only on the process being depicted in an individual image, but also the way in which one event is linked with another in successive images (in Painter et al.'s term "INTER-EVENT" options). Firstly, the visual processes represented in the whole book are classified in Table 5 – 2. As the table shows to us, there is a predominance of material actions over other types of visual processes in the story book. The images in which material actions are represented bring dynamics to the story narration and show the various activities performed by the story's protagonist, Uncle Da Guan and the snowman.

A variety of material actions are depicted in the picture book, such as in the 2nd, 3rd, 4th, 5th, 6th, and 7th double-paged spreads. In the second spread of the book where Uncle Da Guan puts a set of letters into the mail pouch, a material action is depicted and vectors are created by the arm of the protagonist and the letter. The reader sees directly the action that is carried out by the protagonist and is then reminded of the narrative event being progressed: delivering those letters to the given addresses. By the similar token, the material action depicted in the recto image of the 3rd spread is carried out by the protagonist who is riding on the bicycle to deliver letters. The different actions depicted in the successive image thus realise the option of [unfolding: succession: between sequence], clarifying the relations between the two processes of actions. The material action of putting letters in the mailbag is included in the activity sequence of preparing to deliver letters which precedes the action of riding a bike on the following page. It is remarkable that the essence of the story narrative lies in such kind of "temporal sequence" (Painter et al. 2013: 73). It plays a vital role in advancing and progressing the narration of story events. Despite the dominated occurrences of material processes (especially actions) in the picture book, there are still several mental processes concerning the perception of protagonist, such as in 2rd and 8th double-page spreads. Both the two instances deploy the structure of transactional reaction in which vectors are created by line of gaze from the protagonist to the mailbag or to the mysterious letter. Nevertheless, the difference between the depictions of perception lies in the diverse moods represented in the two images. While the former provides a sense of depression and loneliness, the latter creates a mood of curiosity and suspicion.

Considering the relations established between the depicted actions in successive images, the realisations of unfolding relations in the picture book are mostly identified as that of between sequences. A noticeable exception in the picture book occurs in 11th double page spread (see Illustration 5 – 9) where five little snowmen stand one by one, passing the baskets of gifts to one another. The verso image of the spread depicts an older snowman looking at the very young snowmen with smiles while a little snowman carrying a basket to pass to the next. In the recto, other four snowmen are carrying baskets happily and feverishly. Thus a choice of [unfolding: succession: within a sequence] is applied in this double spread to remind the reader to focus on their feelings of excitement and gratitude in receiving the gifts for New Year. Another INTER-EVENT relation between successive images in this picture book is that of projection when the reader simply observes that Uncle Da Guan is looking at a mysterious letter in one image. He/she is then shown immediately what the protagonist sees in the following page (the recto of the 8th double spread). Combined with the visual technique of zoom in, it is clearly shown to us the information about what the letter says, what purpose the letter expects to achieve, and where the letter comes from. In this respect, it is important for the illustrator to employ the strategy of [unfolding: projection: real] to represent the reader a sense of mystery and inquisitiveness, and to make the narration of story events more cohesive. In a nutshell, the picture book depicts a majority of material actions to bring dynamics to the story and exhibit the different activities carried out by the represented participants. Correspondingly, a large number of temporal sequences are embedded in the images of the picture book to fulfill the essence of the story narrative.

Illustration 5 – 9   from *The Adventure of the Postman* (2014)

> ➤ **Circumstantiation**

Circumstantial meanings in the story image deal predominately with the depiction of details of spatial location. Corresponding to the generic feature of narrative, the reader is required to focus on both the circumstantiation in a single image and the relations between the circumstantial backgrounds in successive images.

Therefore, when we consider the story pages from the point of view of the circumstantiation in successive images, it is noticeable that there is a striking feature related to the varying degrees in the circumstances depicted. That is, it is no surprise to notice that the picture book is taken up by a majority of movements from less to more circumstantiation (and vice versa). The visual strategy for varying the degrees in circumstantial details are used in a series of double page spreads such as the 3rd, 4th, 5th, 6th, 9th and 10th spreads. Take the succession of variation from the 3rd to 6th double spreads as an example, the course of the story in this period has been taken up by a swift shift to decontextualise or recontextualise the degrees of circumstance details. A choice of [vary degree: recontextualise] has been employed in the 3rd spread after a brief depiction of Uncle Da Guan and his work with a decontextualised background in the preceding image, returning our attention to the story event and imagined world. When the page turns, a contrast strategy of [vary degree: decontextualise] is used by removing the circumstantial background, bringing the represented characters (in this case, the reappearance of postman and the first depiction of the snowman) into focus. Therefore the reader's attention is attracted by the representation of the characters, and he/she is engaged with the depicted character to share a sensation of surprise in the adventure to meet a virtuous snowman on the special day. Nevertheless, as the page turns again, a recontextualisation of the circumstantial background is repeated in this spread by increasing circumstantial degrees, which facilitates the narrative plot of the story and shifting our emphases to the imagined story-world. It is interesting to observe that the recontextualisation of the circumstantiation in the picture book is always combined with the use of different ambience to highlight the depiction of the background context of story world; whereas the strategy of decontextutalisation is applied with the options of FOCALISATION to achieve a strong engagement between the reader and represented character, and to forge the identification of them via the foregrounding depiction of facial expressions or bodily postures. To facilitate a full understanding of ideational options in relation to the images within this picture book, a graphic representation of these options is given in the Table 5 – 3.

Table 5 – 3 Visual ideational choices in *The Adventure of the Postman*

Page	Ideation	Character manifestation	Character appearance	Process type	Inter-event	Intercir-cumstance
1	a boy platting a "FU" character; two women make dumplings; a number of houses	Complete	Appear	Material actions (boy plats, two women make)		
2	a postman, namely, "Uncle Da Guan" (UDG) standing beside a bike with a baggage; a house in a snowy day	Complete	Appear	Material actions (UDG puts the letters in the baggage); perception (looks at the baggage)		Change context: relocate

Continued

Page	Ideation	Character manifestation	Character appearance	Process type	Inter-event	Intercir-cumstance
3	UDG riding the bike, a number of snow covered tress and houses	Metonymic	Reappear/ immediate: varied: status: recede	Material actions (UDG rides)	Unfolding: succession: between sequence	Vary degree: recontextualise
4	Snowman pushing the bike, UDG looking back at snowman	Complete	Appear (snowman); Reappear/ immediate: status: increased	Material actions (snowman pushes); Behavioural(UDG-looks back)	Unfolding: succession: between sequence	Vary degree: decontextualise
5	UDG bidding farewell in foreground, two men look at UDG, a number of trees and houses in a heavy snow in the background	Complete	Reappear/ immediate: unchanged	Material actions (UDG bids goodbye to others, and shakes his hand)	Unfolding: succession: between sequence	Vary degree: recontextualise
6	Snowman sitting on the bike; snowman riding the bike; UDG	Complete	Reappear/ immediate: unchanged (UDG) Reappear/ later: unchanged (snowman)	Material actions (snowman rides; UDG sits)	Unfolding: succession: between sequence	Vary degree: decontextualise
7	UDG arriving at home; UDG and his house in foreground; a number of other houses in background	Complete	Reappear/ immediate: unchanged	Material actions	Unfolding: succession: between sequence	Vary degree: recontextualise
8	UDG staring at a letter; the content of the letter	Complete	Reappear/ immediate: unchanged	Behavioural (UDG looks); perception (inferred)	Projection: real	Maintain context: new perspective

Continued

Page	Ideation	Character manifestation	Character appearance	Process type	Inter-event	Intercir-cumstance
9	UDG smiling and preparing; UDG standing besides the bike and waiting; five small baskets and a plate of dumplings on table	Complete	Reappear/immediate; varied; attribution; decrease/descriptive detail	Behavioural (UDG smiles and stands) Material actions; (UDG takes)	Unfolding; succession; between sequence	Vary degree; decontextualise
10	baskets hanged over the bike;			Static image		Vary degree; recontextualise
11	Snowman taking a baskets; a dark night	Complete	Reappear/later; unchanged	Material actions; (Snowman takes); Behavioural; (Snowman smiles)	Unfolding; succession; within a sequence	Vary degree; decontextualise
12	Basket on the backseat of bike; bike in front of houses				projection; real	Change context; relocate
13	UDG looking up and smiling; people smiling and playing firecrackers	Complete	Reappear/immediate; varied; attribution; decrease/descriptive	Material actions; (People play); Behavioural; (UDG smiles and looks up)	Unfolding; succession; between sequences	Maintain context; new perspective

5.3.3 The analysis of ideational intersemiotic complementarity

As mentioned earlier in Section 3.4, Royce (1999, 2007) proposes an intersemiotic complementarity framework on page-based multimodal texts to explore the cohesive relations between both the verbal semiotics and visual semiotics within a multisemiotic text. In the analysis of ideational intersemiotic complementarity, Royce (1996, 2007) firstly discusses the experiential meanings of verbal texts and visual images. Regarding the ideational meanings of verbal text, he examines the transitivity features by categorising a set of parameters on the basis of systemic functional grammar: *process types*, *participants*, *attributes* and *circumstances*. Correspondingly, as for visual images, Royce brings forth the essential concept of Visual Message Element (VME or VMEs) to refer to the visual components of an image. As a semantic unit in the framework, VMEs are primarily classified into *Identification* (represented participants), *Activity* (what action), *Attribute* (qualities or characteristics of the represented participants), and *Circumstance* (represented context) (Royce 1999: 223 – 228).

In order to examine the ideational intersemiotic complementary relations, this section selects two types of pages (an image including actions versus a static image) as the exemplar to explore the ideational cohesion by analysing the semantic links established by the verbal elements and VMEs (Royce 1999).

When it comes to the first image (see Illustration 5 – 10) that contains actions, we are going to commence with an analysis of the VMES. Since VMEs "carry semantic properties which are realized by a range of visual techniques at the disposal of the writers (i. e. drawers, graphic designer etc.)" (Royce 1999: 139), they form the reference point for exploring the verbal aspect of the bimodal text. As far as verbal text is concerned, the activity, identification, circumstances as well as attributes of lexical items which bear semantic relevance to VMEs will be explored.

Participant VMEs

The analysis begins with the identification of the represented participants in the image, accounting for the questions about who (or what) is in the visual frame and who (or what) they interact with. It is safe to say that the most salient represented participants are explicitly offered to the viewer via the visual representations of their facial expressions and bodily postures. Obviously, there are two main depicted characters shown to the reader within the double-page spread: a snowman and a postman with their facial expressions clearly portrayed. Apart from the two depicted characters (the protagonists inferred

Illustration 5 – 10   from *The Adventure of the Postman*(2014)

from the story narrative), two relevant participant VMEs are illustrated in the visual frame: a bicycle and a green mailbag hung over its back seat. The identification of the represented participants in this visual frame can be mainly identified as Uncle Da Guan, the snowman, the bicycle and the mailbag, which will be glossed as the VMEs "UDG", "snowman", "bicycle" and "mail pouch".

Activity VMEs

With regard to the activity in a visual image, the attention is placed on what action is taking place between the depicted actors and the recipients (or objects). We can see a snowman sitting on a bicycle and offering an invitation to the postman (inferred from preceding image) for getting a ride in the verso. Another action depicted in the spread is the action of the snowman riding the bike with the postman sitting at the backseat. In a similar vein, the activity depicted in the visual frame is going to be glossed as the VMEs "sitting" and "riding" (as shown in the visual frame, both of the two actions are taking place on the bicycle).

Circumstance VMEs

The circumstance depicted in the visual frame is mainly concerned with the represented context in which the action is taking place between different represented participants. The postman and the snowman as represented characters in this visual frame are placed on a snowy day when the snowman is riding a bicycle with the postman sitting on the back. As discussed earlier, the verso page of the spread adopts an option of [vary degree: decontextualise] in the depiction of circumstantial details, shifting our attention from the circumstantiation context to the depicted participant. As a result, the prime circumstance VME in the visual frame can be identified as "snowy day".

Attribute VMEs

As the last important factor related to the representation of message elements in visual images, attribute VMEs refer to the characteristics or qualities of the participants, focusing on any important characters, properties or qualities attributed to the depicted participants in the visual frame. In the double-paged spread, the circumstantial setting is depicted as a snowy day in winter, and a snowman is demonstrated in the visual frame as the main character of the story, all of which contribute to the inference of "cold" attributes. Another attribute VME in the visual composition is "fast" speed inferred from the riding bicycle and the relatively small houses and trees against the background setting. Therefore, the attribute VMEs in the visual frame can be summarised as "cold" and "fast". The ideational intersemiotic complementarity analysis of the bimodal text is demonstrated in Table 5 − 4. Table 5 − 4 The ideational intersemiotic complementarity in a narrative image

As illustrated in the Table 5 − 4, the most salient intersemiotic cohesive relation is conducted via the uses of repetitions and collocations between two different semiotic systems. In the first place, there are a good number of lexical items linking semantically with the experiential meanings represented by the VMEs in the visual image. For instance, the lexical items "大关叔叔" (Uncle Da Guan) and "雪人" (snowman) are repeated for several times to refer to the identification of the same visual represented participants in the visual frame. The repetitions of the depicted characters in both two modes enable the reader to pay his/her attention to the main protagonist and the adventure happening between

Table 5 –4 **The ideational intersemiotic complementarity in a narrative image**

	Participants				Processes		Circumstances	Attributes	
		snowman	mail pouch	bicycle	sitting	riding	snowy day	fast	cold
1	UDG①								
2	大关叔叔 (R)② UDG		一封信 (C) a letter			回家 (C) go home			
3	他 (R) he			自行车 (R) bicycle		走到 (C) walk			
4		雪人 (R) snowman		前面 (M) front seat	坐到 (R) sit on		雪人 (C) snowman		雪人 (C) snowman
5		雪人 (R) snowman		后座 (M) back seat			雪人 (C) snowman		雪人 (C) snowman
6	他 (R)				坐上去 (R) sit on				
7		雪人 (R) snowman		摩托车 (A) motorbike		骑 (R) ride	雪人 (C) snowman	还快 (R) faster	雪人 (C) snowman
8	大关叔叔 (R) UDG				伸出手 (C) hold out hands				

① UDG refers to the main protagonist of the story: Uncle Da Guan.

② R = repetition; S = synonymy; M = meronymy; C = collocation.

Continued

	Participants	Processes	Circumstances	Attributes
9	雪人 (R) snowman 腰 (M) waist	抱住 (C) embrace	雪人 (C) snowman	雪人 (C) snowman 好冰 (R) very icy
10	他 (R) he	坐上去 (R) sit on		

them, thus playing a metafictive role in the narration of the story to bring the reader into focus. Another important visual technique meriting our attention is that an option of [FOCALISATION: contact] is adopted to engage the reader with the depicted character, which supports the metafictive essence of the narrative and complements the verbal introduction ("发现雪人坐到了前面"; [he] finds the snowman sitting on the front seat of [the bicycle]) of the snowman sitting on the bicycle. It is found that the postman as the protagonist does not appear in the verso, which is not corresponded to the verbal text. However, a more experiential reader can easily infer from the bodily gesture (e. g. pointing to the backseat) as well as facial expression (e. g. smiling) of the snowman that he is inviting the postman to sit on the backseat of the bike so as to give him a ride. And consequently, it construes an intersemiotic cohesive relation between verbal text and visual text. In a similar vein, intersemiotic repetitive relation is applied to the activities which are taking place between the two represented characters in the visual frame. A series of verbs in the verbal text are repeatedly used to identify the activity VMEs such as "坐到了前面" (sit), "坐上去" (sit), "骑" (ride), reminding the reader to focus on the activities happening between the protagonists and to figure out the sequence of the depicted activities within the visual composition. It is shown to us that the snowman in the verso making an invitation to the postman to sit on the bike and take him a ride. It involves an expectation of the reader to see the postman accepting the invitation. The following page then portrays a scene that the postman sits on the backseat of the bike while the snowman riding. A choice of [unfolding: between sequences: + fulfilled] is adopted to realise the inter-event relations between the activity sequences as the story unfolds, which in turn reinforces the cohesive intersemiotic sense relation between the visual image and verbal text and enables the reader to achieve a better understanding of the picture book narrative.

Aside from the intersemiotic cohesive relation via employing repetitions, there are also plenty of collocations applied to establish intersemiotic sense relation. The first use of collocation appears in the opening clause "送完最后一

封信" (Having delivering the last letter). The lexical item "letter" forms an intersemiotic collocative relation with visual element of the mail pouch, emphasising the wonder journey happening to the postman on the day of Spring Festival. The snowman in the visual frame is depicted as the main protagonist whose appearance is closely related to the circumstantial setting of "snowy day" and the attribute VME of "cold" property. Meanwhile, the visual option of [vary degree: decontextualise] in the depiction of circumstantial setting attracts our attention to the appearance of the snowman from the background setting, strengthening the attribute (cold in this case) of the snowman and provoking the reader's appraisal towards the snowman. Although cold in his body, the snowman is a kind-hearted character who is ready to help others.

> **The ideational intersemiotic complementary analysis of the static image**

The characters depicted in picture books are usually involved in some kind of action, as shown in Illustration 5 – 10, engaging the reader with the represented participants within a particular picture book story. However, the characters may also be represented to the reader in a more static image which may serve as a pause on the rhythm of the depicted story. Illustration 5 – 11 is drawn as an example of the static image in the picture book narrative. It is a double page spread with a static depiction ofa bicyclein front of a house on a winter night (it is inferred from the previous depiction as the night of Spring Festival) in the left image, and of a basket filled with a number of "*niangao*" (a traditional Chinese food made of glutinous rice flour during the Spring Festival) in the recto. Having examined the ideational intersemiotic complementarity within a visual frame consisting of "narrative processes" (in Kress and van Leeuwen's term), it comes to the analysis of ideational intersemiotic cohesive relations between verbal text and visual text within the static visual frame.

Participant VMEs

As for the represented participants depicted in the visual frame, the bike is placed in the foreground of the circumstantial setting with a basket on its backseat. In the recto image, the depiction of basket is highlighted via emplo-

Illustration 5 – 11   from *The Adventure of the Postman* (2014)

ying a decontextualisation of the circumstantiation of the image. Through the use of zooming in, the reader can clearly see the basket is put on a red paper, and inside the basket are a great many *niangao* made of ice. Thus the Identification VMEs in this example can be categorised as "bicycle", "basket", "*niangao*", and "red paper".

Circumstance VMEs

Although there is no character appearing in the image, the circumstantial setting also plays an important role in offering to the reader a good deal of information about the background setting of the depicted scene of the story. It is on a night in the depth of winter that a bicycle in parked in front of a variety of houses. A basket remaining on the backseat of the bicycle encourages the reader to make a series of guesses on it such as: what is it in the basket; what is the basket for; or is the basket left by its owner or being sent as a gift by someone else? The circumstance VMEs is therefore identified as "house".

Attribute VMEs

With regard to the property and attributes associated with the represented participants, niangao as the represented participant is signified as auspicious and lucky. In Chinese culture, niangao is perceived as a traditional Chinese food prepared on the day of Spring Festival, connoting a meaning of a lucky and better life in the coming year. By the similar token, the paper painted in red is also attributed to the auspicious connotation. For Chinese, the most favored choice of colours during the Spring Festival is red colour, which symbolises a wish for the fortunate and happy days in the next year. Another attribute represented in the visual frame is related to the basket, concerning the depicted size of the basket. The attribute VMEs in the visual frame can be then summarised as "auspicious" and "big". The ideational intersemiotic sense relations of verbal and visual texts within the static visual frame are illustrated in Table 5 −5.

Table 5 −5   The ideational intersemiotic complementarity in a static image

Page	Participants				Circumstances	Attributes	
	bicycle	basket	niangao	red paper	house	auspicious	big
1							
2					屋 (R)		
3	自行车 (R) bicycle	小竹篮 (S) small basket			house		小 (A) small
4		大竹篮 (S) big basket					大 (R) big
5		竹篮 (R) basket					
6			年糕 (R) niangao				
7			年糕 (R) niangao 冰块 (C) ice				
8				红纸 (R) red paper		红 (C) red	
			年糕 (R) niangao			年年高 (C) more prosperous year after year	

As demonstrated in the visual frame, there are a majority of repetitions applied between the verbal text and visual depiction to achieve an intersemiotic cohesive sense relation. For example, a set of repetitive use of the lexical word "年糕" (niangao) serves to identify the visual represented participants in the image, bringing the represented participant into focus. The visual strategy of [vary degree: recontextualise] by removing any depicted circumstantiation strengths the effect of shifting our attention to the choice of niangao as a gift for New Year and to the reason underlying this choice. It is motivated by the fact that the cultural connotations attributed to the niangao enables the reader (especially Chinese reader) to better understand the connections between the represented participant and the Chinese New Year. And the repetition of "红纸" (red paper) is also used to identify the represented participant in the visual image, which leads the reader to focus on the depiction of the paper and on the partly ambiguous characters written on it. Complemented with the verbal text, the reader can completely make out the Chinese characters. The verbal text is shown as follows:

年糕年糕生活年年高。
May you be more prosperous year after year by eating niangao.

The verbal text supports the visual representations of "niangao" by providing an explanation of the cultural connotations that niangao carries, facilitating the reader's recognition of its "symbolic attribute" (Kress & van Leeuwen 2006). Another important intersemiotic cohesive device applied in the visual composition is the use of collocation. For instance, the symbolic attribute of niangao and the red coloured paper contribute to construing the collocative sense relation with the Attribute VME in the visual image. The intersemiotic collocation leads the reader to grasp the implied meanings represented in the visual image rather than merely knowing what is put inside the basket. In a nutshell, although viewed as a static image without any depicted characters, it presents to the reader a pause of the story rhythm. By utilising ideational intersemiotic devices such as repetition and collocation, the author/illustrator expects to teach the young reader to achieve a full understanding of the cultural connotations of the Spring Festival.

This section examines how different semiotic systems in two divergent visual frames cohere with one another in construing complementary ideational meanings as a coherent whole. It is found that repetition and collocation are the most widely used intersemiotic cohesive devices in both the "narrative" visuals and "static visuals".

5.3.4   Analysing the ideational commitment

This section is mainly concerned with the commitment of ideational meaning of verbal and visual semiotics. To this end, the section selects Illustration 6 – 9 as the exemplar. In order to compare the different commitment of meaning between verbal and visual semiotics, the complementary systems of both two semiotics are provided by Painter et al. (see Table 5 – 6)

Table 5 – 6   **Complementary ideational meaning systems across image and language (Painter et al. 2013: 138).**

	Visual meaning Potential	Visual realisations	Verbal meaning potential	Verbal realisations
Action	Visual action	Depicted action with:	Actional figure	Tense, phase, etc with transitivity structures:
	Action	Vectors		Marterial, behavioural processes
	Perception	Gaze vectors		Mental perception processes
	Cognition	Thought bubbles, face/hand gestures		Verbal, behavioural processes
	Inter-event relations	Juxtaposition of images (+/ – change of setting or participant)	Conjunction, projection	Logico-semantic relations of expansion and quoting/reporting
Character	Character attribution	Depiction of physical attributes	Participant description, classification, identification	Relational transitivity nominal group structures, deixis
	Character manifestation and appearance	Character depiction		
	Character relations	Adjacent/symmetrical arrangement of different participants	Participant classification, description	Comparative epithets classifying clauses, etc.

Continued

Visual meaning Potential	Visual realisations	Verbal meaning potential	Verbal realisations
Circumstantiation	Depiction of place, time, manner	Circumstantiation	Specification of time, place, cause, manner, matter, contingency, role, etc.
Inter-circumstance	Shifts, contrasts continuities in locations		Logico-semantic relations of enhancement

(Setting)

Through a lens of ideational meaning committed in the visual composition, we can discover a set of various depicted actions, for instance, a snowman sitting on the bicycle and making an invitation, as indicated by the positions of his hands and invisible gaze vector in the first image. Although the given receiver (the postman that can be read from the verbal text) does not appear in the image, it can be inferred from the vectors of actions created by his arms and gaze directions that he is making a invitation to someone to sit on the backseat of the bicycle. In the following image, we can observe that the snowman is riding a bike while a postman is sitting on the backseat of the bicycle with his arms round the waist of the snowman. The facing adjacent images suggest a temporal inter-event relation between the two activity sequences which can be recognised as a kind of fulfilled relation. An expectancy about the next action to come between activity sequences is achieved in the successive images. The different depicted actions in the two images reinforce the cohesive relation between the two main protagonists (the snowman and the postman), catering to child's expectation about the narrative and highlighting a close affiliation between them in the adventure. With regard to the verbal text, there are various types of processes applied for construing ideational meaning. For instance, some of verbs are used to identify the activities happening in the story, such as "坐" (sit), "走" (walk), "骑" (ride) and "抱" (embrace), committing ideational meanings with respect to action to remind the reader of what is going on at the moment. Even the verbiage commits some kinds of ideational meanings unavailable to the image. The verbalisation of the actions taken by the postman (e. g. walking to the bicycle, and watching a snowman sitting on his bicycle) has no complementary visual expression in the composition. The reader has to infer such kind of meaning from the bodily gesture and the invisible gaze vectors of the snowman depicted visually. However, in the image there is no verbalisation of the expansion relations between different actions that are visually committed and interpreted.

When it comes to the description of character, both the postman and the snowman are portrayed in a complete depiction, and the latter reappears immediately, contributing to the maximal accessibility for the child reader to identify the main protagonist of the story. The reader can infer more information (e. g. age, race, occupation, or even social class) about the depicted characters on the basis of their depicted attributes of clothing, colours of wearing, size and so on. For a Chinese reader, it is easy to infer the occupation of the main protagonist via the depiction of green suit and hat, and the green coloured mail pouch. Noticeably, the postman and the snowman are portrayed in a close adjacent arrangement, showing a friendly relation between them and laying a foundation for the following narrative. As far as setting of the image is concerned, the circumstantiation of the verso page is decontextualised, removing the background setting to highlighting the depicted characters to the child reader. The recontextualisation of circumstantial background in recto has the function of bringing the reader into the story world to participate in the narrative events. A swift shift in the depiction of circumstantial setting manages the reader's attention and involves a varying degree of commitment of ideational meaning. In comparison to the visual image, there are differing commitments of ideational meaning in the linguistic text. The visually depicted characters are not described verbally at all except from a verbal expression of attribute of the snowman through an implicit mental projection "哟, 好冰哦" ([the snowman feels] icy). This projection is emanated by the postman to share his feeling towards the warmth of the snowman when he is embracing the snowman. In the visual image, we can only infer this attribute from the gaze vector of the postman and our experiential cognition of the snowman. It is hardly impossible to deduce such mental projection from the visual depiction of character. In terms of circumstantiation in verbal text, there is a specification of time about when the action is taking place. The verbal clause "大关叔叔准备回家了" (Uncle Da Guan is ready to return home) indicates a relatively specified time of the depicted actions with no complementary commitment of the same meaning through visual expression. However, the inter-circumstantiation relations are not elaborated verbally so that the reader can only infer from the visual images the cohesive relation between a series of different actions as well as the varying degrees in the two different circumstantiations.

Therefore, with regard to the differing commitments between visual and verbal text in relation to ideational meanings, it can be concluded that there is more ideational meaning committed in the image than in the verbiage in terms of attribution, character manifestation, relation, inter-event relation, and inter-circumstantiation; and also that the verbal text commits some degrees of ideational meaning which have not been expressed in the visual text (e. g. in terms of action and circumstantiation). The divergence in the commitment of ideational meaning between the verbal and visual semiotic systems exhibits an uneven and differing degree of sharing of semantic load within the visual composition. The schematic representation of different commitment of ideational meaning in the two modalities is outlined in Table 5 – 7 related to action, character and setting.

Table 5 – 7　　　　　**Degrees of commitment of ideational meaning in Illustration 5 – 10**[①]

	Image	Commitment	Verbal text	Commitment
Character	Attribution	Full (Snowman and UDG) dress, figure, size, age, weight and etc.	Attribution	Partial: attributes of snowman
	Manifestation & reappearance	Full: complete manifestation reappearance/immediate	Identification	Partial: verbal naming choices
	Relations	Full: (Snowman and UDG) via adjacent arrangement	Role Specification	

---

　　① Shading in the cell is employed to facilitate the analysis of areas of commitment. Dark shading indicates no commitment, while light shading signifies minor degree of commitment.

Continued

	Image	Commitment	Verbal text	Commitment
Action	Action	Partial: action depicted with vectors	Material/ behavioural	Full: Material/ behavioural process
	Perception	Partial: gaze vectors and bodily posture (inferred only)	Mental	
	Inter-event (across images)	Succession: between sequences/fulfilled	Expansion	
Setting	Circumstantiation		Circumstantiation	Full: (verso) specification of time
	Inter-circumstance (across images)	Full: vary degree: recontextualisation	Circumstantiation	

5.4　Summary

This chapter has conducted a comprehensive account of ideational choices available to the writer/illustrator to represent the narrative reality and different participants within Chinese picture books. In accounting for the processes of making meaning carried out by both visual and verbal modes within picture books, the analysis consists of several parts. In the first part, the visual analysis of images along the database applies Painter et al's (2013) visual narrative framework to identify the visual features and techniques employed by the author/illustrator to represent participants, processes and circumstances. It is concluded that the verbal text and visual text share a common feature in highlighting the actions through the high occurrences of material processes (or material actions depicted in image), providing the reader an immediate sense of activity and involving him/her in the development of the story plot.

Based on Royce's (1999, 2007) intersemiotic complementarity, it then moves on to an account of ideational cohesive relations between verbal text and visual texts within the exemplar picture book. In order to explore the collaboration of the two modalities in the creation of ideational meaning, the chapter examines how the verbal and visual texts within the two divergent visual frames (a "narrative" versus a "static" one) cohere with each other in construing complementary ideational meanings via the utilisation of a range of intersemiotic cohesive devices such as *repetition*, *synonymy*, *meronymy*, and *collocation*. Among them, it is found that *repetition* and *collocation* serve as the effective and repeatedly used intersemiotic devices in both the narrative and static visuals.

The chapter also conducts an account of the difference between two semiotic resources in the way in which ideational meaning is commited. Through the comparison, a summary is reached that the divergence in the commitment of ideational meaning between the verbal and visual semiotic systems results in an uneven and differing degree of sharing of semantic load within the visual composition.

The next chapter is mainly concerned with the textual meaning construed by visual and verbal semiotics, probing into the ways in which both semiotics are co-deployed to form coherent messages within Chinese picture books.

Chapter Six The Interplay of Visual and Verbal Semiotics in Creating Messages

6.1 Introduction

The primary focus in this chapter is placed on the textual meaning that is realised in both visual and verbal semiotics within Chinese children's picture books. In this chapter, the textual features of visual components are first identified throughout the database, and examined through the parameters of INTERMODAL INTEGRATION, FRAMING, and FOCUS. It then moves to the analysis of compositional intersemiotic complementarity between verbal and visual semiotic systems to create coherent messages, using the picture book *Reunion* as an exemplar. This chapter concludes with an analysis of different commitment of meaning for verbal and visual semiotics in the book and their relative contribution to the overall meaning.

6.2 Composing visual space in picture books

The previous two chapters have examined the ideational meanings and interpersonal meanings represented in Chinese picture books. While the former deals with the ideational representations of participants and processes in various circumstances, the latter is concerned with the relationship between different types of participants (e.g. interactions between the depicted character and the reader). When it comes to the textual meanings, the focus is shifted to the integration of ideational meanings and interpersonal meanings as a meaningful and coherent whole. Extrapolating from the textual meaning of language,

Painter et al. (2013) propose the concept of "focus group" to refer to a unit of information, which means the visual elements grouped together as some kind of "eyeful" to which the reader is attending. Based on the basic unit of compositional information, they further elaborate on three fundamental dimensions of construing textual meanings in visual narratives: INTERMODAL INTEGRATION, FRAMING, and FOCUS. Drawing on Painter et al.'s (2013) analytical framework, this section conducts an analysis of textual meanings encoded in the visual images of Chinese picture books, exploring how visual elements in compositional space are framed.

6.2.1   Investigating the layout

As a significant dimension in considering the textual function in Chinese picture books, the integration of visual and verbal composition accounts for the arrangements of page or double page spread in which both verbal and visual semiotics are framed. The first type of intermodal integrated layout is termed as "complementary" layout where each visual and verbal semiotic resides in its own space. It means that both visual and verbal modes in a visual composition may play a distinct role in meaning-making, depending on the varying semantic weight of each semiotic. When an image occupies most of the visual space within a single page (or spreads across the gutter of a double page frame), it is viewed as being privileged when compared to the verbiage; while when an image takes up equal visual space with the verbal text in the visual frame, they are regarded as being carrying the same semantic weight (see Illustration 6-1). In this case, the double page spread is conceived of as a "macro" frame (Painter et al. 2013) where each modality facing each other carries equal semantic weight by apportioning image and text the same visual space. The verbiage on the left side of the spread describes an important plot of the story through the talk between three main protagonists. And the visual image on the recto depicts three characters eating and talking, giving a support to the verbiage on the verso. Thus the visual composition is a complementary layout with verbal text and visual image adjoined horizontally.

Illustration 6 – 1   from *A Battle with Nian*(2015)

Despite the facing layout of visual compositions, there are also a number of complementary layouts in Chinese picture books organised alongside the vertical axis with verbiage and image adjoined to each other in descending layers. In the type of descending layouts, the image in the visual composition may be placed above the verbal text, or vice versa. However, the upper part of the visual layout is usually considered to have more semantic weight (e. g. Arnheim 1982, Kress & van Leeuwen 1996, 2006) than the lower part, no matter which modality is framed on the upper part. According to Kress and van Leeuwen (2006), the visual elements which are placed in the upper part within a vertical layout play an essential role of representing "Ideal" information value.

If, in a visual composition, some of the constituent elements are placed in the upper part, and other different elements in the lower part of the picture space or the page, then what has been placed on the top is presented as the Ideal, and what has been placed at the bottom is put forward as the Real. For something to be ideal means that it ispresented as the idealized or generalized essence of the information, hence also as its, ostensibly, most salient part. The Real is then opposed to this in that it presents more specific information (e. g. details), more 'down-to-earth' information (e. g. photographs as documentary evidence, or maps or charts), or more practical information (e. g. practical consequences, directions for action).

(Kress & van Leeuwen 2006: 186 – 187)

Obviously, elements in the upper proportion of a visual composition, according to Kress and van Leeuwen (2006), are ostensibly most salient part of the visual layout. And they further extend that if the upper part is taken up by the visual image (one or more) and the lower part by the verbiage, then the visual image plays the role of representing ideologically foregrounded message while the text serves to provide elaboration on it; inversely, if the verbal text occupies the upper part of a visual composition, it then plays a dominating role while the images in a subservient role (Kress & van Leeuwen: 187). However, Painter et al. (2013) emphasise the amount of visual space taken up by each modality as an indicator of salience in the visual composition, rather than depending on the orientation of axis alongside which the visual layout is organised. The present research follows Painter et al. 's (2013) perspective to the analysis of Chinese picture books, with a particular focus on distinguishing the foregrounded part of a visual composition via the amount of visual space it occupies.

Apart from the complementary organisation of visual image and verbal text, there is the alternative kind of layout commonly used in picture books where image and verbiage are integrated to form a more unified frame rather than having the two modalities in demarcated parts of the visual compositions. The verbal text and visual image can be organised to form a unified arrangement in two ways. When a visual composition is arranged with the verbiage represented in a bubble of speech or thought, it presents an option of [integrated: projected] which comprises a represented projector as well as a projection of verbal text. Another differentiated integrated layout in picture books is the choice of [projected: sound] which projects only the non-speech sound such as "Cracking" or "Bang". Illustration 6 - 2 provides an example which depicts an image of playing firecrackers, projecting the non-speech sound of "Cracking" in the central of the visual composition.

It is noticeable to the reader that the verbiage in projecting relation is integrated to the represented participant so as to offer a full meaning which has to be interpreted as a unity. In this sense, the verbiage of the sound is regar-

Illustration 6 – 2   from *Happy New Year* (2011)

ded as a visual unit that is overlaid onto the visual image, serving as a symbolic attribute of the celebration of Spring Festival to highlight the mood of jollification at this important moment of the story. Combined with the interpersonal choice of [WARTH: warm], it provides a positive mood to involve the reader in the significant moment of the story to share with the delightful and light-hearted feeling with the main protagonist.

6.2.2   Establishing visual framing

While INTERMODAL INTEGRATION as a vital parameter considers the layout of visual composition (e. g. single page or double page), the system of FRAMING moves the foci to the image itself, taking into account whether and how the image is framed within the composition. In considering the framing devices applied in picture books, there are two major choices realising pictorial framing within visual compositions, relying on whether the image extends to the edge of page (as an "unbound" frame) or whether there exists a margin enclosing (partly or fully) the image (as an "bound" image). In an unbound image, there is no boundary between the depicted world and the child reader, which enables the reader to establish a kind of affinity with the represented characters within the image.

Illustration 6 – 3, for instance, adopts the option of [FRAMING: unbound] in the image to construe a close link between the world of the child reader and the represented story world, inviting the reader to engage with the main protagonist at the selected moment of defeating the monster Nian. Coupled with the interpersonal choice of [graduation: quantification: up], the child reader is then invited to the story world to share with the depicted character's feeling of extraordinary happiness for achieving the success. The unbounded frame encourages the reader to identify with the child protagonist via sharing the positive feeling of happiness and easiness invoked in him.

Illustration 6 –3   from *Nian* (2015)

In comparison to the type of unbound images, bound images demarcate the world of child reader from the depicted story world at a relative remote distance, with a margin of space or border confining the represented character. Generally speaking, the margin of a particular bound image would afford some kind of interpersonal meaning through the use of colour. Since the default choice of colour for the depiction of margin is white (and black for border), a variety of bound images in picture books are likely to employ different colours to make a prevailing background ambience within the image. The visual is viewed as a bound image where the child protagonist is enclosed by a rounded border. Instead of the default choice of black colour for the border, the image makes a differentiated choice of red hues to decorate the margin, and therefore, the depicted character is confined by a red margin. The unmarked choice of colour enables a positive background ambience to be foregrounded, encouraging the reader to share the surge of positive attitude invoked by the warm ambience, and also the mood of happiness of the depicted character when he has found ways to defeat the monster Nian. The colours used for the margin or border have played a significant part in contributing to the ambience of the image. Nevertheless, regardless of the functions of colours in construing visual frame, there is another type of frame via ultilising a set of simple lines to separate the image from a minor frame built on the experiential content.

An example of this type can be found in the 8th double spread of *The Monster Nian is Coming* (see Illustration 6 – 4) where the depicted characters are enclosed in a house portrayed by several simple lines. The house emerges on the central place of the image, which constitutes the visual frame for the picture on the basis of the experiential content, emphasising that it serves a shelter for the depicted characters to hide from being attacked by the monster Nian, and also that its iconic status is highlighted to facilitate the nursery rhyme.

Illustration 6 – 4   from *The MonsterNian is Coming* (2013)

6.2.3 Mapping out focus groups

Unlike framing devices applied for delimiting boundaries of an image, the system of Focus is concerned with the visual elements enclosed within the boundaries, or in Painter et al. 's term, "focus groups" that constitute a plus of information and placed within a visual composition as "eyeful" (Painter et al. 2013). The textual meanings in picture books account for the organisation of meaning in a visual composition through placing various visual elements in different visual space to attract and control the reader's attention. To this end, the concept of focus group is essential for the analysis of visual elements in compositional relations. According to the data of picture books, there are two basic types of focus groups. A focus group may be composed of a series of identical or similar ideational visual elements which are repeated in the visual composition; or it may be emplaced around the centre of the image in different ways. The former instance refers to the visual composition where a set of visual elements are repeated along vertical, horizontal or slanted lines.

An instance is presented in Illustration 6 – 5 where an option of [iterating: aligned] is adopted to present a row of human characters, distracting the reader's attention from any individuated character in the image. Combined with the choice of minimal style of character depiction, the iterating focus groups illustrated in the visual image contribute to the management of the reader's attention, enabling the child reader to identify the depicted characters as collective groups.

A central focus group may occur in picture books when its visual elements are placed around a centre of the visual composition. The choice of [centred: simple] is seen as the most straight forward form in picture books where the central space of visual image is filled with one single (or a group of) visual element (s).

An example can be found in the first spread of *The Monster Nian is Coming* (Liu 2013). The image depicts a introduction of the monster Nian-

Illustration 6 – 5　from *Nian*（2007）

which attracts the reader's attention to the represented character in a relatively direct way, creating a static moment of the story narrative. In this sense, it serves as a significant way to introduce the depicted character as the main protagonist of the depicted story. Through the choice of a simple centrifocal focus group, the image encourages the reader to attend to the single depicted character (the monster Nian in this case) without potential dispersal of his/her attention. Apart from the most simple and straight forward central focus groups, there are some other complex types displaying extended centred focus groups. Analogous to the "centre-margin" composition (Kress & van Leeuwen 1996, 2006), the choice of [extended: circular] describes the image where the central element (or the central space) is ranged around by a set of additional visual elements in a circular pattern.

　　In our data of Chinese picture books, an example can be found in Illustration 7 – 6 from *On the Spring Festival* (2012) where the central space is occupied by a round table and a group of family members are placed around the centre in a circular fashion. In the image, a table of Spring Festival dinner as the central element is highlighted as the principle focal point of meaning. By contrast, different family members are placed on the edge of the image which indicating their status at this moment of the story as just members of a collective group rather than an individuated protagonist that deserves somewhat longer looking. Furthermore, the image shifts our attention to the harmonious atmosphere of the family reunion, and correlates the family reunion with the Spring Festival so as to teach the child reader a lesson of Chinese traditional culture.

Illustration 6 – 6   from *On the Spring Festival* (2012)

As a very common choice for Chinese picture book, the [polarised] compositions intend to place different represented characters along a horizontal, vertical or diagonal axis, balancing or opposing them within a visual composition. An example can be found in Illustration 5 – 3 in Chapter 5 (*The adventure of the Postman*) where the two depicted characters (the snowman and the postman) are located in a polarisation. In the composition, both of represented participants are viewed as the main focal points of ideational meaning, suiting their status in the story as the primary protagonist. In this regard, the polarised focus group within the composition comprises a human participant and an anthropomorphised participant. The compositional organisation can realise some particular interpersonal meaning by the depicted orientation and proximity between them. The represented characters are depicted in an intimate contact by placing them in a face-to-face position and also via the deictic vectors between the two represented participants. The deictic vector is created through the eye contact between the depicted characters, which in turn symbolises a close relationship and intimacy between them.

6.3   The interplay of image and verbiage in composing visual space

In this section, the focus is placed on the synergy between words and images to create textual meaning. In the first place, this section selects the picture book *Reunion* (Yu & Zhu 2008) as the main objective to explore the intersemiotic cohesive relations between the two modalities with respect to textual meaning. It conducts an account of the textual aspect of language by analysing thematic structure of the verbal text (Halliday 1994/2000; Halliday & Matthiessen 2004) , and then explores the compositional features of the visual images on the basis of Painter et al. 's (2013) analytical framework.

In order to illustrate the textual choices with respect to the verbal and visual texts we will provide a brief introduction of *Reunion* (Yu & Zhu 2008). It is a prizewinning ("Feng Zikai" award for children's picture books) Chinese picture book which has gained an extensive readership. As a well-known picture book, it tells a story about the annual reunion of a father and a daughter. In the visual images of the book, it is clear that an endearing little girl is the main protagonist who is expected to see her father on the holiday of the Spring Festival. However, the verbal text uses the first pronoun "我" (*I*) to refer to the little girl, reinforcing the engagement between the girl protagonist and the child reader. We are then invited to share with her a mood of deep sadness in bidding farewell to her father after a "transitory" reunion during the holiday of Spring Festival.

6.3.1   Textual analysis of the tale

The textual metafunction of language is concerned with the linguistic resources for creating coherent texts, enabling the interpersonal and ideational meanings to be configured as a meaningful whole with relevance to the contexts in which they are produced and interpreted. In SFL, the thematic structure that gives the clause its character as a message can be generally regarded as a structure comprising thematic element and rhematic element (Halliday 1994/ 2000, Halliday & Mattheiseen 2004). Theme is considered to be "the starting point of the message", referring to "what the clause is going to be about" (Halliday 1985a: 39). Apart from the Theme of the clause, the rest of the message is labelled as Reheme, which usually follows the initial element in the clause.

By utilising different thematic structure, the writer/speaker intends to project a same message from divergent points of view. Theme in this sense serves as a meaningful choice that "sets the scene for the clause itself and positions it in the relation to the unfolding text" (Halliday & Matthiessen 2004: 66). Within these concepts, we are moving to the verbal analysis of *Reunion*, with specific reference to the typology of themes that predominates in the verbiage, aiming to see how this picture book story is structurally organised. As shown in Table 6 − 1, both simple and multiple themes have been identified, with simple type of theme appearing more frequently (88.8%).

Table 6 − 1   **Simple and multiple themes in *Reunion***

Theme	Number	Percentage
Simple theme	79	88.8
Multiple theme	10	11.2
Total	89	100%

Evidence of this fact is shown in most of the clauses within this picture book where the thematic slots of them tend to be realised by the type of sole ideational elements that makes reference to the two main protagonists within the book, I (the little girl protagonist) (26.7%) and the father(24%). The choices of themes in the verbiage and focus groups in the visuals are demonstrated in detail in Table 6 − 2.

Table 6 – 2   Themes and focus groups in the bimodal text of *Reunion*

Page	Themes (in verbal text)	Focus groups (in visual text)
1	爸爸 father	
2	我 I 爸爸 father 妈妈 mother 看 look 爸爸 father 妈妈 mother	
3	吃过中饭 having lunch 爸爸 father 走 go 我 I	
5	包 make 爸爸 father 谁 who 这天夜里 on the night 我 I 我 I	
6	第二天 The following day 突然 suddenly 好运硬币 lucky coin 我 I 毛毛 Mao Mao 爸爸 father 妈妈 mother	
7	路上 on the street 毛毛 Mao Mao 我 I 我 I 这 this 我 I 我 I 爸爸 father	

Continued

Page	Themes（in verbal text）	Focus groups（in visual text）
8	大年初二 the 2nd of the Lunar Year 一大早 early in the morning 呀 ah 走 walk 爸爸 father 太好了 fantastic	
9	哈 aha 咦 gee 噢 oh 爸爸 father 在哪儿 where 我 I 爸爸 father 看 look	
11	大年初三 the 3rd of the Lunar Year 下午 afternoon 我们 we 然后 after then	
12	天快黑 it's getting dark 我 I 我 I	
13	毛毛 Mao Mao 爸爸 father 不要 do not 我 I 晚上 on the evening 叮当 ding dong 硬币 coin 爸爸 father	

Continued

Page	Themes（in verbal text）	Focus groups（in visual text）
14	那天夜里 on that night 早上 in the morning 爸爸 father	
15	爸爸 father 他 he 他 he 下次回来 next time you come back 不 no 我 I 我 I	
16	我 I 这个 this 爸爸 father 他 he	

For instance, the first clause of the picture book story introduces the father as one of the main protagonists as he is located in the thematic position of the clause and continues in such slot in the following clauses. The rhematic parts of the two clauses inform the child reader of his occupations and hard work outside. A number of similar uses of thematic structure have been found in the picture book story. The thematic positions of these clauses are taken up by two major types. The first type in which thematic position is occupied by the girl protagonist（including the pronoun "我" "I" and the nickname "毛毛" "Maomao"）occurs in the story to represent the activities taken by her on the holiday of the Spring Festival, conveying some interesting Chinese customs to the child reader. In this sense, the status of the girl protagonist within the verbal text is highlighted and the reader's attention is attracted by the foregrounding of the protagonist to share the feelings and moods of her.

The high utilisation of simple theme in language plays an essential role in bringing the child reader's attention to the major protagonists as well as their activities in which they jointly participate during the precious time of reunion. Coupled with the high frequency of simple choices, there are frequently-adopted options of unmarked themes identified in the verbal text where the verbal component of themes is able to fulfill the syntactic function of the subject of that clause. Consequently, the unmarked realisations of themes in language complement the purpose and strategy of facilitating the child reader's interpretation of the narrative plot and his/her understanding of the empathising stance.

Standing on the shoes of the girl protagonist and her father, we are likely to experience two differentiated kinds of emotions: happiness for the annual reunion and sadness for the departure.

6.3.2　Visual analysis of the images
➤ INTERMODAL INTEGRATION

As for the choice of layout in the story, the book is composed of sixteen double-page openings and two single image (one is depicted in the initiated page as a lead in, and another for a closing), which create a set of two contrastive arrangements for the pattern of layout within the picture book story. With few exceptions in the whole book, the pattern of intermodal integration employs a complementary choice of layout, comprising a single image and a single chunk of verbal text. Among those complementary arrangements, there is a predominance of choices for complementary vertical layout where the upper part of a visual composition is occupied by an image and lower part by a chunk of verbiage. A salient feature of the complementary layout in the story is that the visual image and verbal text have separate and distinct visual space. For instance, the second double spread of the picture book adopts a choice of [complementary: descending: equal] where the image placed at bottom depicts the reunion of the girl protagonist and her father, while the verbal text elaborates in detail on the situation of the first reunion between them (see Illustration 6 – 7). In this sense, the verbal text on the lower part of the story page serves to complement the visual image in a detailed way, providing the reader with a combination of equally important visual constituents of the composition. In addition, it can be noted that a choice of focalising contact is applied in the image where the girl protagonist stares at the reader while the father looks straight at her. Thus the reader is engaged with the girl protagonist to share a feeling of delight and shyness at the first reunion in a whole year. The story page draws our attention to the moved scene of the father and girl protagonist and to their affect via the focalisation as well as their facial expressions and bodily gestures.

我远远地看着他，不肯走近。
爸爸走过来，一把抱起我，用胡子扎我的脸。
"妈妈……" 我吓得大哭起来。
"看我给你买了什么！" 爸爸赶紧去掏他的大皮箱——
哦，好漂亮的帽子！
妈妈也换上了爸爸买的新棉袄。

Illustration 6 –7   from *Reunion* (2008)

The expanded integrated layouts as exceptions in the story are occasional applied where the verbal text and visual image share the white space of the page, with the verbiage integrated to the image that contributes to a construal of harmonious layout. These exceptions present themselves in the first single image of the book and the opening double-page spread. For example, the first single image of the book adopts a choice of [integrated: expanded: co-located: balanced] to highlight the meaning-making of both image and verbiage as a unity. The image at the upper part illustrates a scene of the little girl and her mother waiting for the family unification, and the verbiage supports the image by narrating the background of the coming story. When the page turns, an option of [integrated: expanded: co-located: unbalanced] is applied in the visual composition to depict the father returning home and the girl protagonist waiting beside the door. The reader is therefore encouraged to read the image and verbiage as a comprehensive unity, even though the image which occupies a larger amount of space may convey sufficient meaning by itself to indicate the depicted participants and events taking place in the page. However, although taking up a relatively small amount of visual space, the verbal text also plays a significant part in reinforcing the ideational meanings presented by the image so as to involve the reader in the depicted story world. Through the use of integrated layout, the reader's attention is attracted to both the image and verbiage, which in turn contributes to construing a harmonious organisation of bimodal text as a coherent whole.

➤ Framing

In terms of framing devices, there is a distinct comparison between unbound images and bound images in the picture book *Reunion*. The former deals with the visual composition where the image extends to the edge of the page, narrowing the distance between the depicted story world and the world of the reader. The book repeatedly utilises the contrast between unbound images (usually on the verso page) and bound images (usually on the recto) within the frame of double-page spread, exploiting some kind of special meaning. A striking example is the ninth spread of the picture book (see Illustration 6 – 8) in which a unbound image on the left side of the composition welcome us to enter the depicted story world to participate into the family activity with the represented participants. When it comes to the recto, we are then introduced to a bound image where the represented participants are enclosed by several lines with the edge of white colours. This format shifts our attention to the depicted characters rather than the circumstantial details. Coupled with a choice of the generic style of character depiction, the bound image makes it easier for the reader to identify with the represented characters (in this case, the daughter sitting on the shoulder of her father). Taking them as individuals, the reader is then expected to stand in the character's shoes and sympathetically feel their emotions and needs. Furthermore, it can be inferred from the previous image that the successive image sustains the same context but removes the circumstantial setting with a strategy of zooming in, and consequently, foregrounding the depicted characters within the bound image. This format enables the child reader to be engaged in the surge of positive of affect inscribed in the bound image and also the affinity invoked in the represented characters. In a nutshell, the shift not only conveys a sort of message like "doing family activity with your father" but also invokes the reflection on the affection and preciousness in spending time with your family.

Illustration 6 – 8   from _Reunion_ (2008)

Experiential frame as another type of bound image is adopted in the picture book to demarcate the image as against a frame formed by the experiential elements within the image. An example of experiential frame can be found in the fourteenth spread, where the represented characters are shown within a bedroom with the door as its edge. The image depicts the father packing up and going to leave in the bedroom. Serving as the experiential frame, the door with suntan lines has the function of symbolic attribute, indicating the imminent departure between the father and the girl protagonist.

> **Focus**

With regard to the choices of FOCUS in the picture book story, this section explores in detail the visual elements placed in frames to manage the reader's attention. The focus groups are defined as some kinds of eyefuls constituting a pulse of message. Within the story, the choices made from the system of FOCUS in effect emphasises experiential meaning and highlight several focus groups which deserve repeated looks. A typical example as such can be found in the eighth double-page spread, where the choices of focus groups have been schematically analysed in Figure 6 – 1. In this visual composition, there appears a [centrifocal: plorised: orthogonal: horizontal] relationship between the image on the verso page and the visual composition composed of an image and a verbal text on the right. On the verso page, the various versions of the father in conducting different kinds of housework form an [iterating: aligned] manifestation, emphasising that the laborious father involved in a series of activity sequences is brought to the reader's notice as a principal focal point. The ideational meaning is reinforced by the ongoing process of various activity sequences taken by the depicted character in a successive relation. On the recto page, there is obviously a choice of [plorised: orthogonal: vertical] connecting the image and verbiage, each of which occupies the same amount of visual space and thus affords equal semantic weight. By utilising such choice of focus groups, the visual composition stress two primary focal points in a coherent way in which the verbiage supports the image by elaborating on it. In the upper image, the ideational meaning is strengthened by the deictic vectors between the represented participants. In this case, the deictic vectors are formed by the orientationand gaze interaction between the father and the girl protagonist, which serves as an important means in realising interpersonal meanings of proximity. A social contact has been established by the face-to-face placement of the two depicted characters, and a close intimacy can be indicated from the close social distance and the embracing posture between them, as well as by their facial expressions of care and delight.

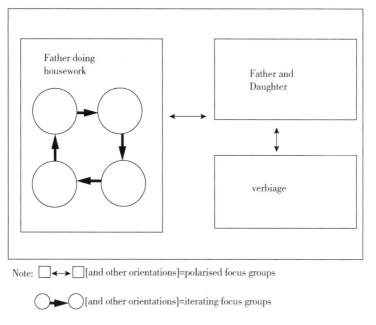

Note: ☐◄─►☐ [and other orientations]=polarised focus groups

⭕─►⭕ [and other orientations]=iterating focus groups

Figure 6 – 1   Focus groups represented in the eighth spread in *Reunion*

It is observed that the FOCUS choices in the picture book rely heavily on the narrative theme of the story. To be specific, the father and the girl protagonist are regarded as the principle focal points of ideational meaning, which are often brought to the reader's attention. The most frequent choice of focus groups within the story is polarization that place the girl protagonist and her father on a horizontal or vertical axis, representing a close intimacy between them and also various activities they are taking part in (such as in the double spreads 2, 5, 8, 9, 13, 15 and 16). Despite the overwhelmingly uses of polarised focus groups, there are some other choices of focus groups applied within the book, such as the option of [centred: extended: triptych] in the recto page of the second spread, where the central space is occupied by the mother as accompanied by the girl protagonist and the father on either side. The family members are organised as a close "triptych" (Kress & van Leeuwen 2006: 197). The emphasis is then turned onto the focus group of the family members and the reader is expected to align with those depicted characters to enjoy the important moment of family reunion on the Spring Festival. The analysis of the main FOCUS choices within the book is demonstrated in Table 6 − 3.

Table 6 − 3   **Analysis of main options of FOCUS in *Reunion***
(**Focal elements within the focus group are indicated in brackets**)

Spread		Focus		
1	whole	centrifocal: plorised: orthogonal: horizontal (streetscape & familyreunion)		
	verso	centrifocal: plorised: orthogonal: horizontal (children & motorbike) centrifocal: plorised: orthogonal: vertical (lanterns & old man on boat)	recto	centrifocal: plorised: orthogonal: horizontal (parents & daughter and dog) centrifocal: plorised: orthogonal: vertical (lanterns & ducks)
2	whole	centrifocal: plorised: orthogonal: horizontal (a number of houses & the family)		
	verso	centrifocal: plorised: orthogonal: vertical/ + deceit vector (image & verbiage)	recto	centrifocal: centred: extended: triptych (father-mother-daughter)
3	whole	centrifocal: plorised: orthogonal: horizontal (father + daughter & image + verbiage)		
	verso	centrifocal: centred: extended: circular/ + filled (father + barber + daughter)	recto	centrifocal: plorised: orthogonal: vertical (image & verbiage)
4	whole	centrifocal: plorised: orthogonal: horizontal (x 2) (trees & house; a small visual frame & mother) centrifocal: plorised: orthogonal: vertical (houses as background & protagonists' house)		

Continued

Spread		Focus		
5	whole	centrifocal: plorised: orthogonal: horizontal (father + daughter & image + verbiage)		
	verso	centrifocal: plorised: orthogonal: horizontal/deictic vector (father & daughter)	recto	centrifocal: plorised: orthogonal: vertical (image & verbiage)
6	whole	centrifocal: plorised: orthogonal: horizontal (family members & image + verbiage)		
	verso	centrifocal: centred: extended: circular/ (father + mother + daughter)	recto	centrifocal: plorised: orthogonal: vertical (image & verbiage)
7	whole	centrifocal: plorised: orthogonal: horizontal (people & image + verbiage)		
	verso	centrifocal: centred: extended: circular/ (daughter + mother + neighbors)	recto	centrifocal: plorised: orthogonal: vertical (image & verbiage)
8	whole	centrifocal: plorised: orthogonal: horizontal (father & verbiage)		
	verso	iterating: aligned (doing housework)	recto	centrifocal: plorised: orthogonal: vertical (image & verbiage)
9	whole	centrifocal: plorised: orthogonal: horizontal (father & image + verbiage)		
	verso	centrifocal: centred: extended: triptych (cat-father-daughter)	recto	centrifocal: plorised: orthogonal: vertical (image & verbiage)
10	whole	centrifocal: centred: extended: circular/ (dragon dancing + sightseers + houses) centrifocal: plorised: orthogonal: horizontal (housein left & right house)		
11	whole	centrifocal: plorised: orthogonal: horizontal (image + verbiage & children)		

Continued

Spread		Focus		
	verso	centrifocal: plorised: orthogonal: vertical (image & verbiage)	recto	centrifocal: centred: extended: circular/ (snowman + children)
12	whole	centrifocal: plorised: orthogonal: horizontal (image + verbiage & daughter)		
	verso	centrifocal: plorised: orthogonal: vertical (image & verbiage)	recto	iterating: aligned (searching for lucky coin)
13	whole	centrifocal: plorised: orthogonal: horizontal (image + verbiage & mother + daughter)		
	verso	centrifocal: plorised: orthogonal: vertical (image & verbiage)	recto	centrifocal: plorised: orthogonal: horizontal (mother & daughter)
14	whole	centrifocal: plorised: orthogonal: horizontal (image + verbiage & family members)		
	verso	centrifocal: plorised: orthogonal: vertical (image & verbiage)	recto	centrifocal: centred: extended: circular (family members + cat)
15	whole	centrifocal: plorised: orthogonal: horizontal (father + daughter & image + verbiage)		
	verso	centrifocal: plorised: orthogonal: horizontal (father & daughter)	recto	centrifocal: plorised: orthogonal: vertical (image & verbiage)
16	whole	centrifocal: plorised: orthogonal: horizontal (& image + verbiage)		
	verso	centrifocal: plorised: orthogonal: horizontal (father & daughter)		

6.3.3 The interplay of words and images at the textual level

Having respectively examined the verbal and visual semiotic resources within this picture book, I now move to the analysis of compositional intersemiotic complementarity between the verbal and visual semiotic systems to create coherent messages. The attention of this section is placed on the way verbal and visual semiotic resources are combined to create textual and compositional meaning.

The analysis of the synergy of the verbal and visual semiotics at textual level is conducted by comparing the verbal and visual semiotic resources chosen by the writer/illustrator to make the information flow of the story and foreground the most relevant parts of the picture book story. Through the analysis, there are a range of important visual-verbal compositional aspects in the picture books. The textual analysis of verbal text reveals that there is a correlation between the departure of the clauses as messages and the two primary protagonists, "I" (the little girl protagonist) and the father. The visual textual patterns seem to have a correspondence with the verbal text within the picture book narrative. This kind of correspondence can be realised by the choices of focus groups within the images of this tale. In the images, the girl protagonist and her father are perceived as the principle focal point of ideational meaning, which are often brought to the child reader's attention. For instance, the most widely used choice of focus groups within the tale is polarization (in double spreads 2, 5, 9, 13, 15 and 16) which places the girl protagonist and her father on a horizontal or vertical axis, indicating a very close intimacy between them and also various activities they are taking part in. Despite the choices of polarised focus groups, there are some other choices of focus groups to reinforce the correspondence to the verbal text. In the recto of the second double spread, for example, the central space is occupied by the mother as accompanied by the girl protagonist and the father on either side. The family members in this case are organised as a close triptych. The emphasis is then shifted to the focus group of the family members and the reader is encouraged to align with those depicted characters to enjoy the big moments of family reunion on the Spring Festival. According to the analysis, the verbal and visual semiotic resources are combined to highlight the two primary participants in the story which indicate the important and valuable reunion of family.

6.3.4 The analysis of different commitment of meaning

With the ideational and interpersonal meaning completed in previous chapter, this section conducts an integrated analysis on the different meanings committed by verbal and visual semiotics within the tale with respect to ideational, interpersonal and textual meaning. To facilitate the analysis, the last spread of the picture book has been drawn on to explore the different commitment of both two modes. It selects Illustration 6 − 9 as the exemplar to investigate the commitment of meaning related to verbal and visual semiotic resources.

Illustration 6 − 9　from *Reunion*（2008）

Concerning the ideational meaning committed in the visual image, we can observe an action depicted（a little girl putting a coin onto the hand of a man）, as indicated by the vectors informed by her arm and the coin, and the middle-aged man looking down at her（with invisible gaze vector towards the little girl, indicating a perception process）. As far as the character manifestation is concerned, we are provided a complete depiction of the man but only the profile of the little girl. Through their depicted attributes（e. g. dress, size, hair, skin colour）, we can also infer a variety of factors related to them such as the age, race, or even social class and social relationship. The represented participants within the image are depicted in a very close social distance (e. g. the girl being held tightly by the arms of the man) , suggesting a kind of family role as "daughter and father". Although the reappearance of the girl protagonist at this moment is portrayed with profile, the child reader is able to make an identification of the character through the "marked attributes" of her (e. g. red coat and pink-grey hat). In view of the ideational meanings instantiated by the linguistic text, some of actions (e. g. putting the coin, nodding, hugging) are described verbally and a verbal action is taken by the girl protagonist to his father, with the projection of the direct speech. However, there are no cues to deduce that the depicted characters are illustrated visually as talking to each other (e. g. mouth closed, without speech bubble). The manifestation of character is not construed verbally at all except from the identification of the familiar role as daughter and father.

Looking at the visual composition through an interpersonal lens, the reader is offered an image where a little girl being held tightly by her father. As for the visual focalisation, the depicted characters have no eye contact with us and hence we are kept outside of the story world. Nevertheless, we are positioned to see the profile of the girl protagonist with the father's eyes, since the father is looking straight at his daughter. A choice of mediated viewing has been encoded into the image so that we are placed temporarily in the stance of the father to make a vicarious contact with him. We are then encouraged to get involved in the important moment of the story to share with the father a mood of sadness and being reluctant to part with his daughter. Unlike the commonly accepted choice of minimal character depiction in picture books, the represented characters are depicted in a generic style, indicating an empathic role in evoking attitudes in the child reader. Different from the minimalist depiction keeping the reader as detached observer outside the story, the generic style in the image invites the reader to see themselves in the focalising character's view, creating alignment and affinity between the reader and the represented characters. When it comes to the involvement, combined with the generic style of character depiction which creates an empathetic pathos, we are kept at a close social distance with the depicted characters by a close shot to see clearly their facial expression. In terms of the affiliation between the depicted characters in the image, the father looking down at his daughter symbolises the former's power or authority. Furthermore, the two represented characters are in a close proximity to each other, and the father's posture in the image (embracing the girl protagonist in arms) ensures an actual physical touch between the two, reinforcing the interpersonal affinity between them as well as evoking a mood of sadness in the child reader.

Turning to the visual expression of feeling, we are likely to share an emotion of sadness in view of the facial expressions and their bodily postures. This feeling is underlined by the ambience of the image where the represented characters are suited in a both cool and familiar ambience through using of a full palette of dark hues despite that the girl protagonist is wearing a red cloth (the red colour in this case serving only as the maintenance of character depiction). The choice of vibrant and cool ambience thus contributes to building a depressed and sad emotion for the father in parting with his daughter. The verbal text by comparison commits some differing meanings in relation to the interpersonal aspect. The interpersonal meaning systems in play are those of proximity between the two represented characters, realised via choices in naming (爸爸, Dad) and verbal projection. Through the projected direct speech and a series of feedbacks given by the father (e. g. promising by nodding his head), a more experiential reader is able to infer the feeling of sadness and upset.

Lastly, with regard to the textual meaning encoded in the image, we need to consider prominence in terms of framing, focus group and intermodal integration. The double-page spread is regarded as a kind of "micro" frame where the verbal text is framed off from the image by being placed on a separate page. A choice of complementary layout is adopted in the spread where the verbal text and visual image reside in its own space with equal semantic weight. In this sense, we are introduced to the picture book story by reading separately the visual and verbal semiosis in the spread. In view of framing device used in the spread, an option of [unbound: decontextualised: individu-ated] in framing encourages the reader to enter the story world. The decon-textualsion choice has a strong effect in highlighting the affect or behaviour of the depicted characters, facilitating some of the interpersonal meanings by shifting our attention to the depicted characters. Within the unbound image, a removal of circumstantial setting narrows the distance between the depicted story world and the reader's world, so that the represented characters are less constrained by the unnecessary circumstantial details. As for the focus group, the represented characters are arranged in a polarised relation, implying that both of them are viewed as principal focal point of ideational meaning. In ad-dition, interpersonal meanings are expressed by the deictic vectors between the two characters formed by the face to face orientation and gaze interaction, indicating the close proximity and affiliation between them. Thus the choice of focus group within the image encourages our immediate apprehension of the two characters as a pair of focal points rather than focusing merely on any one of them. Thus the visual textual choices contribute to organising the ideational and interpersonal realisations and all three metafunctions are co-patterned in the visual text. However, as for the verbal text at textual level, there is no such commitment of meaning to help to build primary focal points.

Through the analysis of the differing commitment of meaning between vis-ual and verbal text, it is noticeable that there is more ideational meaning com-mitted in the visual text than the verbal one in respect to the depiction of the characters (in terms of attribution and manifestation). On the contrary, the verbal text commits a few meanings that have not been found in the visual text (e.g. the projected direct speech). The two modalities within the composition exhibit an uneven degree of sharing of the ideational semantic load. When it comes to the interpersonal meaning, there is a sharing of similar meaning be-tween the image and verbiage in respect to the affiliation. However, the image and verbiage do not share such similarities in the feeling. Textually, there is more meaning committed by the visual semiotic than the verbal one, without complementary meaning choices realised in the verbiage.

**Table 6 – 4①   Degrees of commitment of three strands of meaning
related to Illustration 6 – 9**

	Image	Commitment	Verbal text	Commitment
Character	Attribution	Full (daughter and father) size, age, dress, hairstyle…	Attribution	
	Manifestation	Full: complete manifestation (daughter): profile of the face	Identification	
	Family role	Partial: inferred only	Role Specification	Full: her father
Action	Action	Full: action depicted with vectors	Material/ behavioural	Full: Material/ behavioural process
	Perception	Full: gaze vectors via facial expression	Mental	
	Talking		Projection	
Feeling Setting	Visual affect	Full: (father) sadness	Verbal affect	Partial: implied only
	Ambience	Full: cool, dark, familiar	Attitude, tone	
	Evoked judgement	Full: sadness, sympathy	Attitude	
Affiliation Setting	Pathos	Full: generic style of character depiction	Characterisation	
	Social distance	Full: via a close shot; (daughter and father) in close proximity to each other	Social distance	
Prominence Setting	Framing	[unbound: decontextualised: individuated]	Tonality	
	Focus	centrifocal: polarised focus group	Information flow	

6.4   Summary

This chapter is primarily concerned with the way in which verbal and vis-

---

① Shading in the cell is employed to facilitate the analysis of areas of commitment. Dark shading indicates no commitment, while light shading signifies minor degree of commitment.

ual semiotic resources are co-deployed to form coherent messages within Chinese picture books. Based on Painter et al. 's (2013) visual narrative framework, it first identifies the compositional features of visual elements through the picture books. In order to explore the compositional cohesive relations between verbal and visual semiotics, the chapter selects the picture book *Reunion* as the exemplar for analysis. The analysis demonstrates that the thematic structures of most clauses within the verbal text are realised by the type of simple theme with particular reference to the two protagonists of the story: I (the little girl protagonist) and father (the girl's father). This feature is complemented and reinforced by the visual text through the dominating uses of polarised focus groups which place the two protagonists as the most salient and foregrounding focal points in images. Both the verbal and visual strategies adopted by the writer/illustrator are subjected to the theme and metafictive nature of the story.

This chapter concludes with an analysis of different commitment of meaning for verbal and visual semiotics in the picture book. It is observed that there is more textual meaning committed by the visual text, without the complementary meaning choices realised in the verbal text. The choice of focus groups in visual text is influenced by the topic and development of the story, which in turn enhances the prominence of the important represented participants and strengthens the management of the reader's attention.

Chapter Seven   Conclusion

7.1   Introduction

The overall aim of the book is to account for visual and verbal choices available to the author/illustrator to construct ideational meanings, to shape/reshape depicted identities and negotiate interpersonal relations, and to make the story narratives coherent and interesting within children's picture books. The theory that underpins the present study is Systemic Functional Linguistics (SFL) which has been extended to various multimodal studies to examine the process of meaning making by different kinds of semiotic resources (e. g. Kress & van Leeuwen 1996, 2006; O'Toole 1994, 2004) and to explore the collaboration and synergy among different semiotic systems (e. g. O'Halloran 2005, 2008; Royce 1999; Painter & Martin 2011). In order to achieve a full understanding of the ways in which visual and verbal semiotic resources complement each other to synergistically making meaning, Royce's (1999, 2007) framework of intersemiotic complementarity is extended to investigate on the collaboration between the two modalities within the exemplar books.

As a new development in the field of image analysis, Painter et al. 's (2013) analytical framework for visual narrative has been applied and extended to the systematic analysis of visual semiotic resources in our database of Chinese children's picture books. Moreover, informed by the SFL dimension of instantiation (Halliday & Matthiessen 2004) and Martin's articulated notions of "commitment" (Martin 2008, 2010), the present research conducts a comparative study on the different commitments of meaning between the two semiotic systems within Chinese children's picture books, aiming to track the way in which each of them is instantiated in the bimodal text and to compare their relative contributions to the overall meanings at ideational, interpersonal and textual levels.

This chapter is intended to present the major findings by revisiting the research questions formulated in the first chapter. The findings of the book are followed by the contributions for further research and identification of some limited areas that require further research.

7.2   A recount of the research findings

As mentioned in the first chapter, the book conducts a systemic functional analysis of the visual and verbal semiotic resources to systematically and comprehensively explore the meaning making process in Chinese children's picture books. The systemic functional semiotic approach and its metafunctional framework, that underpins the theoretical construct of the present research has proved to be powerful and effective in accounting for the texts involving more than one semiotic system ("bimodal" text in the present research). In considering the research aims proposed in the introductory chapter of the thesis, this section would summarise the major findings of the research via addressing the following research questions:

(1) How are the three strands of meanings construed by choices from both verbal and visual semiotic systems in Chinese children's picture books?

(2) How are cohesive relations construed between visual and verbal semiotic systems within Chinese picture books?

(3) To what degrees are meanings in verbal system and visual system taken up in the process of creating the story as a meaningful whole? And what are the differences between the commitments of verbal and visual semiotic resources in Chinese picture books?

In order to achieve a better understanding of each question, studies and theories that are relevant to the present research have been reviewed, followed by the analyses carried out in Chapters 4 to 6. As mentioned earlier, the book is informed by SFL theory and its metafunctional framework, thus analyses in Chapters 4 to 6 are metafunctionally oriented and organised, each of which is mainly concerned with one specific strand of meaning. In order to facilitate the analyses, three well-designed picture books are carefully examined. In this section, the major research findings are summarised in terms of (1) the identification of the three strands of meaning realised by verbal and visual choices; (2) the analysis of intersemiotic cohesion between visual and verbal semiotics and (3) the analysis of different commitment of meanings for each semiotic in the process of co-instantiation.

7.2.1 The cohesive relations between the verbal and visual semiotics within Chinese children's picture books

To answer the first two questions, Chapter 4 deals with the interpersonal meanings construed by both visual and verbal semiotic resources and the way in which each modality complements another to create engagement and affinity between different kinds of participants, with a particular focus on the construal of the relationship between the represented participants and the child reader. The interpersonal meanings construed by the visual semiotic resources are primarily examined through four parameters. (1) From the perspective of focalisation, it is found that the options of contact (73.6%) are preferred by the author/illustrator to achieve a forceful engagement between the child reader and the depicted characters, and to forge a deep identification of the reader with them within the story. (2) Considering the use of colours, the picture book adopts activated ambience throughout the story narration to please the child reader and employs some contrastive colours as the strategy to facilitate a comparative reading of disparate emotions represented by the depicted participants. (3) As far as the visual affect is concerned, the use of minimalist style predominates in the picture book which is highly schematic and iconic to vividly express the degrees of sadness or happiness of the represented participants. (4) In the respect of visual graduation, we have found that the options of upscaled and downscaled quantification take almost the same proportion, which in combination contribute to strengthening attitudinal meanings and provoking the child reader's emotional feedback. In order to examine the interpersonal meanings encoded in the linguistic resources of the exemplar, the Mood structure of the verbal text is analysed clause by clause. Through the analysis, it can be observed that an objective narrative voice has been construed via the relatively high occurrences of declarative clauses (68.1%), and scarce uses of interrogative clauses and imperative clauses. Thus the linguistic choices serve to advance the story narrative and manage the reader's attention to the story per se, while the visual choices intend to establish a strong engagement and affinity between the reader and the picture book. The different features represented by the verbal and visual modalities indicate a collaboration to communicate interpersonal meanings that are beyond the scope of the sole modality.

With regard to interpersonal intersemiotic complementarity (Royce 1997, 2007), an analysis of the cohesive relations between visual and verbal semiotic systems is carried out to probe into the various intersemiotic ways of relating the child reader with the picture book. The interpersonal cohesion is then examined in terms of *attitudinal congruence*, *attitudinal dissonance*, and *reinforcement of address*. According to the analysis, *attitudinal congruence* takes place when both verbal and visual semiotics cooperate to present similar interpersonal content and parallel kinds of attitude. There is evidence to confirm that the interpersonal cohesions between visual and verbal semiotics are mainly realised through *attitudinal congruence* and *attitudinal dissonance*. The verbiage and images within the book are generally organised in a convergent attitudinal fashion, which complement each other to synergistically make interpersonal meanings. For instance, an interpersonal congruence is realised by the interplay of the verbiage and image within the tenth spread of the book where the verbal text made up of some declarative clauses realises the unmarked speech function of offering a statement to the reader; and the image also addresses the reader from a far distance (and lack of eye contact with us) without requiring him/her to react or give a response. Through the analyses, it can also be observed that *attitudinal dissonance* is sometimes adopted in children's picture book to construean ironic attitudinal meaning. The two semiotic systems within the picture book complement and reinforce one another in establishing various kinds of engagement as well as building interpersonal cohesive relations.

Chapter 5 places the attention to the ideational meaning realised by the visual and verbal semiotics and the way in which each modality coheres the other to represent the narrative reality as well as the depicted participants in the story. Throughout the analyses of verbal and visual texts in the exemplar book, one can note that the verbal and visual texts share a similarity in the dominating uses of material processes (47.9 % and 52.6 %) which provide the reader an immediate and intense sense of activity and movement as well as helping to drive the development of the plot. Apart from the material processes, some relational processes are adopted to identify the represented participants and their attributes. Besides the single action depicted in images, the visual analysis takes into account of the relations between various events in successive images. It shows that the "temporal sequence" as the most used option plays a key role in building and keeping the story narrative of the picture book.

As for the ideational intersemiotic complementarity, an account of the cohesive relations between verbal text and visual elements is conducted in two divergent types of visual frames: a "narrative" image (Kress & van Leeuwen 2006) involving actions that are formed by vectors and a "static" image (Painter et al. 2013) without such actions. The verbal text coheres with the visual message elements (VMEs) in construing complementary ideational meanings via the utilisation of a range of intersemiotic cohesive devices such as *repetition*, *synonymy*, *meronymy*, *collocation* and so on. Among these cohesive devices to construct ideational cohesive relations, it is found that the frequently-adopted devices of *repetition* and *collocation* are often indicative of the complementary relation between verbal and visual semiotic systems in both the narrative and static visuals.

In Chapter 6, the textual meaning realised by visual and verbal semiotics is scrutinised to explore how the visual and verbal modes collaborate to make the story a meaningful and coherent whole. An analysis of verbal text in the exemplar is conducted in relation to the typology of themes to examine the structure organisation of the picture book. According to the analysis, the thematic structures of most clauses within the picture book are realised by the type of simple theme with particular reference to the two protagonists of the story: I (the little girl protagonist) (24%) and father (the girl's father) (26.7%). The two participants are foregrounded via being located in the thematic position, which account for more than 50% of the clauses counted in the story. Furthermore, by analysing the focus group in the visual text, we can find that the visual text places a particular emphasis on the girl protagonist and her father as the principal focal point through the frequent choices of polarised focus groups which arrange the little girl and her father on a horizontal/vertical axis, suggesting a close intimacy between them. The intersemiotic relation between the two modalities is thus complementary, in that both the choices of verbal and visual semiotic systems rely heavily on the narrative theme of the story, and reinforce each other to give prominence to the two protagonists and to involve the reader to perceive the sincere emotion between them. The choices of thematic structure (in verbiage) and focus groups (in image) are influenced to a large extent by the topic and development of the picture book narrative, which on the other hand strengthen the management of the reader's attention and position him/her in a well designed reading stance.

7.2.2 Different commitment of meaning related to the verbal and visual semiotics

Having identified and examined the features represented by the choices of verbal and visual semiotic systems and the collaboration between them, the book delves into the different affordance of meaning related to each mode by focusing on the SFL dimension of instantiation (Halliday & Matthiessen 2004). Instantiation refers to the relation between the meaning potential that inheres in the system and the particular instance. In the cases relevant to children's picture books, it is manifested as a relation between the language or image (in general) as a totality of systems and the specific text (linguistic or visual) as instance of that totality. Drawing upon Martin's (2008) notion of commitment, the present study explores the different commitments as manifested in verbal and visual semiotic systems, and to compare how meanings of verbal system and visual system are taken up and the degree of delicacy selected within the systems.

In the exploration of different commitments of interpersonal meaning between visual and verbal semiotic systems, an analysis is conducted by drawing on Painter and Martin (e. g. Painter & Martin 2011; Painter et al. 2013) complementary meanings systems, to be more specific, the commitment of interpersonal meaning is examined through the parameters of Affiliation and Feeling. Through the analyses, it can be summarised that there is more interpersonal meaning committed in the image than that in the verbal text. In the exemplar, the visual text is more responsible for establishing interpersonal relationship than the verbal text, not only in terms of the visual space it occupies, but also in terms of the meanings manifested in the visual choices. While there are some degree of meaning committed in visual systems related to affiliation and feeling (such as pathos, social distance, ambience, and visual graduation), no commitment at all has been found in the complementary meaning system within the verbiage. The visual image thus plays a more fundamental part in establishing engagement between the child reader and the represented characters as well as in constructing identification of the former with the depicted characters.

Based on the complementary meaning systems for verbal and visual semiotics, the analysis of differences in commitment of ideational meaning is examined through parameters of Character, Action and Setting (Painter & Martin 2011; Painter et al. 2013). On the basis of the analysis, the observation is reached that there is more ideational meaning committed in the visual text than in the verbal text in terms of attribution, character manifestation, relation, inter-event relation, and inter-circumstantiation in the exemplar. By contrast, the verbal text also commits some degrees of ideational meaning which have

not been co-instantiated in the visual text (e. g. in terms of action and circumstantiation). The divergence in the commitment of ideational meaning exhibits
an uneven and differing degree of sharing of semantic load by each semiotic
system. Textually, the analysis of commitments of meaning is conducted
through the parameter of Prominence. Through the analysis, it can be found
that there is more meaning committed by the visual semiotic system (such as
framing and focus) than the verbal semiotic system, without complementary
meaning choices realised in the verbal text.

The analyses conducted in Chapters 4 to 6 provide different perspectives
on analysing the meaning making of both visual and verbal semiotic systems in
Chinese children's picture books. Apart from the collaboration between the two
modalities in construing different stands of meaning, the difference in commitment of meaning afforded by each semiotic has also been scrutinised to shed
light on a comprehensive account of how each semiotic contributes to the overall meaning as well as how they are collaborated to make the picture book a
meaningful, coherent and attractive one.

7.3　Contribution of the study

The bookdraws enlightenments from a number of previous studies in multimodal discourse studies and systemic functional approach, and enriches multimodal studies by adopting a social semiotic perspective to the analysis of Chinese children's picture books. The significance of the research lies in both theoretical and practical grounds.

In the first place, the book contributes to the theoretical orientation by
extending the social semiotic account of the visual semiotic resources and exploring how visual semiosis complement the verbal text to synergistically construe different kinds of meaning in Chinese children's picture books.

Secondly, the book contributes to the practical orientation by enriching
the linguistic studies of Chinese picture books with a complementary study on
visual narratives. Although there are some new emerging studies on picture

books (e. g. Painter et al. 2013; Tian 2011), the foci of attention given to Chinese picture book narratives are rare, thus the present study will fill in the gap by providing a systematic account ofverbal and visual semiotic resources and the interplay between them in Chinese picture books.

As reiterated in this research, a primary focus is placed on the cooperation and interplay of verbal and visual semiotics to construe meanings. In this regard, this book endeavours to provide insights useful for developing a comprehensive account of the intersemiotic complementarity between visual and verbal semiotics, and also for pushing the boundaries of current theorisation of multimodal studies by analysing the differences in the commitment of meaning in relation to each semiotic. This book aims to shed light on how each semiotic contributes to the overall meaning and how they are collaboratedto make meaning and contributes to a better understanding and interpretation of contemporary multimodal resources.

Furthermore, in SFL sense, over the past decades, most work in SFL has focused on the development of two hierarchies (realisation and rank) and two complementaries, and the study on other complementary hierarchies (instantiation and individuation) is relatively less developed (see Martin 2008). With this consideration, the present research examines the different commitment (as a perspective on the cline of instantiation) of meaning afforded by both verbal and visual semiotic resources when they are co-instantiated in the picture book story, consequently, expanding and broadening the application scope of the SFL. Since the studies on the SFL dimension of instantiation are primarily centred upon the relation between the meaning potential that inheres in the of system of language and the actual linguistic text, this research extends the analysis of instantiation to the non-verbal semiotic system, shedding useful insights as well as suggesting new directions for further studies on the instantiation of verbal and non-verbal semiotci resources.

7. 4 Limitations and suggestions for future research

Despite the arduous efforts that are made in the book, there are still some limitations in the research andseveral suggestions for further study.

Firstly, the book is primarily concerned with the multisemiotic nature of Chinese picture books, however, there are undoubtedly a number of other types of multimodal communication outside picture book discourse. Today's world has witnessed a rapid development in communication technology, and the studies of multimodal discourse are not limited to the page-based discourse. The multimodal resources infused every aspect of our lives, such as three-dimensional artefacts, online resources, and audio-visual devices, call for further attention from the analysts who focus on the social semiotic studies and multimodal research. Therefore, more work should be done in the future research to explore and describe the process of meaning-making by these types of "hypertexts" (e. g. Djonov 2007) to bring a knowledge of the collaboration between different semiotic systems and their contributions to the construct of overall meaning.

Secondly, the analysis and research findings are based on Chinese picture books. The interplay and collaboration of visual and verbal semiotic resources are examined through Chinese children's picture books. In order to gain a better understanding of the ways in which different semiotic resources complement one another to making meaning, more research needs to be done to examine various characteristics manifested in the process of making meaning by picture books from outside China. In the further research, a complementary analysis will be conducted to investigate both Chinese children's picture books and English picture books, comparing their similarities and differences between the two types in creating multiple meaning.

In addition, since the book takes a social semiotic approach to the analysis of children's picture books, the major interpretations in this research are qualitative analysis. The analyses within the research are unavoidably somewhat subjective.

References

Baldry, A. P. 2004. Phase and transition, type and instance: Patterns in media texts as seen through a multimodal concordancer. In O'Halloran, K. L. (ed.). *Multimodal Discourse Analysis: Systemic Functional Perspectives.* London: Continuum, 83 – 108.

Baldry, A. P. & Thibault, P. J. 2006. *Multimodal Transcription and Text Analysis.* London: Equinox.

Barthes, R. 1977. Rhetoric of the image. In Barthes, R. *Image-Music-Text.* Heath, S. (trans.). London: Fontana, 32 – 51.

Bateman, J. A. 2008. *Multimodality and Genre: A Foundation for the Systematic Analysis of Multimodal Documents.* Hampshire: Palgrave Macmillan.

Bateson, G. 2000. *Steps to An Ecology of Mind: Collected Essays in Anthropology, Psychiatry, Evolution and Epistemology.* Chicago: Chicago University Press.

Bosmajian, H. 1999. Reading the unconscious: psychoanalytical criticism. In Hunt, P. (ed.). *Understanding Children's Literature.* New York: Routledge, 81 – 99.

Bowcher, W. L. 2007. A multimodal analysis of good guys and bad guys in "Rugby League Week". In Royce, T. and W. L. Bowcher (eds.). *New Directions in the Analysis of Multimodal Discourse.* Mahwah, New Jersey: Lawrence Erlbaum Associates, 239 – 274.

Bowcher, W. L. 2012. Multimodality in Japanese anti-war placards. In W. L. Bowcher (ed.). *Multimodal Texts from Around the World: Cultural and Linguistic Insights.* Basingstoke, New Hampshire: Palgrave Macmillan, 217 – 245.

Bowcher, W. L. (ed.). (2012) *Multimodal Texts from Around the World*: *Cultural and Linguistic Insights*. Basingstoke, New Hampshire: Palgrave Macmillan.

Bradford, C. 1998. Playing with father: Anthony Browne's picture books and the masculine. *Children's Literature in Education*, 29 (2): 79 –96.

Butt, D. (2001) Firth, Halliday and the Development of Systemic Functional Theory. In Auroux, S., Koerner, E. F. K., Niederehe, H-J., and Versteegh, K. (eds.). *History of the Language Sciences*, 1806 – 1838. Berlin and New York: Walter de Gruyter.

Caple, H. 2009. *Playing with Words and Pictures: Text-image Relations and Semiotic Interplay in a New Genre of News Reportage*. Unpublished PhD thesis, University of Sydney.

Caple, H. 2010. Doubling-up: allusion and bonding in multisemiotic news stories. In M. Bednarek, M. & Martin, J. R. (eds.). *New Discourse on Language: Functional Perspectives on Multimodality, Identity, and Affiliation*. London: Continuum, 111 – 133.

Chang, C. G. (常晨光) 2004. *English Idioms and Interpersonal Meanings*. Guangzhou: Sun Yat-sen University Press.

Chang, C. G. (常晨光) 2011. Commitment in parallel texts: A study of *Pride and Prejudice* and its adaptations. *Studies in Functional Linguistics and Discourse Analysis*, 3 (1): 159 –173.

Chen, Y. M. (陈瑜敏). 2013. Review of "Multimodality in practice: Investigating theory-in-practice through methodology. *Discourse & Society*, 224 (2): 254 –256.

Chen, Y. M. (陈瑜敏) 2014. Exploring the attitudinal variations in the Chinese English-language press on the 2013 air pollution incident. *Discourse & Communication*, 8 (4): 331 –349.

Chatman, S. B. 1978. *Story and Discourse: Narrative Structure in Fiction and Film*. Ithaca, NY: Cornell University Press.

Cleverley, J. & Phillips, C. D. 1987. *Visions of Childhood: Influential Mod-*

els from Locke to Spock. New York: Teachers College Press.

Crago, H. 1999. *A Circle Unbroken: The Hidden Emotional Patterns that Shape Our Lives.* Sydney: Allen & Unwin.

Demers, P. & Moyles, G. (eds.). 1982. *From Instruction to Delight: An Anthology of Children's Literature to* 1850. Toronto: Oxford University Press.

Djonov, E. 2007. Website hierarchy and the interaction between content organization, webpage and navigation design: A systemic functional hypermedia discourse analysis perspective. *Information Design Journal*, 15 (2): 144 – 162.

Dong, L. 2006. Writing Chinese America into words and images: storytelling and retelling of The Song of Mu Lan. *The Lion and the Unicorn*, (30): 218 – 233.

Doonan, J. 1996. The modern picture book. In Hunt, P. (ed.). *International Companion Encyclopedia of Children's Literature.* New York: Routledge, 231 – 241.

Economou, D. 2009. *Photos in the News: Appraisal Analysis of Visual Semiosis and Verbal-visual Intersemiosis.* Unpublished PhD thesis, University of Sydney.

Ekman, P. (ed.). 1973. *Darwin and Facial Expression: A Century of Research in Review.* New York: Academic Press.

Fairclough, N. 1995. *Critical Discourse Analysis. The Critical Study of Language.* London: Longman.

Feaver, W. 1977. *When We Were Young: Two Centuries of Children's Book Illustrations.* London: Thames and Hudson.

Fowler, R. 1986. *Linguistic Criticism.* Oxford: Oxford University Press.

Goffman, E. 1963. *Behavior in Public Places.* New York: Free Press.

Goffman, E. 1981. *Forms of Talk.* Philadelphia: The University of Pennsylvania Press.

Gumperz, J. J. 1982. *Discourse Strategies.* Cambridge: Cambridge University Press.

Gumperz, J. J & Hymes, D. 1972. *Directions in Sociolinguistics: The Ethnography of Communication.* New York: Holt, Rinehart, and Winston.

Hall, E. 1964. Silent assumption in social communication. *Disorders of Communication*, 42: 41 – 55.

Hall, E. 1966. *The Hidden Dimension.* New York: Doubleday.

Halliday, M. A. K. 1973/2003. The functional basis of language. In Bernstein, B. (ed.). *Applied Studies towards a Sociology of Language* (Vol 2): *Class, Codes, and Control.* London and New York: Routledge, 343 – 366.

Halliday, M. A. K. 1978/2001. *Language as Social Semiotic: The Social Interpretation of Language and Meaning.* London: Arnold/Beijing: Foreign Language Teaching and Research Press.

Halliday. M. A. K. 1985a. *An Introduction to Functional Grammar.* London: Arnold.

Halliday, M. A. K. 1985b. *Language, Context and Text: Aspects of Language in a Socio-semiotic Perspective* (Part A). Geelong, Victoria: Deakin University Press.

Halliday, M. A. K. 1990. Some grammatical problems in scientific English. *Australian Review of Applied Linguistics Series* 6: 13 – 37.

Halliday, M. A. K. 1994/2000. *An Introduction to Functional Grammar* (2nd edn.). London: Arnold/Beijing: Foreign Language Teaching and Research Press.

Halliday, M. A. K. 2007. Computing meanings: Some reflections on past experience and present prospects. In Webster, J. (ed.). *Collected Works of M. A. K. Halliday* (Volume 3): *Computational and Quantitative Studies.* London: Continuum.

Halliday, M. A. K. 2008. *Complementarities in Language.* Beijing: Commercial Press.

Halliday, M. A. K. & Hasan, R. 1976. *Cohesion in English.* London: Longman.

Halliday, M. A. K. & Matthiessen, C. M. I. M. 1999. *Construing Experience Through Meaning: A Language-based Approach to Cognition.* London: Continuum.

Halliday, M. A. K. & Matthiessen, C. M. I. M. 2004. *An Introduction to Functional Grammar* (3rd edn.). London: Arnold.

Halliday, M. A. K. & Matthiessen, C. M. I. M. 2009. *Systemic Functional Grammar: A First Step into the Theory.* Bilingual edition, trans. by Huang, G. W and Wang, H. Y. Beijing: Higher Education Press.

Halliday, M. A. K. & Webster, J. 2009. Keywords. In Halliday, M. A. K. & Webster, J (eds.). *Continuum Companion to Systemic Functional Linguistics,.* London and New York: Continuum, 229 – 253.

Hasan, R. 1984/1996. The nursery tale as a genre. In Cloran, C. Butt, D & Williams, G. (eds.). *Ways of Saying: Ways of Meaning.* London: Cassell, 51 – 72.

Hasan, R. 1985. *Language, Context and Text: Aspects of Language in a Socio-semiotic Perspective* (Part B). Geelong, Victoria: Deakin University Press.

Hasan, R. 1988. Language in the process of socialization: home and school. In Gerot, L. ; Oldenburg, J. & van Leeuvan, T. (eds.). *Language and Socialization: Home and School.* North Ryde, NSW: Macquaire University.

Hasan, R. 1995. Theconception of context in text. In Fries, P. H & Gregory, M. (eds.). *Discourse in Society: Systemic Functional Perspectives.* Norwood, NJ: Ablex, 183 – 296.

Hjelmslev, L. 1961. *Prolegomena to a Theory of Language.* Madison, Wisconsin: University of Wisconsin Press.

Hood, S. 2004. *Appraising Research: Taking a Stance in Academic Writing.* Unpublished PhD thesis, University of Technology, Sydney.

Hood, S. 2008. Summary writing in academic contexts: implicating meaning in processes of change. *Linguistics and Education,* (19): 351 – 65.

Huang, G. W. (黄国文) and Ghadessy, M. 2006. *Functional Discourse Analysis.* Shanghai: Shanghai Foreign Language Education Press.

Hunt, P. 1994. *An Introduction to Children's Literature.* Oxford University Press.

Iedema, R. 2001. Analysing film and television. Invan Leeuwen, T. & Jewitt, C. (eds.) *Handbook of Visual Analysis*. London: Sage, 183 – 204.

Jewitt, C. 2002. The move from page to screen: The multimodal reshaping of school English. *Visual Communication*, 1 (2): 171 – 195.

Jewitt, C. (ed.). 2009. *The Routledge Handbook of Multimodal Analysis*. London: Routledge.

Jewitt, C. & Oyama, R. 2001. Visual meaning: A social semiotic approach. In van Leeuwen, T. & Jewitt, C. (eds.). *Handbook of Visual Analysis*. London: Sage, 134 – 156.

Jones, R. 2005. You show me yours, I'll show you mine: The negotiation of shifts from textual to visual modes in computer mediated interaction among gay men. *Visual Communication*, 4 (1): 69 – 92.

Kress, G. 2000. Design and transformation: New theories of meaning. In Cope, B & Kalantzis (eds.). *Multiliteracies: Learning Literacy and the Design of social Futures*. Melbourne: Macmillan, 153 – 161.

Kress, G. 2010. *Multimodality. A Social Semiotic Approach to Contemporary Communication*. London: Routledge.

Kress, G. & van Leeuwen, T. 1996. *Reading Images: The Grammar of Visual Design*. London: Routledge.

Kress, G. & van Leeuwen, T. 2001. *Multimodal Discourse: The Modes and Media of Contemporary Communication*. London: Arnold.

Kress, G. & van Leeuwen, T. 2006. *Reading Images: The Grammar of Visual Design*. (2nd edn.). London: Routledge.

Labov, W. 1972a. *Language in the Inner City: Studies in the Black English Vernacular*. Philadelphia: University of Pennsylvania Press.

Labov, W. 1972b. The transformation of experience in narrative syntax. In Labov, W (ed.). *Language in the inner city: studies in the Black English vernacular*. Philadelphia: University of Pennsylvania Press, Chapter 9.

Labov, W. & Waletzky, J. 1967/1997. Narrative analysis: oral versions of personal experience. In J. Helm (ed.). *Essays on the Verbal and Visual Arts* Seattle: University of Washington Press, 12 – 44.

Lewis, D. 2001. *Reading Contemporary Picturebooks : Picturing Text.* London: Routledge.

Lim, F. V. 2004. Developing an integrative multi-semiotic model. In O'Halloran, K. L (ed.). *Multimodal Discourse Analysis : Systemic Functional Perspective.* London: Continuum, 220 – 246.

Lim, F. V. 2007. The visual semantics stratum: Making meaning in sequential images. In Royce, T. D. and Bowcher, W. L. (eds.). *New Directions in the Analysis of Multimodal Discourse.* Mahwah, New Jersey: Lawrence Erlbaum Associates, Publishers, 195 – 214.

Martin, J. R. 1986. Grammaticalising ecology: The politics of baby seals and kangaroos. In Threadgold, T. Grosz, E. A. , Kress, G. and Halliday, M. A. K. (eds.). *Semiotics, Ideology, Language.* Sydney: Sydney Association for Studies in Society and Culture, 225 – 268.

Martin, J. R. & Plum, G. A. 1997. Construing experience: Some story genres. *Journal of Narrative and Life History*, 7: 299 – 308.

Martin, J. R. 1992. *English Text : System and Structure.* Amsterdam: Benjamins.

Martin, J. R. & Rose, D. 2003. *Working With Discourse : Meaning beyond the Clause.* London; New York: Continuum.

Martin, J. R. & Rose, D. 2008. *Genre Relations : Mapping Culture.* London: Equinox.

Martin, J. R. & White, P. 2005. *The Language of Evaluation : Appraisal in English.* New York: Palgrave Macmillan.

Martinec, R. & Salway, A. 2005. A system for image-text relations in new (and old) media. *Visual Communication*, 4 (3): 337 – 371.

Matthiessen, C. M. I. M. 2007. The multimodal page: A systemic functional exploration. In Royce, T. & Bowcher, W. (eds.). *New Directions in the Analysis of Multimodal Discourse.* Mahwah, New Jersey: Lawrence Erlbaum Associates, 1 – 62.

Matthiessen, C. M. I. M. 2009. Multisemiosis and context-based register typology: Registerial variation in the complementarity of semiotic systems. In E. Ventola & Guijarro, A. J. M. (eds.). *The World Told and the*

World Shown. Basingstoke, Hampshire: Palgrave Macmillan, 11 – 38.

Matthiessen, C. M. I. , Teruya, K. and Lam, M. 2010. *Key Terms in Systemic Functional Linguistics*. London and New York: Continuum.

Moebius, W. 1986. Introduction to picture book codes. *Word and Image* 2: 141 – 151.

Nesbitt, C & Plum, G. 1988. Probabilities in a systemic-functional grammar: the clause complex in English. In Fawcett, R. P. & Young, D. (eds.). *New Development in Systemic Linguistics*, Vol 2: theory and application. London: Pinter, 6 – 38.

Nichols, S. 2002. Parents' construction of their children as gendered, literate subjects: A critical discourse analysis. *Journal of Early Childhood Literacy*, 2 (2): 123 – 144.

Nikolajeva, M. & Scott, C. 2000. The dynamics of picturebook communication. *Children's Literature in Education*, 31(4): 225 – 239.

Nikolajeva, M. & Scott, C. 2001. *How Picturebooks Work*. New York: Garland Publishing.

Nodelman, P. 1988. *Words about Pictures: The Narrative Art of Children's Picture Books*. Athens and London: The University of Georgia Press.

Nodelman, P. & Reimer, M. 2003. *The Pleasures of Children's Literature*. (3rd edn.). Boston: Allyn and Bacon.

Norris, S. 2002. *A Theoretical Framework for Multimodal Discourse Analysis presented via the Analysis of Identity Construction of Two Women Living in Germany*. Unpublished PhD thesis, Georgetown University.

Norris, S. 2004. Multimodal discourse analysis: A conceptual framework. In LeVine, P. and Scollon, R. (eds.). *Discourse and Technology: Multimodal Discourse Analysis*. Washington, D. C. : Georgetown University Press, 101 – 115.

Norris, S. 2005. Habitus, social identity, the perception of male domination—and agency? In Norris, S. and Jones, R. H. *Discourse in Action: Introducing Mediated Discourse Analysis*. London: Routledge, 183 – 196.

Norris, S. & Jones, R. H. 2005. *Discourse in Action: Introducing Mediate*

Discourse Analysis. London: Routledge.

Norris, S. 2009. Modal density and modal configurations: Multimodal actions. In Jewitt, C. (ed.). *The Routledge Handbook of Multimodal Analysis.* London: Routledge, 78 – 90.

O'Halloran, K. L. 2000. Classroom discourse in mathematics: A multi-semiotic analysis. *Linguistics and Education*, 10(3): 359 – 388.

O'Halloran, K. (ed.). 2004. *Multimodal Discourse Analysis: Systemic Functional Perspectives.* London: Continuum.

O'Halloran, K. L. 2005. *Mathematical Discourse: Language, Symbolism and Visual Image.* London: Continuum.

O'Halloran, K. L. 2008. Systemic functional-multimodal discourse analysis (SF-MDA): Constructing ideational meaning using language and visual imagery. *Visual Communication*, 7(4): 443 – 475.

O'Halloran, K. 2009. Historical Changes in the Semiotic Landscape: From Calculation to Computation. In Jewitt, C. (ed.). *The Routledge Handbook of Multimodal Analysis.* London: Routledge, 98 – 113.

O'Toole, M. 1994. *The Language of Displayed Art.* London: Leister University Press.

O'Toole, M. 2004. Opera Ludentes: The Sydney Opera House at work and play. In O'Halloran, K. L. (ed.). *Multimodal Discourse Analysis: Systemic Functional Perspectives.* London: Continuum, 11 – 27.

O'Toole, M. 2011. *The Language of Displayed Art* (2nd edn.). London: Routledge.

Painter, C. 2001. *Learning through Language in Early Childhood.* London: Continuum.

Painter, C. 2007. Children's picture books: Reading sequences of images. In A. McCabe, A., O'Donnell, M. & Whittaker, R. (eds.). *Advances in Language and Education.* London: Continuum, 38 – 57.

Painter, C. 2008. The role of colour in children's picture books: choices in ambience. In Unsworth, L. (ed.). *New literacies and the English curriculum.* London: Continuum, 89 – 111.

Painter, C. & Martin, J. R. 2011. Intermodal complementarity: modelling affordances across image and verbiage in children's picture books. In Huang, G. W. (ed.). *Research in Functional Linguistics and Discourse Analysis*, *Vol* 3. Beijing: Higher Education Press.

Painter, C., Martin, J. R. & Unsworth, L. 2013. *Reading Visual Narratives: Image Analysis of Children's Picture Books*. London: Equinox.

Plum, G. A. 1988. Text and contextual conditioning in spoken English: A genre approach. *University of Sydney Linguistics*, 1988.

Poynton, C. 1985/1989. *Language and Gender: Making the Difference*. Geelong, Victoria: Deakin University Press. / Oxford: Oxford University Press.

Rothery, J. 1990. *Story Writing in Primary School: Assessing Narrative Type Genres*. Unpublished PhD thesis, University of Sydney.

Rothery, J. & Stenglin, M. 2000. Interpreting literature: The role of Appraisal. In Unsworth, L. (ed.). *Researching Language in Schools and Communities: Functional Linguistic Perspectives*. London: Cassell, 222 – 244.

Royce, T. 1998. Synergy on the page: Exploring intersemiotic complementarity in page-based multiomodal text. *JASFL Occasional Papers*, (1): 25 – 50.

Royce, T. 1999. *Visual-Verbal Intersemiotic Complementarity in the Economist Magazine*. Unpublished Ph. D. dissertation. The University of Reading.

Royce, T. (2002) Multimodality in the TESOLclassroom: Exploring visual-verbal synergy. *TESOL Quarterly*, 36 (2): 191 – 205

Royce, T. 2007. Intersemiotic Complementarity: A Framework for Multimodal Discourse Analysis. In Royce, T. and W. Bowcher (eds.). *New Directions in the Analysis of Multimodal Discourse*. Mahwah, New Jersey: Lawrence Erlbaum Associates, 63 – 109.

Royce, T. & Bowcher, W. (eds.). 2007. *New Directions in the Analysis of Multimodal Discourse*. Mahwah, New Jersey: Lawrence Erlbaum Associates.

Sarland, C. 2005. Critical tradition and ideological positioning. In Hunt, P (ed.). *Understanding Children's Literature: Key Essays from the Second Edition of the International companion encyclopedia of Children's Litera-*

ture (2nd edn.). New York: Routledge, 30 – 49.

Scollon, R. & Scollon, S. 2004. *Nexus Analysis: Discourse and the Emerging Internet*. London: Routledge.

Sipe, L. R. 1998. How picture books work: a semiotically framed theory of text picture relationships. *Children's Literature in Education*, 29 (2): 97 – 108.

Spitz, E. H. 1999. *Inside Picture Books*. New Haven & London: Yale University Press.

Stegling, M. Space and communication in exhibitions: Unraveling the nexus. In Jewitt, C. (ed.). *The Routledge Handbook of Multimodal Analysis*. London: Routledge, 272 – 283.

Stephens, J. 1992. *Language and Ideology in Children's Fiction*. New York: Longman.

Stephens, J. (ed.). 2002. *Ways of Being Male: Representing Masculinities in Children's Literature and Film*. New York: Routledge.

Schwarcz, J. H. 1982. *Ways of the Illustrator: Visual Communication in Children's Literature*. Chicago: American Library Association.

Thomas, M. 2009. Developing multimodal texture. In Ventola, E. and A. J. M. Guijarro (eds.). *The World Told and the World Shown*. Basingstoke, Hampshire: Palgrave Macmillan, 39 – 55.

Thompson, G. 1996. *Introducing Functional Grammar*. London: Arnold.

Thompson, G. 2001. Interaction in academic writing: Learning to argue with the reader. *Applied Linguistics*, 22 (1): 58 – 78.

Tian, P. 2011. *Multimodal Evaluation: Sense and Sensibility in Anthony Browne's Picture Books*. Unpublished PhD thesis, University of Sydney.

Toolan, M. 1988. *Narrative: A Critical Linguistic Introduction*. New York: Routledge.

Unsworth, L. 2001. *Teaching Multiliteracies across the Curriculum: Changing Contexts of Text and Image in Classroom Practice*. Buckingham: Open University Press.

Unsworth, L. 2005. *E-Literature for Children: Enhancing Digital Literacy Learning*. London: Routledge.

Unsworth, L. 2006. Towards a metalanguage for multiliteracies education: Describing the meaning-making resources of language-image interaction. *English Teaching: Practice and Critique*, 5 (1): 55 – 76.

Unsworth, L. 2008. *New Literacies and the English Curriculum: Multimodal Perspectives*. London: Continuum.

Unsworth, L. & Cleirigh, C. 2009. Multimodality and reading: the construction of meaning through image-text interaction. In Jewitt, C. (ed.). *The Routledge Handbook of Multimodal Analysis*. London: Routledge, 151 – 164.

van Leeuwen, T. 1999. *Speech, Music, Sound*. London: Macmillan.

van Leeuwen, T. 2005. *Introducing Social Semiotics*. London: Routledge.

Van Leeuwen, T. 2009. Parametric systems: The case of voice quality. In Jewitt, C. (ed.). *The Routledge Handbook of Multimodal Analysis*. London: Routledge, 68 – 77.

van Leeuwen, T. & Jewitt, C. (eds.). 2001. *Handbook of Visual Analysis*. London: Sage.

Ventola, E. & Guijarro, A. J. M. (eds.). 2009. *The World Told and the World Shown*. Basingstoke, Hampshire: Palgrave Macmillan.

Welch, A. 2005. *The Illustration of Facial Affect in Children's Litearture*. Unpublished BA honours thesis, University of Sydney.

White, P. R. R. 2000. Dialogue and inter-subjectivity: reinterpreting the semantics of modality and hedging. In Coulthard, M., Cotterill, J. & Rock, F. (eds.). *Working with Dialogue*. Tubingen: Neimeyer, 67 – 80.

常晨光:《英语习语的人际意义》,《外语与外语教学》2002 年第 12 期。

常晨光:《系统功能语言学的社会符号视角》,《当代外语研究》2013 年第 3 期。

冯德正、亓玉杰:《态度意义的多模态建构——基于认知评价理论的分析模式》,《现代外语》2014 年第 5 期。

顾曰国:《多媒体、多模态学习剖析》,《外语电化教学》2007 年第 4 期。

黄国文:《系统功能语言学研究中的整合》,《中国外语》2009 年第 1 期。

胡壮麟:《社会符号学研究中的多模态化语言》,《教学与研究》2007 年第 1 期。

李德志:《广告类超文本多模态的视觉语法分析》,《外语学刊》2013 年第 2 期。

李战子、陆丹云:《多模态符号学:理论基础,研究途径与发展前景》,《外语研究》2012 年第 2 期。

刘宝根、李林慧:《早期阅读概念与图画书阅读教学》,《学前教育研究》2013 年第 7 期。

裴永刚:《儿童绘本的现状、问题及发展趋势》,《中国出版》2005 年第 9 期。

宋国云:《浅析经典图画书主题的儿童性设计特点》,《出版发行研究》2013 年第 3 期。

王蕾:《图画书与学前儿童语言教育》,《学前教育研究》2008 年第 7 期。

王文璐:《浅谈儿童图画书插图的叙事性》,《中华女子学院学报》2014 年第 1 期。

王玉:《儿童阅读图画书的基本特征》,《中华女子学院学报》2012 年第 5 期。

肖静:《儿童图画书的阅读流程设计》,《美术学报》2007 年第 4 期。

杨信彰:《多模态语篇分析与系统功能语言学》,《外语教学》2009 年第 7 期。

张德禄、丁肇芬:《外语教学多模态选择框架探索》,《外语界》2013 年第 3 期。

张霞:《论儿童绘本的题材与图画表达》,《内蒙古教育》2013 年第 2 期。

Appendix

The Monster Nian（2007）Xiongliang

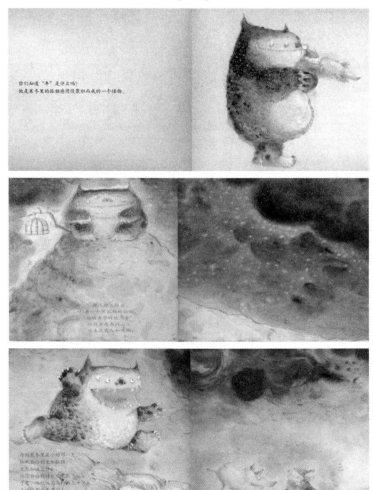

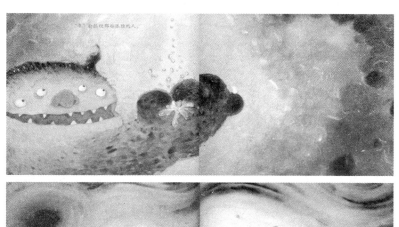

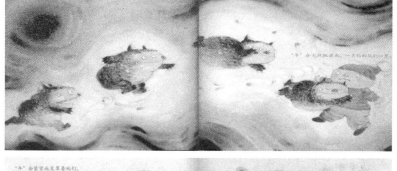

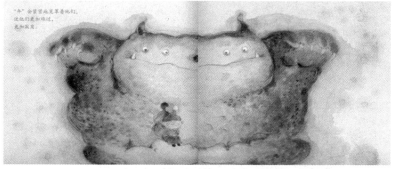

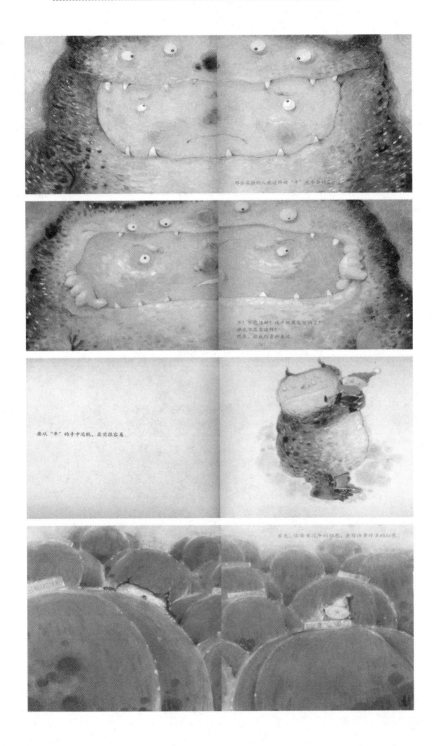

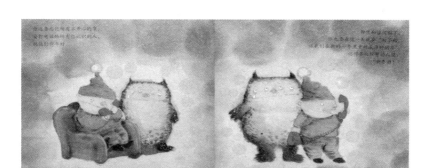

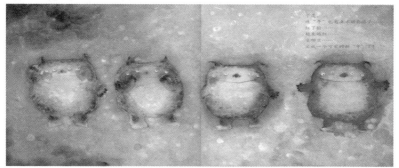

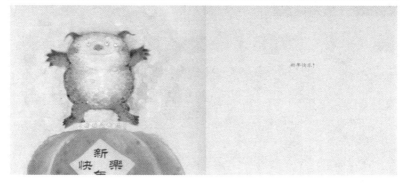

Reunion (2008) Yu Liqiong Zhu Chenliang

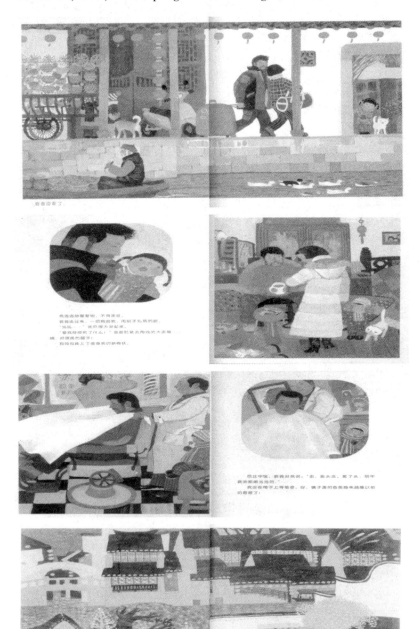

包法面糊，爸爸把一枚硬币包进饺馅里，"谁吃到它，来年就会交好运嘞！"

这天夜里，猫行"辞旧迎新"这碗个不停，我俯伏在爸爸身构中间睡着了，迷迷糊糊地，我仿不想还缩着身等好的奇店，就们识破说着……

第二天一大早，妈妈就流上了热腾腾的饺子，爸爸用刀个捐给我的。

爸爸，我的牙咬一个硬东西地了一下。

"好运硬币！好运硬币！"我叫起来

"毛毛真棒！快查到完度，好吃就不会搭糊糊糊！"爸爸比我这片心慰。

哈妈你就就上了新棉袄，要去开年嘞！

路上，我遇到了大春。

"毛毛，你去哪儿啊？"

"我邮爸爸去拜年！"

"我也是，爸，我有大红包！"

"这有什么稀奇！"我从兜里掏出那枚硬币，"我有好运硬币！爷爷把在这路里沙，指我远到了！"

大年初二，天刚刚亮亮，要下雪了，一大早，爸爸就忙了起来，补完户级，我却门拿，轻奸打扫——

咦，屋里一下子空得真室了。

"爸，叶爷送走嘞！"爸爸冲我拼了拼翼。

太好了！那儿童呐儿从来不是和统一个人上念的倒办呢。

"毛毛熊呢，我再给你一个，喏，跟这个一样。"医生
掏出一枚硬币。

"不要不要，我就要那个！"我一动第一边叫。

床上，我挽过胳膊上床，跟姐姐的时候——"叮当"，
那个东西掉到了地上。

医生！我的硬币硬币！

"赶快快乐看，好吗没跑。它一直在我身上了"

那天夜里，我搂搂待抱着——

早上一起来，我就看见妈妈在为爸爸收拾东西——
爸爸今天要走了。

爸爸很快就收拾好了。他走到我身边，蹲下来用力抱住我
趴在他肩头上爸爸说，"下次我爸来，我就给你带一个漂亮的。
好不好？"

"不！"我使劲摇头，"我要把这个给你——"

我把那枚攥了很久的硬币塞进爸爸的手心里：
"这个给你，下次回来，我们还把它包在冰激凌里堆。"

爸爸没说话，他用力地点点头，接着我不由手——

Happy New Year (2008) Sun Zhaozhi

On the Spring Festival (2012) Wang Zaozao Li Jian

The Monster Nian is Coming (2013) Liu Longsha

老人不在乎热身冷脚时，吃下滚烫的饺子烫死了，可怜地："唉
公公，我们家想有一些热乎热乎的东西，您喝碗吧。"

老人一听，一把一把地是摆了客家的孩子，沈福吃水较
纪夫口吃起来 吃完，她狠狠就来，问道："奇怪，你们三样
东仁连服热热地红在盆上烫烫。"

下客每吃口气，连着闪红年客言人的茅檐就在来，最后
说法："今春就奉来了，我这就先下场了，其根留下来，您吃吧。"
找起这来些呀！呀到这念呀呀，就完好了。

洗海后，新人吵哈起起说："我们再过许客完就了的客，当
善是这个经众，是善善，你料这 今天地上的有我找物担心。"

下客每醒天了缝缝，说。"如今、热茶稍稍暖哦吃大年客，
奈人真暴原上翻下来，说："只要你善养手把红衫了哈我吃，
就被肴不法把完年客，等一会儿，你只要我网那如就就哈我，将
给我一地大红花，其地时等然完哈去。"

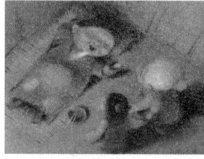

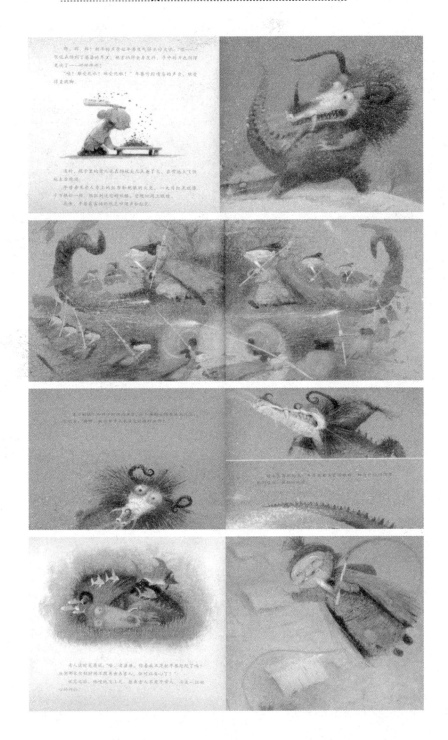

第二天，当村民们回到村子，发现了客客和孙子争吵之事，都很好奇了。丁爷爷一户一户挨地前一致的事就出来。

村民们高兴地说："太好了，以后每年都很累的这一天，我们改变剃剃字的儿、穿红衣、麻起来、挂什子起来了，再也不用害怕外面吃人啦！"

The Spring Festival (2013) Zhu Shifang Hua Xiaowu

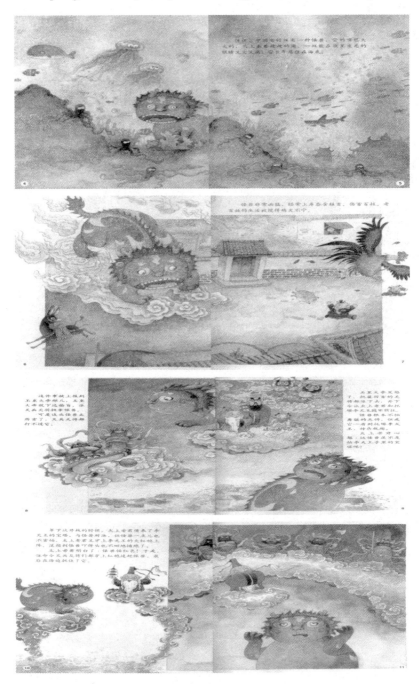

Nian (2013) Gao Jinnan Wang Fang

The Adventure of the Postman（2014）Zheng Chunhua Zhao Xiaoyin

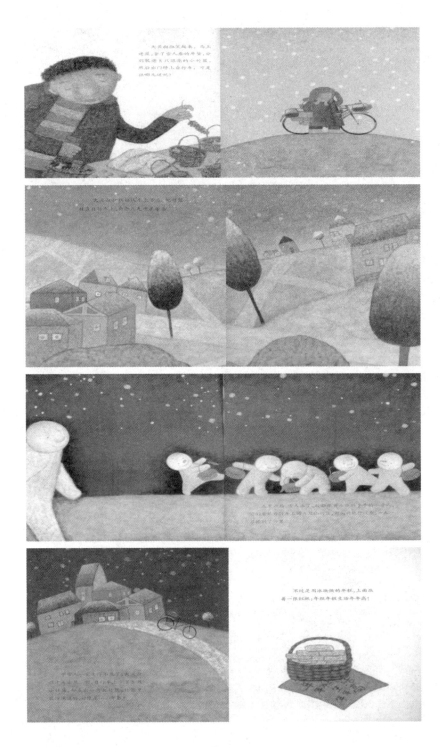

Nian（2015）Zhu Huiyin

很久很久以前，有一只巨大的怪兽叫年，
它平时在很深的大海里，偶尔翻个天换地。

与普通那条大灾难的行径，
它怕阳光，晚上等夜时看到。

年到村子里吃村里人
它一来，人们都被吓得慌忙逃走。

人们非常害怕年，
每逢年快要出现时，都提前逃到离远山里躲起来。

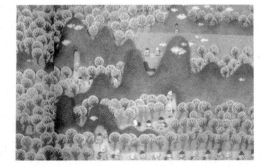

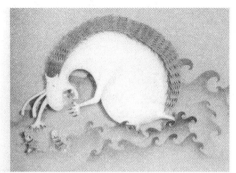

村里有个男孩，他本来是第一个拿糖的家。
有意他问妈妈想想和爷爷奶奶的模样。
但是，上一次年夜的钟响，他们消听了，原有的亲人都做年夜神
只有男孩独自拉灯得很了。

忽然了年快来到的脸，男孩头心寒下来社业了。
令人们随后寻积的忙累。
只是，他只是一个走丢失错的孩子，怎样才能起走年吧？
他缓缓的想想啊啊

第二天，老人随悲伤对男孩说。
"醒醒吧，善良的孩子。
我告诉你一个起来身的办法。
这个秘密，搅搅放的多啦……"
说完，老人就消失了。
男孩抬头一看，
只见一只七彩蝴蝶闲闲飞舞——

男孩连忙跑去搬家，
陌生人的魔示，
记年做了起来。

男孩像从梦中惊醒，起紧订开书包，一首红彤彤的歌谣展现在眼前。

我我那一起红彤彤成火红火红的灯笼。

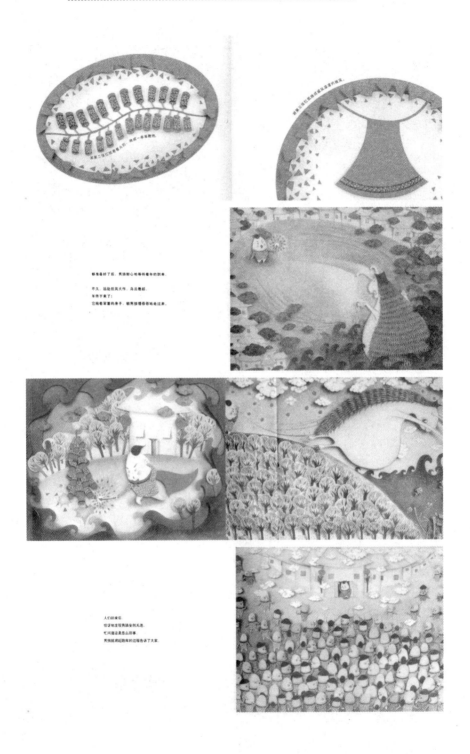

从此，人们再也不用害怕年了。
每年除夕，
人们就会穿红衣，戴红帽，
家家门前挂灯笼，放鞭炮。
中国人开始欢欢喜喜过大"年"了!

A Battle with Nian（2015）Liu Jialu

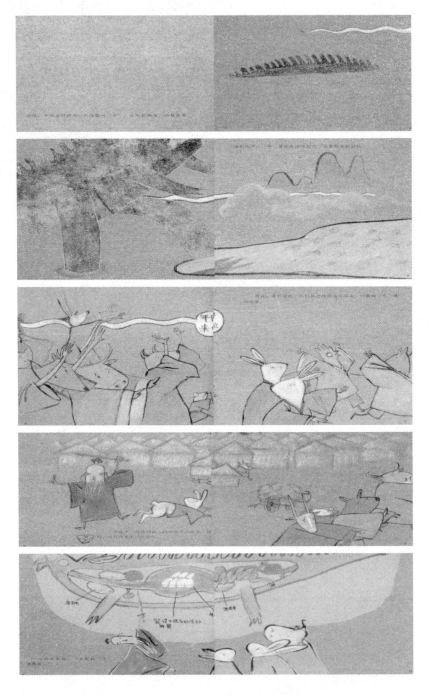